WILD KIDS

How youth has shocked its elders – then and now!

WILD KIDS

FRANK R. DONOVAN

STACKPOLE BOOKS

Wild Kids

Copyright © 1967 by
STACKPOLE COMPANY

Published by
STACKPOLE BOOKS
Cameron and Kelker Streets
Harrisburg, Pa. 17105

Library of Congress Catalog Card Number 67-21671. Printed in U.S.A.

Contents

One generation passeth away,
and another generation cometh:
but the earth abideth forever . . .

The thing that hath been, it is
that which shall be; and that which
is done is that which shall be done:
and there is no new thing under
the sun.

Ecclesiastes 1: 4 and 9

1

What Are Kids?
And What Is Wild?

SOCRATES WAS A WISE GREEK WHOSE PHIL-
osophical pronouncements have endured for some twenty centuries. In his later years the old philosopher made what he probably
considered a profound observation when he proclaimed that
children did not behave as they had in his youth. They were more
unmannerly, more disobedient, more defiant of authority. In short,
they were wilder. Socrates probably did not know that this opinion
was already an ancient cliché; Confucius, for one, had made the
same complaint about the younger generation five centuries earlier.
And surely many others had said it during the intervening 500
years—as it has constantly been repeated for some 2,000 years
since.

Every older generation since the dawn of history has denounced
the rising generation as being inferior in terms of manners and
morals, ethics and honesty. Whether this is because of the way
the kids behaved or because, in the words of Jane Addams, "every
generation clings with an almost romantic fervor to the aims of its
own age," is an open question. But seldom in the past has youth

been accused of delinquency more loudly, more frequently and by more varied sources than are the youngsters of the mid-twentieth century.

"Delinquency, National Crisis," "Wild Youth," "School Crime Wave," "My Name is Barbarian," "Tense Generation," are typical of titles that have recently headed articles by psychologists, psychiatrists, sociologists, ministers, educators, welfare workers, doctors, and law enforcement officers who make sensational charges that kids are running wild today as never before. The antics, misdemeanors, immoralities and crimes of youth are prime news. Press, podium, pulpit and television combine to accuse the modern younger generation of conduct that defies all authority—parental, school, church and police. In a *single* year in the 1960's there were four times as many articles on juvenile delinquency in the nation's magazines as were published during the final *ten* years of the last century. Yet during the Gay Nineties there were some who decried the current increase in juvenile delinquency.

Going back another half century, we find a British magazine proclaiming: "The tales of juvenile depravity which are commonly circulated give a very faint notion of its fearful amount. The youthful imagination, once perceived, seems to exercise itself in the invention of all monstrous, horrible and ineffable crimes." A religious publication, reporting on juvenile behavior in the mid-nineteenth century, commented on "the constantly increasing record of crimes, the defiance of all repressive institutions, the utter disregard for the police." And a third journal succinctly expressed its view of the current situation with the headline: "Society in Danger from Children."

One hundred years ago in the United States there were some who believed that youngsters of the 1860's were as bad as or worse than we now consider the youth of the 1960's. In a report of New York's Board of Metropolitan Police, one member said: "For the last ten years I have been a close observer of what has passed among the rising generation in this great metropolis, and I cannot suppress the humiliating conviction that even pagan Rome under Augustus never witnessed a more rapid and frightful declension in morals, nor witnessed among certain classes of the young a more utter disregard of honor, of truth and piety, and even the commonest decencies of life."

One hundred and fifty years ago the "wave" of juvenile delinquency in London was considered so appalling that a society was formed to investigate its extent and causes and make recommendations to the Parliament for its control. The society's report said:

"1stly. The members of the committee believe, from their inquiries, that there are some thousands of boys under seventeen years of age in the metropolis who are daily engaged in the commission of crime.

"2ndly. That these boys associate with professed thieves of mature age, and with girls who subsist by prostitution.

"3rdly. That such characters frequent houses of the most infamous description, where they divide their plunder and give loose to every vicious propensity."

In the light of today's expert opinion on the causes of increased juvenile delinquency, the findings of this investigating committee 150 years ago are interesting. Today we are told that broken homes are a factor. The 1816 committee cited "the prevalence of improvident marriages." Today, parents do not set a good example or exert the proper authority. A century and a half ago it was found that "the first circumstances which are allowed to operate in the formation of character flow from the exercise, or neglect, of parental authority and love. It is apprehended that, in many cases which have come before this Society, the number of boys is very small whose original tendencies to do wrong have not sprung from the improper conduct of their parents."

The high school dropout is frequently mentioned as a factor in modern delinquency. This aspect of the problem was slightly different in 1816, for the committee reached the following conclusion: "It appears that a considerable number of boys have received no instruction whatever and that few have been able to read or write with tolerable accuracy. The want of education is a powerful cause of the alarming depravity which prevails."

As a solution, the committee had a forward-looking proposal: "Thus depredations are often occasioned by the want of an industrious occupation. The Committee cannot, therefore, too warmly recommend the formation of Public Establishments in the most populous districts of the metropolis for the suitable employment of distressed youth." Today, of course, we have the Job Corps.

THROUGH THE CENTURIES CHILDREN HAVE expressed a rebellious attitude toward the disciplines of the adult world in their desire for freedom, excitement and adventure, and this has led to the accusation of wildness by the mature societies against which they have rebelled. But to determine whether today's kids are more or less wild than those of yore we must first consider the changing conception of a juvenile and of what constitutes delinquency. The words "juvenile," "youngsters" and the colloquial "kids" are not subject to exact definition. In this book they are used interchangeably to denote young people from the later elementary school years through high school age.

The legal definition of a juvenile varies in different states. In a few, all cases involving minors (except capital crime) are under the jurisdiction of the juvenile courts. In most states the maximum age at which cases are automatically referred to the juvenile court is eighteen, in some sixteen, but cases involving youngsters above these ages, and still in their teens, are frequently transferred to juvenile courts by the court of first jurisdiction. According to the Children's Bureau of the Department of Health, Education and Welfare the peak ages for juvenile delinquency are sixteen and seventeen. The classification of youngsters of this age as juveniles was not generally accepted until well into the twentieth century. When making his *bar mitzvah* at the age of thirteen, a Hebrew boy starts his traditional speech by saying: "Today I am a man," and throughout most of Jewish history, this was interpreted literally. The wisdom of Solomon's saying, "Foolishness is bound up in the heart of a child," was recognized, but childhood ended at puberty; among the poor, at an earlier age when children were physically capable of doing productive work.

In medieval Europe boys of ten started their adult careers as pages. Middle-class youths were apprenticed starting at the age of twelve. Girls went into domestic service as young as fourteen up to the early years of this century, when most middle-class American families had teen-age "servant girls." In America throughout the eighteenth and nineteenth centuries boys of sixteen were treated as men. In post-Revolutionary days they paid taxes and were required to join the militia. Boys entered Boston Latin school, equivalent to today's high school, as young as eight and went to college at fourteen. Admiral Farragut went to sea at the age of twelve as a midshipman—the equivalent of an Annapolis cadet in this day—and he was with his "peer group," few of whom were over sixteen when they started their service. In short, the exhortation of St. Paul to "put away childish things," and at the earliest possible time, was the general rule applied to children growing up.

The acceptance of teen-agers as adults in previous times is indicated by marriage customs. Today if a girl marries before she finishes high school there is much sad wagging of heads because "she isn't even eighteen." In the French Canadian colonies a father was fined if his daughter had not married by the age of sixteen. In the last century if a girl was not married or engaged by eighteen her parents started to worry and by twenty-five she was definitely considered as a confirmed spinster. Throughout most of history puberty has been considered as determining a marriageable age; child brides were the custom rather than the exception. Letters of twelve-year-old American girls in the eighteenth and early nineteenth centuries indicate a universal preoccupation with thoughts of marriage; brides of thirteen were not unusual and marriage at fifteen or sixteen was commonplace.

The difference in marriage customs has a bearing on sexual juvenile delinquency which was pointed up by a professor of sociology at Princeton thusly; "Among most peoples of the world, at least until recently, there was some variation of a recurrent pattern. Either marriage occurred shortly after puberty or premarital intercourse prevailed. The choice of a marital partner was generally in the hands of parents or kinsmen. . . . By way of contrast American society is unusual in the following ways: It maintains the ideal of premarital chastity in the face of a long period of postponement of marriage after puberty. In connection with this, it upholds the freedom of marital choice and fosters competition . . . in courtship. . . . As a consequence, the adolescent period becomes one of considerable strain. The young person is permitted to associate closely with the opposite sex but is put on his honor to remain virtuous, is supposed to choose his own mate independently but is in many ways still under the authority of the parents."

An interesting example of the changing attitude toward juvenile love is the extent to which teen-agers were involved in many of the great romances of literature. Achilles had a son by Deidamia when he was fifteen; the love affair between Acis and Galatea started when he was sixteen; Chione was reported to have had "a thousand suitors when she reached the marriageable age of fourteen"; Narcissus was sixteen when "many youths and many maidens sought his love"; Helen was twelve years old when Paris carried her off from Sparta; in a great pastoral romance Daphnis was fifteen and Chloë was thirteen; Heloise was eighteen when she fell in love with Abelard; Tristan was nineteen when he first met Isolde; and Juliet was fourteen when Romeo made love to her. By today's standards all of these love affairs would have been at least frowned upon, and most of the participants would have been considered juvenile delinquents.

In comparing wild kids today with wild kids of yesteryear it must be understood that most juvenile delinquents of the twentieth century would not have been juvenile delinquents in previous centuries simply because they would not have been considered as juveniles. There was no differentiation between teen-age and adult criminals. The British Annual Register tells how many murders were committed in each year of the eighteenth century, but says nothing of the age of the murderers. Be he thirteen or thirty, a murderer was a murderer, a thief was a thief, and all received equal treatment.

As the concept of a juvenile has changed, so has the concept of what constitutes delinquency. Fighting is a case in point. From the earliest times until the fairly recent past, to be a fighter was considered a virtue in youth. Wrote William James: "Our ancestors have bred pugnacity into our bone and marrow." A boy's competence in physical combat was a matter of pride, not disorderly conduct. Spontaneous juvenile fighting in the village streets of a bygone America was a common occurrence—a form of recreation for the combatants and entertainment for the spectators. One who would have been considered as a juvenile delinquent by today's standards was Abraham Lincoln.

The attitude toward premarital adolescent sex has also varied widely at different times and in different places. By modern American standards nothing could be more delinquent than a fifteen-year-old girl who has intercourse with three boys in an evening. In some cultures—that of Samoa, for instance—such conduct was accepted as normal and natural. In ancient Athens there was nothing reprehensible about a thirteen-year-old *dicteriade* (a juvenile prostitute), unless she was the daughter of a citizen. For base-born or foreign girls this was an acceptable way to make a living. The modern fifteen-year-old miss who pets in a parked car is thought to be well on the road to ruin. Her Puritan forebear of like age who bundled with a boy in a bed was on the road to marriage; this was accepted premarital conduct.

Drinking is another aspect of youthful behavior on which the attitude of society has changed. In many cultures, and in colonial America, most children drank. Until the early years of this century a sixteen-year-old boy in most American cities could stop on his way home from work and bend an elbow at the bar with adult workers. He was not considered delinquent, nor was he considered a juvenile.

The right of boys to gather in gangs was generally accepted until recent years, although it was recognized that boys could misbehave more wildly in groups than as individuals. Today the words "gang" and "delinquent" are associated like "ham and eggs." The social unit of the gang has always been basic to a boy's world. Sociologist Frederic Thrasher, who made an exhaustive study of the subject says: "Gangs represent the spontaneous effort of boys to create a society for themselves where none adequate for their needs exists. What boys get out of such association that they do not get otherwise under the conditions that adult society imposes is the thrill and zest of participation in common interest, more especially in corporate action, in hunting, capture, conflict, flight and escape. Conflict with other gangs and the world about them furnishes the occasion for many of their exciting group activities. . . . The quest for new experience seems particularly insistent in the adolescent, who finds in the gang the desired escape from, and compensation for, monotony."

Running away from home, in an earlier America, was almost considered as a part of growing up. The youngster who rebelled against his stern parents and sought to show them the error of their ways by packing his few belongings in a bundle and leaving his unreasonable home was an American legend. When older juveniles left home in their mid-teens to make their way in the world, it was generally considered as commendable rather than delinquent.

Much of the minor wildness of youth was not considered as delinquency in most past societies. Kids who upset outhouses fifty years ago were considered bad or mischievous boys, not vandals. Much conduct that is today sternly repressed as "disturbing the peace" or "disorderly conduct" was formerly considered as youthful pranks or mischief and more or less shrugged off on the basis that "boys will be boys."

Despite the popular concept that standards for juvenile behavior used to be more rigid, young people in an earlier America actually had more freedom than they have today. Then the important traits of character were considered to be those that would tend to prepare a child to produce in the adult world—to make him materially successful. He should conform to the rules laid down by Benjamin Franklin's *Almanac* for diligence, honesty and thrift, and the moral code of the Bible. If he followed these clear criteria it did not much matter how he conducted himself otherwise. Neither parents nor society knew or cared about his psychological makeup. His social adjustment to the adult world was less important than his ability to make a material contribution to it, and he had a certain freedom to be different, provided that he did his work well.

Kids have always behaved more wildly in cities. Most types of what is now considered delinquency were rare in an agrarian or frontier society where, in general, children had too much to do to have time to be bad. In comparing the wildness of today's youth with youngsters of the past it must be remembered that the frontier disappeared in America during the last half of the nineteenth century, and the great shift of population from the farm to urban areas took place in the twentieth, accelerating after World War I.

IN AMERICA, UNTIL THE DAWN OF THE CURrent century, the state had little interest in how most youngsters behaved. Unless he committed a major crime, the only contact that a kid had with a restrictive or guiding state agency was through the cop on the beat. The first juvenile court did not come into existence until 1899, in Chicago, and its purpose was primarily to protect the child from the more stringent punishments of adult criminal courts, not to check closely on all aspects of his misbehavior.

After the laws of the Puritan theocracy in New England passed away, the state did not start to make special rules concerning children until about one hundred years ago. These were part of the general humanitarian movement of the mid-nineteenth century, and the early rules were designed to protect the juvenile rather than restrain him. The first child labor laws did not make their appearance in America until after the Civil War and, for a long time, they were mainly honored in the breach. True, the American colonies had child labor laws, but their purpose was to compel children to work rather than prevent them.

The attitude of the state toward its youthful members in bygone days is indicated by the story of the formation of the Society for the Prevention of Cruelty to Children. In 1874 a mission worker, visiting a sick woman in a New York tenement, heard a child crying piteously in the next room. The woman told her that the child was brutally beaten every day and, when she was not screaming, she cried and moaned constantly. Miss Wheeler, the worker, went to the police and was told that, unless an actual witness complained that the child's life was in danger, they could not intervene. A city magistrate proved to her by a law book that he had no right to interfere. Several charitable societies assured her that they had no authority to act, and everywhere she was cautioned that it was a serious matter to interfere between parents and a child. Finally, Miss Wheeler bethought herself of an institution that had been organized eight years earlier—The Society for the Prevention of Cruelty to Animals. Here she went and convinced the director that a child was an animal. The SPCA swore out a complaint and secured a conviction against the child's foster parents. As a result of the publicity accorded the Mary Ellen case, the SPCC came into being. This has nothing to do with delinquency, but it does indicate the attitude of the state toward the child in years past.

During the last half of the nineteenth century several other children's agencies came into being: children's aid societies, child welfare leagues, juvenile protective associations and others. All of these were organized primarily to protect and help children, not to control their behavior. And they were all private philanthropies, not state agencies.

At about the same time the first groping steps were being made in child psychology and studies of child behavior, but those who believed that the behavior of children, particularly children past puberty, was a subject for special study were considered radical. When Sigmund Freud wrote, as recently as 1925, "The child has become the main object of psychoanalytical research and in this respect has replaced the neurotic with whom the work began," he was saying something that would have been completely incomprehensible a few years earlier and which was still thought to be rather "far out" by most people. The child "expert" did not start to come into his own until after World War I, and it was in this era that state agencies—youth boards, social workers, etc.—first started to make their weight felt.

Several factors have a bearing on what constitutes wild kids: the age at which they are considered to be kids; the attitude of the society of which they are a part towards various aspects of youthful behavior; the extent to which the state interferes with or seeks to control such behavior. In a sense, trying to determine whether this is the wildest generation by comparing the behavior of today's youth with that of youngsters of yore is comparing oranges to apples. But the standards that we live by are the standards that we judge others by and the only valid judgment on youthful wildness is one that interprets wildness in terms of the rules by which today's youth are governed. In sixteenth-century Europe a fifteen-year-old thief was not regarded as a juvenile delinquent; at many times and in many places a thirteen-year-old prostitute was not considered reprehensible. Today, such are surely wild kids—and are so presented herein.

2

Young Savages

LIKE BEAUTY, EVIL IS OFTEN IN THE EYE
of the beholder, and this applies with great force to juvenile delinquency. Whether or not juvenile behavior is delinquent depends
largely upon the social code by which it is judged. In terms of the
Hebraic-Christian code which guides Western civilization, most
youngsters in primitive societies—and in many pagan cultures—
were very wild kids indeed, although their conduct was condoned
and approved by the societies of their times and places.

In general, primitive kids had a great deal more freedom than
modern youngsters and were not compelled to submit to adult
authority in all things. This was particularly true of boys. The
cliché "boys will be boys" was recognized as a fact of life by most
primitive peoples, and boys were allowed to develop naturally and
freely from childhood through adolescence to manhood. Reverence
and respect for elders was general practice in most cultures, but
not to the extent of curbing the child's every instinct and thwarting
its natural desires. If a young American Indian boy struck his
father, the parent's reaction would be one of pride rather than

condemnation; the youngster was showing a fine, independent spirit and would grow into a good brave.

Little stress was laid upon total filial obedience in most primitive cultures. Sociological and cultural anthropological studies of such varied peoples as tribes of Africa, natives of the Pacific islands, Indians of North and South America, aborigines of Australia and the Eskimos of the Arctic confirm this. In these societies punishment of children for what we would consider gross misconduct toward their parents was rare or non-existent; when complete submission to the adult will is not required—as it is not in most primitive societies—most occasions for punishment melt away. Many members of primitive societies, when exposed to Western disciplinary measures for children, come to the conclusion that European and American parents do not love their offspring.

Primitive peoples seemed to realize, perhaps better than civilized ones, that children were not naturally social animals, and had more patience in letting them become socialized as they matured. If a Polynesian boy took a "joy ride" in a village canoe, or an American Indian boy made unauthorized use of a horse, such acts were not considered theft. The child would probably be reproved by its father, or perhaps a village or tribal elder, but the child's action would be considered natural, not delinquent. And, in most cases, if an Indian boy stole a horse from another tribe, he would be praised rather than condemned.

The natural tendency of boys to form gangs and to fight with their peers was recognized in most primitive cultures and encouraged in many. Although fighting within the tribe, clan or village was frowned upon by most societies, if a gang of boys from one African tribe which met a gang of boys from another tribe did *not* have a bloody rumble they would have to answer to the chief when they got home. In some cases gang fights were encouraged even within the tribe. The parents of Maori boys in New Zealand, for instance, organized their offspring into two gangs to stage mock battles, using light reeds instead of spears as striking and thrusting weapons. When the contest got hot, the boys usually discarded these ineffective implements in favor of clubs and stones which were more damaging.

So far as major crime is concerned, the primitive juvenile seems to have had a better record than the modern youth. Of course, it must be remembered that acts against other tribes or villages were not usually considered as crimes. Murder, major theft, arson or vandalism *within* the tribe were so viewed, and studies of primitive peoples indicate that such crimes by juveniles were relatively rare and, when committed, were punished with more severity than in our culture. Murder has been a crime in every culture (always excepting the murder of an enemy), and juvenile murderers were punished as adults. A typical primitive response to such crime was described by the captain of a Coast Guard cutter which visited an Eskimo village and found a dead missionary. Three boys who were sent to his school had acted in their normal, undisciplined manner. To teach them the white man's more civilized ways the missionary had spanked them. The boys had never been spanked before and, to them, it was an intolerable insult, so they got harpoons and killed him. The Coastguardsmen were shown three graves. Two of the youthful murderers had been stoned to death by the tribe. The third had been treated more leniently. He was permitted to dig his own grave and lie down in it. Then he was shot.

In most cultures boys started to feel their oats when they were little past infancy and became progressively more free from adult supervision and control. A study of the Zuñi Indians of New Mexico states: "There is an early period in the life of the child, especially of the small boy, that is marked by great freedom. Small boys of four or five roam the countryside on horseback." A similar report on the Iroquois says that "boys between the ages of eight and eleven wandered in the forest for days at a time, sleeping in the open, eating wild roots and fruits and the small animals that they could snare or shoot with their blow guns."

In many societies boys left home at an early age, sometimes as young as seven. In some tribes they stayed with relatives to get away from parental supervision. More frequently, by the time boys reached puberty, they had huts or club houses of their own in which they lived as they saw fit without much supervision. They usually had communal duties to perform: tending goats, cattle or horses; helping to fish or hunt; learning to fight. They were expected to respect the taboos of their tribe and were considered delinquent when they violated them, but in the main they were wild, outlaw gangs by the standards of modern civilization.

Most primitive peoples seem to have recognized adolescence, particularly male adolescence, as a distinct stage of development. Centuries before Western civilization started to understand that teen-agers were neither children nor adults, less civilized peoples were not binding them to the disciplines of childhood or expecting them to conform to the codes of adults. They accepted the adolescent for what he was, a creature in a formative stage who was feeling the urges and instincts of manhood without the experience to control them. Except as the welfare of the tribe required it, or in connection with the taboos and other religious superstitions, they did not seek to make the juvenile behave like a grown-up. At some time in their formative years boys were usually initiated, frequently by stages, into various adult social activities and customs, and from that point on, they were expected to act their age. Then, as now, they usually grew up to be responsible members of the society of which they were a part, but without going through a period of juvenile delinquency, because most things that juveniles had an urge to do as a natural part of growing up were not considered delinquent.

As regards social control of behavior, the primitive girl lived by rules that were closer to those that control her civilized sister. Her right to freedom was not so widely recognized as that of boys, principally because most societies did not recognize the right of females of any age to freedom. Nevertheless, in some cultures girls had their own means of combating parental control. Among many African tribes, for instance, girls usually became unmanageable when they reached puberty. They defied their mothers, refused to do housework, stayed away from home. To any threat of punishment the defiant miss replied: "If you hit me, I'll elope." This was a potent weapon against parents, because the girl had reached an age when she might soon be traded in marriage for from eight to thirty cattle. If she eloped, the parents got no cattle.

THE PRINCIPAL DIFFERENCE BETWEEN PRIMitive girls and modern girls has to do with sex relations. In some cultures all girls were, by our standards, sex delinquents. Among other peoples great efforts were made to keep girls chaste until marriage, to the extent of confining them in huts after they reached puberty or, in extreme cases, in cages. Most primitive peoples placed some value on virginity; at least, the girls' parents did. The basis of this was usually economic rather than moral. The girl was a piece of merchandise who would bring a "bride price" in whatever goods, commodities or monetary symbols the tribe valued. Because there was no difference between the primitive and the civilized male ego, the virgin bride commanded a better price. However, the girl got no part of the bride price and had no incentive to accept the adult code.

In many cultures there were taboos against premarital sex for girls, and for boys within the tribe. Virtually no primitive people saw anything wrong in a boy having sex relations outside the tribe or village. In some cultures the girls were impressed with the great shame they would bring on their families and relatives by sexual misconduct. In other cases chastity was required only of girls who would become the mates of chiefs. And in still others the matter was of concern only to the girls' parents; the society had no rules.

Regardless of taboos, shame, or paternal disapproval, the young savages (even as civilized youth) had their own, different ideas about sex. A more or less typical situation among many primitive peoples is described in this excerpt from a study of the Ojibwa Indians of Canada: "There is a double standard of morals concerning premarital chastity. Boys are allowed complete freedom, but girls are supposed to be chaste. However, a single standard obtains, for the girls are not supervised, except for rare instances, and then not always effectively. During the summer, the children play together in mixed groups, and part of their play is the imitation of the intimate behavior of adults. Girls are supposed to be passive, and boys are supposed to pursue them. The game of love is a tremendously important preoccupation. . . . At the time of her first menstruation, a girl is reminded that she must be chaste. However, the childhood habits, and the insistence of boys and men, nullify caution, and almost every girl bears one or more illegitimate children."

Premarital chastity was considered desirable by most tribes of American Indians and in some cases loss of virginity was severely punished, wantonness sometimes by death. Yet the Indian virgin of twenty must have been rare because such a feat was the subject for tribal celebration among some groups of redskins. A sociological study of the Dakotas, after stating that a girl could secure prestige by unusual proficiency in beadwork, comments: "The other way in which a woman achieved prestige was by being chaste before marriage and faithful after. The feast of the Virgin Fire would be given by a family in honor of a girl in her early twenties who was pretty and had been courted a good deal and yet had chosen to remain single and chaste. A feast was given in her honor to the whole encampment by her family group. All the other virgins who could so qualify were honored guests, and presents were given them. This was not a religious occasion; it was a happy party to celebrate the individual prestige of a girl and it was made important by the giveaway of property. It was incumbent on any man to tell on any girl who tried to join the honored group if she was there falsely, and he would literally drag such a girl away."

Regardless of their views on chastity after puberty, most primitive societies saw nothing delinquent about sex play among small children. Savage kids learned all of the facts of life very early, not by either formal or gutter sex instruction, but by personal observation. There was little privacy in primitive society. A one-room hut or other structure housed all of the members of a family, sometimes of several generations of a family. Small children could witness everything that went on in the house, including the intimate relations of their parents or of big brother and his wife. If was quite natural that small fry would imitate such acts in their play, just as today's little girls imitate "mommy" dressing up for a party or experiment with her cosmetics. Again, the primitives considered this natural, not delinquent.

In cultures where there was a taboo against sex relations between unmarried adolescents of the same group, girl-hunting outside the tribe or village was a favorite sport of teen-aged boys. Singly or in pairs, they sought to waylay a careless maiden who had strayed from the protection of her own group, sometimes merely to rape her, sometimes to carry her off for later pleasure. A study of the Manuans of the Admiralty Islands tells that adolescent boys "are permitted no role in relation to the women of the community, but are allowed to raid enemy communities to obtain a prostitute. The man who actually captures her can exact fees from the others, but she is essentially a group prostitute. The young unmarried men of a community are united by the common possession of a captured woman, whom they share. She forms a bond of interest among them all, and she is vigorously hated by all the women in the community, from whom she has to be constantly guarded lest they succeed in killing her."

Girl-capturing was a widespread custom among many primitive peoples. Originally, before the practice of purchasing a wife became common, this was the approved way to get one. Many savage peoples had stricter rules on incest than modern civilization, and taboos which prohibited a man mating with any woman in his own tribe or clan. It gave a boy status to drag a girl home from another tribe; she was a prize trophy. Such juvenile kidnapping was not delinquency, it was part of the mores of the primitive culture. History's greatest girl-snatching seems to have been done by the Benjamites. The Old Testament tells of the men of the tribe of Benjamin capturing 400 virgins from Jabesh-gilead and later going to Bethel to "lie in wait in the vineyards" to capture the daughters of Shiloh when they came out to dance.

Selling the girls for prostitution was another common practice among many primitive peoples. In a study of the Papuans the researcher writes: "It is very often the case that the best of the young girls are sold by their parents as courtesans, the native name being *jelibo*. I came across men married and possessing in addition these girls. Young fellows, not having reached puberty, had clubbed together in parties of three or four and had bought young girls from their parents to make courtesans. At feasts these girls are used for the purpose of enriching themselves and their owners."

The custom of girls serving willingly in the club houses of boys of another tribe was widespread in some cultures. In some tribes where an exchange of goods was part of the marriage custom, girls served as prostitutes in the boys' house to earn their shares of the marriage portion. In the Palau Islands such girls were called *armengols*. An *armengol* went to another island and worked as a combination domestic servant and sex companion as part of her education, thus learning to know men and how to influence them. A Palau woman argued with one sociologist that this was a good custom: it gave the girl a chance to see other islands and taught her how to serve and obey men. She added that any girl who did not go abroad as an *armengol* would not be performing her duty, would get the reputation of being stupid and uncultivated, and would get no husband.

The Nyansongo of Kenya, Africa, are one tribe that has strict laws prohibiting marriage within the clan. The men must buy wives from outside the immediate social group. Here sex play among small children is a normal activity, and this period lasts until the girls are circumsized, usually at age eight or nine. After the child is so initiated she is secluded in a hut for a month with a bevy of older friends who have already been initiated. This is supposed to be an all-female activity, but the boys have a part in it with the connivance of the girls, who perform nude dances with phallic symbols at which the boys peek. The principal part played by the boys is called "taking by stealth," in which the youngsters sneak into the hut after dark and have intercourse with the hand-maidens of the new initiate.

When the newly initiated girl returns to her job of minding cattle with other children, she has a problem. Under her new status she may not continue the sex play of her earlier days with uncircumsized boys. Boys are not initiated until about the age of twelve, and ten-year-old boys are resentful that a younger girl will not continue the accustomed play of earlier days with them. If an uninitiated boy tries to coerce an initiated girl she runs home screaming and the boy is punished. This seems to be the only taboo on juvenile sex relations.

After the boy is circumsized, there are no restrictions, and male juveniles between the ages of twelve and eighteen spend much time seducing female juveniles between the ages of ten and fifteen. Frequently the girl is willing; if she is not, the boys pal up in raping her. A sociologist studying this tribe made the flat statement, "All girls have sex before marriage. They are very difficult to control after initiation." Before marriage means before the age of sixteen. Girls are usually bought by a boy from another tribe by the time they are fifteen. Boys, by the age of eighteen, borrow cattle from a relative to acquire a mate.

Incredible as all this seems in terms of our culture, it is not a figment of a dark past. Such sexual freedom is still part of the mores of many African tribes, except that some modern teen-agers now leave the compound and go to the metropolis to become prostitutes. As recently as 1962 the East African Institute of Social Research issued a report titled "Juvenile Prostitutes in Nairobi." Of fifty-five prostitutes of all ages studied, thirty-nine had started their careers at age sixteen or younger. Three started at age ten and thirteen was the age most frequently given. The research team described the juvenile prostitutes as follows:

"Our study in Nairobi has confirmed the existence of certain types of juvenile prostitutes, and these we might classify as follows: (i) the schoolgirl catering for schoolboys. In this group girls as young as nine, ten or eleven may be found, who will hire themselves out to schoolboys for from 10-50 cents, a coloured handkerchief, or any other kind of gift; (ii) the virtually inexperienced girl, fresh from the Reserve, who becomes a short-term concubine but does not make a charge for her services other than food and shelter; (iii) dull, dirty and unintelligent girls ranging from thirteen upwards, who will agree to any kind of arrangement whereby they receive either cash or food or drink or food and shelter for long or short periods in return for their services. They will accept African youths or adults, charge from 2/- to 5/- if they can get cash, but do not cater for other races [i.e., other than their own race]; (iv) the good-time girl who may be at school or may have left school and who uses men not only to earn cash or kind but also in order to have 'fun,' charging up to 10/- plus drinks, etc.; (v) the hardest, most unapproachable and most successful girl is one who will invest a good deal of her earnings in fashionable underwear and smart top clothing and who concentrates entirely on European soldiers and civilians and the wealthier Asians. She charges from 5/-

to 30/- and quite often has a good account at the Bank."

Such formal prostitution is now considered by most contemporary Africans as juvenile delinquency. The tribal society does not endorse it, nor do most parents, if they have any control over the child. The greatest stigma that attaches to the juvenile prostitute is reserved for girls in the fifth class above—the African girls who sink so low that they sell themselves to non-Africans.

The African Institute report summed up the juvenile sexual mores by saying: "According to some very experienced medical officers, it is doubtful if any African girl over the age of nine would be a virgin, partly because, according to some observers, African children freely imitate sexual intercourse as they have observed it among adults and partly because it appears to be quite common for adult males to rape or seduce girls at a very early age. . . . In the very crowded conditions in which many of the girls grow up in the African locations it is inevitable that they will observe the sexual behavior of their parents and other adults and will also, according to our field workers, be subject to considerable experimentation by brothers and others. It would therefore be reasonable to say that an adolescent African girl, whether a prostitute or not, will be thoroughly familiar with and experienced in, sexual activities." They might have added another reason why African girls lose their virginity at such an early age. Many Africans believe that having intercourse with a virgin is a cure for venereal disease.

THE PRIMITIVE JUVENILE SEXPOTS WHO have achieved most fame in modern story and legend are South Sea Island maidens. Many of these Polynesian girls are beautiful by Western standards, and under the sexual mores of their tribes they can freely become delightful companions for white visitors. In fact, under their code, to refuse their favors to a guest would be inhospitable. One of the first accounts of the habits of female teen-agers in this area was written 150 years ago by Captain David Porter of the U. S. Navy. Porter described the Marquesas maidens by writing:

"The girls, from twelve to eighteen years of age, rove at will; this period of their lives is a period of unbounded pleasure, unrestrained in all their actions, unconfirmed by domestic occupations, their time is spent in dancing, singing and ornamenting their persons, to render themselves more attractive in the eyes of man, on whom they indiscriminately bestow their favors, unrestrained by shame or fear of the consequences.

"Virtue among them, in the light in which we view it, was unknown and they attached no shame to a proceeding which they not only considered as natural, but as an innocent and harmless amusement by which no one was injured. Many parents considered themselves as honored by the preference given to their daughters, and testified their pleasure by large presents of hogs and fruit.

"With the young and timid virgins no coercive measures were used by their parents to compel them to make sacrifices, but endearing and soothing persuasions, enforced by rewards, were frequently adopted to overcome their fears.

"With the sailors and their girls all was helter-skelter, every girl the wife of every man in the mess, and frequently of every man in the ship; each one from time to time took such as suited his fancy and convenience, and no one among them formed a connection which was likely to provoke tears at the moment of separation. With the officers the case was different. The connections formed were respectable and, although their fair friends delighted in playing, on every occasion, little tricks of infidelity which they considered as perfectly harmless, still they showed a fondness for the person with whom they were connected and the parting, in several instances I am sure, occasioned tears of real sorrow.

"I must, however, do them justice to say that in practicing the little infidelities above mentioned, they did not appear sensible to doing an injustice to their lover; they were done as acts of retaliation on some of their female acquaintances. They were always flattered by a preference given them, and this preference, enforced by the powerful charm of a whale's tooth, could at all times purchase the favors of the best of them."

That the culture of the South Seas had not changed much in over a century is attested by a study of the Samoans made by Dr. Margaret Mead in 1925. Dr. Mead lived with the tribes on the Samoa Islands solely to study the habits of adolescent and preadolescent children.

Young Samoan children have little adult supervision. Fathers and mothers both fish and work in the fields, babies are guarded by the next oldest girl in the family group, usually a child of six or seven; and the nurse is in turn supervised by an older child, a female relative of any degree. Here the children are more disciplined than in many primitive cultures; the young guardians are not so indulgent as most primitive parents. The children have to conform to a code of behavior that is, perhaps, initially determined by adults but is enforced by a youngster of a slightly older age group. No Samoan mother will ever exert herself to discipline a younger child if an older one can be made responsible.

Unlike many tribes in which sex play among young children is a normal activity, Samoan custom decrees that, from about the age of seven until they pass puberty, youngsters must play and travel in groups of their own sex. At about thirteen or fourteen this starts to break down and the boys and girls mingle very much as ours do at this age; boys are embarrassed or tactiturn in the presence of girls, while girls blush and giggle in the presence of boys. About a year later all of this changes and from that point the relation of the sexes among adolescents is vastly different from that in Western culture. Except for a girl who is to be a *taupo*—the mate of a chief, who must be a virgin—practically all Samoan teen-agers have sexual experience. The regular practice is a night meeting "under the palm trees" with a companion of the same age group.

The clandestine sex relationships of the youngsters are arranged on an almost ritualistic basis. A boy never asks a girl for a date directly. He sends one or more *soas* to sell the young lady on an assignation. The *soa* is a close friend or relative who acts as an ambassador. Unless he has a thoroughly trustworthy friend, a boy has a problem in picking his *soas*. If he selects an inexperienced, inarticulate one, the ambassador may bungle the whole affair. On the other hand if he chooses a fluent, compelling, handsome intermediary, the *soa* may double-cross him and date the girl himself; or the girl may say, in effect, "Why don't you speak for yourself, John?" One boy who badly wanted a particular girl reported that he sent five *soas* to convince her, and four of them got the girl before he did.

There may be *soas* from several different boys working on the same girl at the same time, and she may accept dates at different times on the same night with two or more boys. By the same token, a boy may have *soas* working on several girls at the same time. Samoan parents do not have to worry about their youngsters "going steady." Most of these assignations are short-term or one-time affairs.

Sometimes three or four couples meet under the palms as a group, if either the boys or the girls are relatives, and in such cases they frequently change partners. The girls are not afraid of becoming pregnant, because Samoans think that promiscuity results in barrenness and that only persistent fidelity leads to conception. Says Dr. Mead: "Native sophistication distinguishes between the adept lover whose adventures are many and of short duration and the less skilled man who can find no better proof of his virility than a long affair ending in conception."

Some girls are too timid to have affairs under the palms, where, they believe, ghosts lurk that can do all kinds of horrible things to a maiden. In such cases the young lover must sneak into the girl's house after greasing his body with cocoanut oil to make capture more difficult. Since there are perhaps fifteen other people sleeping in the house, plus several dogs, absolute silence is essential in the lovemaking of such couples. This creates an opportunity for the only type of sex deviant that the Samoans recognize: the *moetolo,* or sleep crawler.

The *moetolo* may be a boy who is too timid to get a date or wants a particular girl who rebuffs him. Sometimes the *moetolo* is a very accomplished lover, able to get girls in the normal way, but prefers the excitement and adventure of sleep crawling. Or he may be a boy who, after waiting in the ghost-haunted grove all night for a girl, seeks revenge by attempting a *moetolo,* particularly if he learns that the girl met some other boy while he was waiting. The *moetolo* operates by sneaking into the home of a girl with whom he does not have a date and silently having intercourse with her. He banks on one of two situations for success: either the girl will be expecting a boy and, in the dark, will accept him as her expected lover, or this particular girl will acquiesce to any boy. If he guesses wrong and the girl raises an outcry, the whole household will arise and give chase. Pursuing a *moetolo* is fine sport, particularly for the women, who resent such surreptitious lovemaking. If caught, he is beaten and loses face in the village. No girl will ever date a known *moetolo* and, after he has been caught and beaten several times, a *moetolo* may become a homosexual. The practice of sleep crawling gives the girl who dates in her own home a convenient "out" if her expected lover arouses somebody in the household. The girl can save herself from being caught in an affair by screaming *"moetolo"* after giving her boy friend a few seconds' head start.

Since the missionaries arrived about a century ago, the Christian Samoans have learned that these good people put a moral premium on chastity (which the natives regard with reverence—and skepticism). Writes Dr. Mead: "The concept of celibacy is absolutely meaningless to them. But virginity definitely adds to a girl's attractiveness, the wooing of a virgin is considered far more of a feat than the conquest of a more experienced heart, and a really successful Don Juan turns most of his attention to their seduction."

None of this teen-age promiscuity is permitted a *taupo*. The *taupo* is usually the daughter of a chief, and must be beautiful and unblemished. She is destined to marry a chief in a ceremony that will have great economic and political importance by uniting the two families. "Virginity is a legal requirement for her," writes Dr. Mead. "At her marriage, in front of all the people, in a house brilliantly lit, the talking chief of the bridegroom will take the tokens of her virginity. In former days should she prove not to be a virgin, her female relatives fell upon and beat her with stones, disfiguring and sometimes fatally injuring the girl who had shamed their house."

Samoan juvenile sex customs have been somewhat modified by Western influence since Dr. Mead made her study, principally because of the influence of the white man during and after World War II. Christian missionaries have been in Samoa since the middle of the last century, and much of the territory has been a United States' dependency since 1899. At the time of Dr. Mead's study there was a large missionary school at Pago Pago and smaller preparatory schools at pastors' houses on the other islands. Christianity, by 1925, had made strides in introducing Western culture to the natives, but not in altering juvenile sex mores. Chastity was a condition of church membership, but pastors did not encourage young people to join the church until they married—except for residents who could be supervised in the missionary school.

When the Samoan juvenile sex delinquents (by our standards) reach the late teens or early twenties, they usually marry and live happily ever after. Sexual fidelity after marriage is possibly as high as in Western civilization, although adultery is not considered a heinous crime. Divorce is simple: if partners disagree, the woman merely goes back to her family and both partners are free to remarry. This system is possible only because children are a part of the large family group, not the exclusive property and responsibility of parents. A child who finds life with its parents uncongenial may go to live with an uncle, a grandfather, a brother-in-law. The relative gives it shelter and provides for it as a matter of course, and the parents cannot, by custom, compel it to return. Although divorce is merely a matter of decision, from the standpoint of the children there are no broken homes in Samoa.

Growing up is easy in Samoa. There is less conflict where no effort is made to force youngsters into a submissive role demanded by parents. Disagreements between parent and child are settled by the child moving across the street. Says Dr. Mead: "The close relationship between parent and child, which has such a decisive influence upon so many in our civilization that submission to the parent or defiance of the parent may become the dominating pattern of a lifetime, is not found in Samoa."

The juvenile sex mores that we would find appalling results in a complete lack of neuroses among the Samoans. "Sex is a natural, pleasurable thing; the freedom with which it may be indulged in is limited by just one consideration, social status. . . . Every one in the community agrees about the matter, the only dissenters are the missionaries, who dissent so vainly that their protests are unimportant. . . . The Samoan girl who shrugs her shoulder over the excellent technique of some young Lothario is nearer to the recognition of sex as an impersonal force without any intrinsic validity, than is the sheltered American girl who falls in love with the first man who kisses her. From their familiarity with the reverberations which accompany sex excitement comes this recognition of the essential impersonality of sex attraction which we may well envy them."

A study similar to that by Dr. Mead among the Samoans was one undertaken among the natives of the Trobriand Islands in Melanesia by Bronislaw Malinowski. The culture of these primitive people is matrilineal, a social order in which kinship is reckoned through the mother only, and succession and inheritance descend in the female line. After the act of fertilization, the Melanesian father is something of an innocent bystander in his relationship with his children, or, more properly, an older companion and playmate. The true head of the household in terms of economics and child discipline is the mother's eldest brother.

At the age of about seven, Melanesian children start to form a small juvenile community within the community. They roam about in bands and play on distant beaches or in secluded parts of the jungle, almost completely independent of adult authority. Their parents never try to keep them from going or interfere in any way, or bind them to any routine, and the child gradually drifts away from the family except for a rather casual contact. Malinowski comments on the lack of tensions in the child under "the Melanesian state of affairs where the process of emancipation is gradual, free and pleasant."

The Melanesians have a strict taboo against any social relationships between brother and sister. From the early age when the girl dons her first grass skirt, she must stay completely apart from her brother. They play in separate groups and, later, must never consort in any social activity. Above all, there must not be the slightest interest on the part of brother or sister in the sex life of the sibling. This is the only juvenile sex taboo in the islands.

From the time that they set up their unofficial juvenile republic until they reach puberty, sex play is one of the main interests of Melanesian youngsters. Their games frequently involve an imaginative re-creation of a real-life situation in which sex plays a part; their interest is in apeing adult life rather than in pure sensuality. When two eight- or ten-year-olds play house, they build a shelter, have a real or fancied meal and a conversation between the make-believe mommy and daddy, even as our youngsters. The Melanesian kids then go to bed together. In a more elaborate game a group may seriously mimic a ceremonial tribal trading or commercial exchange, ending up with sexual activities. Melanesian parents accept completely this aspect of their children's lives. They see nothing immoral or delinquent in it. Sex is a part of life, like eating, drinking or sleeping. A Melanesian mother might worry if her child did not give vent to its natural interest in sex. Such a child would be, to her, acting unnaturally.

After the youngsters pass puberty, sex play becomes more serious. In keeping with the brother-sister taboo, the boys leave home except to eat and perform some work. They move into a *bukumatula,* a bachelors' house, usually owned by an older unmarried boy or a young widower, where from four to seven boys live as a group, each with a sweetheart. This assures that they will be completely apart from their sisters during their sexual pursuits. The girls who share the *bukumatula* usually work at home part of the day, then do their chores at the bachelors' house and return home to sleep after the evening's lovemaking. Extensive promiscuity is more rare among the Melanesians than the Samoans or Marquesans. The relationships of these adolescents might be compared to "going steady" in our society, except for the complete sexual freedom.

An interesting account of what the Melanesians consider extreme juvenile delinquency is the legend that tells how the *sulumwoya* (mint) leaf came to have magical properties as a love potion. A woman in the village of Kumilabwaga had a son and a daughter. One day, to gain the love of a certain girl, the boy undertook to make a love potion of herbs. He crushed the *sulumwoya* leaves in clarified cocoanut oil, boiled the mixture, and recited a spell over it. He then placed it in a receptacle of banana leaves, secreted it in the thatch of their home, and went to bathe.

His sister, while going to the water hole to fill the cocoanut bottles, brushed against the thatch and some of the oil got on her hair. Upon her return from the water hole she asked her mother, "Where is the man. Where is my brother?" The mother was aghast. For the girl to inquire about her brother or speak of him as a man was truly delinquency. The mother sighed to herself, "My children have gone mad."

The girl, under the spell of the love potion, ran to the beach where her brother was bathing, dropped her grass skirt, and tried to join him. In an effort to escape his sister, the boy ran back and forth on the beach, which was confined with precipitous cliffs, until he was exhausted and fell into the shallow waves. Here his sister caught him and they made love. Their shame and remorse were so great that they went to the grotto of Bokaraywata where they remained without food or drink until they died wrapped in each other's arms. Through their linked bodies grew the *sulumwoya* plant. Since that distant day the grotto of Bokaraywata has been a love shrine, consecrated by their great sin of incestuous love, and the sweet-smelling native mint leaf has become a potent ingredient for love potions.

IN MANY OTHER EARLY PRIMITIVE AND PA-gan cultures, juvenile sex was part of religious practice. Most pagan religions had a deity of fertility or reproduction who must be placated to assure the food supply. Originally such gods were wooed by human sacrifice, particularly the sacrifice of babies or virgin maidens. As time passed, sacral harlotry was substituted for human sacrifice; a girl gave herself to the priests or to male worshippers as an offering to the god.

Yale's Professor of Social Science, William Graham Sumner, cited one instance: "Cases occur in barbarism of women consecrated to the gods. Among the Ewe-speaking peoples of West Africa girls of ten or twelve are received and educated for three years in the chants and dances of worship, serving the priests. At the end of the time they become public women, but are under no reproach, because they are regarded as married to the god and acting under his direction. Properly they should be restricted to the worshippers at the temple, but they are not. Probably such was the original taboo which is now relaxed and decayed. . . . The institution is essentially religious in its origin and is intimately connected with phallic worship." He adds, in connection with many pagan cultures, "Sacral harlotry was the only harlotry. It was normal and was not a subject of ethical misgivings. It was a part of the religious and social system. When, later, prostitution became an independent social fact and was adjudged bad, sacral harlotry long continued under the conventionalization and persistence of religious usage. . . . Sacral harlotry, while it lasted, was practiced for one of two purposes—to collect a dowry for the women or to collect money for the temple."

Temple prostitutes were part of most religions in the area around the Mediterranean at the time that Judaism was taking form. It was a social rule that a girl of Babylon, as a sacred duty to Ishtar, go to the temple and offer herself at least once to any stranger visiting the goddess' temple. The historian Herodotus described the grove or park in which this sacrifice took place. Once inside this area no girl could leave until she had found a paying lover and deposited the fee on the altar of the goddess. Some plain girls, said Herodotus, stayed there as long as three years but, since the grounds were always full of eager males in search of pleasure, "the young, the beautiful and the high-born seldom needed to remain more than a few minutes."

In Egypt the most beautiful girls of the noble families of Thebes gained honor and profit as temple courtesans. This was part of a general laxity of moral principles especially, according to Athenaeus, "among young females." In the worship of Anaitis in Armenia, men of rank consecrated their daughters to the goddess. The girls were provided for by their families and had intercourse only with their social equals. In the worship of Ishtar in the Assyra-Babylonian pantheon, there were three grades of temple prostitutes in the sacred prostitution which was a part of her cult. In Phoenicia, at Carthage, and in Syria, she became Ashtart or Astarte, and Aphrodite to the Greeks, with similar voluptuous rites at which maidens prostituted themselves. Originally the sums collected were paid to the priests as offerings to the goddess for upkeep of her temple, but later the girls kept their fees, or part of them, to build a dowry. Among the Persians tales are told of festivals centering around the god Mithra, in which fathers and sons, mothers and daughters, inflamed by wine, lascivious dancing and music, embarked on all-night sex orgies.

Temple or sacred prostitution among the Israelites was a recurrent phase of backsliding against which Moses and some of the prophets raged. To them the *kedeshim,* male and female prostitutes mentioned in the Old Testament, were an "abomination to the Lord." Certain rites of the worship of Moloch and Baal involved temple prostitutes. Apparently the morals of the Hebrews had been corrupted by their stay in Egypt, for Moses commanded: "Do not prostitute thy daughter, lest the land fall to whoredom. . . . There shall be no whore among the daughters of Israel."

The pagan misses who practiced sacral harlotry were, of course, not delinquents, except in the eyes of the Hebrews. Rather they were performing a sacred duty. Under the Hebrew moral code that was adopted subsequently by the Christians, what had been sacred became sinful.

By modern standards, primitive kids were far wilder in most respects than the youth of today. They were disobedient; they roamed away from parental supervision; they "disturbed the peace"; they formed gangs which fought and annoyed the neighborhood; they made unauthorized use of the property of others; and their sexual behavior brings shudders of horror to modern moralists. But, by the standards of their society, they were behaving properly.

Something might be said for some aspects of primitive codes under which children were not required to be submissive to adults in all things and in which their innate right to rebel was recognized. Generally, primitive youngsters grew up to be responsible adult members of the clan, tribe, or village and were perhaps better able to cope with the pressures of their society than are many of their civilized descendants.

3

Greek and Roman Delinquents

THE POET AULUS PERSIUS FLACCUS CASTI-
gated Roman scholars as juvenile delinquents during the reign of
Nero. He bewailed the passing of the "good old days" of the Roman
republic and the slothful, sinful habits of youth that were part of
a "wave of juvenile delinquency" under the Roman Emperors, in
these words:

> I know thee to thy bottom; from within
> Thy shallow center to thy outmost skin;
> Dost thou not blush to live so like a beast,
> So trim, so dissolute, so loosely drest?
> But 'tis in vain: the wretch is drenched too deep;
> His soul is stupid and his heart asleep
> Fatten'd in vice; so callous and so gross,
> He sins and sees not, senseless of his loss.
> Down goes the wretch at once, unskilled to swim,
> Hopeless to bubble up and reach the water's brim.

It should be noted that the poet commented unfavorably on the
dress of youth, which, even as today, did not conform to an adult

concept, and warned them, again as today, that they would never amount to anything if they became dropouts "unskilled to swim."

This is one of very few references to any form of juvenile delinquency except sexual misbehavior in ancient Greece and Rome. The philosophers, poets and dramatists of the day had little to say, good or bad, about children; in all of Homer's writing, a child is mentioned only once. We can only assume how they acted in most things from what historians have recorded of the way they were brought up.

In the Greece of city-states, customs relating to children differed radically in the two principal seats of power, Sparta and Athens. In the former a child was, in effect, the property of the state and was raised for the benefit that it might bring to the state. When a baby was born, public authorities decided whether it should be allowed to live. Any infant that was blemished or deformed was thrown over a precipice or exposed on a mountain; the Spartans reasoned that a less than perfect baby boy would not grow up to be a capable warrior, and that a puny baby girl was not a good prospect for producing warriors in later life.

Spartan boys remained with their parents until the age of seven. From that age until they were eighteen they lived in the Grecian equivalent of a Marine Corps boot camp where, under the strictest discipline, their entire education was physical. The little ones were trained in gymnastics, sports and dancing. Emphasis was placed on toughening them; they slept on pallets of straw without covering and wore little clothing and no shoes summer or winter. They were allowed to steal food to augment their rough diet, but if they were caught they were considered disgraced and severely flogged. The delinquency here was not the stealing, but getting caught.

When they reached their teens boxing and wrestling were their principal interests and they were encouraged to do anything to win. The clean sport that we now call Olympic wrestling was unknown in Sparta. Their boys kicked, scratched, bit and gouged.

In their mid-teens the boys were organized into two companies and taken, once a year, to an island near Sparta where they had a grand gang fight without weapons other than their fists, feet and teeth. At the age of eighteen they went into the army.

Spartan youths were not encouraged to learn to read and write, and their only lessons in ethics and moral conduct came from listening to their adult masters at meals. It would seem that, in a life such as this, they would have little opportunity to be delinquent, except as they were encouraged to be what we now call delinquent as a part of their training as warriors. Here was a class of juveniles who were completely molded to the adult will. One historian wrote: "The state regulated the individual life, and by so doing, crushed out individuality, personal initiative, literary and scientific activity, and ethical freedom."

Spartan girls were better off than most ancient females: they were reared and respected as future mothers. Although they lived at home, their training was similar to that of boys, except for the fighting. Girls were required to perform publicly in the nude in gymnastics and athletic competitions. There was nothing lascivious about this; the body beautiful was something to be admired because it would produce better warriors for the state. Athenaeus wrote: "The Spartan custom of stripping young girls before strangers is highly praised. And on the island of Chios it is very pleasant just to walk to the gymnasia and running tracks and watch the young men wrestling with the girls." One historian claims that "this coming in contact with the males, the great freedom allowed them, and the vigorous training did not spoil the purity of the girls, for adultery was scarcely known in Sparta." Wrestling naked must have given some ideas to teen-aged boys and girls, but if they had desires they seem to have had little opportunity to act on them.

THE TREATMENT AND TRAINING OF CHILdren in Athens was more typical of the other Greek city-states.

Here youngsters were the responsibility of their parents rather than the state. Most Athenians do not seem to have had a very high regard for children. Infanticide, which was fairly common, was at the discretion of the father, and many Athenian fathers who wanted both tranquility and progeny felt that it would be a lot less expensive and troublesome to adopt a boy after his education was completed than to raise one. A Greek proverb says: "Nothing more foolish than to have children," and the philosopher Democritus wrote: "To raise children is an uncertain thing. Success is attained only after a life of battle and disquietude"; a sentiment that might be echoed by many modern parents.

In Athens, boys and girls were kept separate after infancy. Boys lived at home and were sent to school at the age of seven, always accompanied by a male slave who had charge of his manners and morals and had the power to discipline him. This close supervision lasted so long as he remained in school, which might be until he was eighteen. His education was intellectual as well as physical to make him a well-rounded citizen of a state that had regard for the letters and the arts as well as warfare. The boy left for school at daybreak and did not return until sunset. During the day he was under the eyes of teachers who were stern taskmasters not given to sparing the strap or the rod. At other times he was supervised by the slave, who was called a *pedagogue*, although he did no teaching. In such a situation the boy's opportunities for delinquency would seem to be limited except on the frequent holidays and festivals that were part of the Athenian calendar. At the age of eighteen he, like his Spartan counterpart, went into the Army.

The Athenian girl lived a miserable life. Except in Sparta Greek wives and daughters were but a short step above slaves. A wife's duty was to run the house. She did not accompany her husband on any social occasion, was expected to stay off the streets as much as possible, and did not even eat with her husband if he had guests. The Athenian girl was reared for such a life. She lived in her mother's apartments in the back of the house and learned nothing but domestic activities. Wrote one social historian: "The maidens lived in the greatest seclusion till their marriage and, so to speak, regularly under lock and key which had the effect of rendering the girl excessively bashful and even prudish, and so stupid, in all probability, that it is no wonder the men considered marriage a punishment." The girl seldom, if ever, left the back part of her father's house until, at the age of fifteen or shortly thereafter, she was handed over to a husband whom she had probably never seen as a part of a contract that had commercial or political significance. She then spent the rest of her teens—and the balance of her life— in the rear portion of her husband's house. There was little opportunity for juvenile delinquency here.

All of this applies to the offspring of citizens of the Greek city-states. There were, in addition, freemen who were not citizens, and slaves. Nothing is known of the behavior of their kids. Most of the freemen were farmers whose children never saw the city. Juvenile slaves were punished for delinquency with the same extreme brutality that was meted out to adult slaves. A twelve-year-old slave girl who stole her mistress's comb might be flogged, maimed, or sold to a brothel. She could, at her master's discretion, be killed, although this would represent a financial loss to the owner.

Greek writers frequently recorded instances of what would today be regarded as sex delinquency, juvenile and otherwise. Herodotus said of Heracles that he deflowered fifty daughters of Thestius in five days. Hermippus tells of the practice in Lacedaemon of shutting young girls up in a dark room with young men, "and each man led home, as his bride without dower, whichever girl he laid hold of." The poet Eubulus deplored the conduct of youths who had affairs with married women, saying, "Dreadful, dreadful, and utterly intolerable are the practices of the young men of our city. For here there are very pretty lasses in the brothels whom the boys may see basking in the sun, their breasts uncovered, stripped for action and posted in battle-line." Euripides summed up the Greek attitude toward juvenile sex by writing: "Love! I warn the young never to shun it, but enjoy it rightly whensoever it shall come."

Prostitution was a favorite theme of Greek dramatists, and the subject of much comment by philosophers and historians. The first brothels of which there is exact knowledge were the *dicteria* established in Athens under the famed laws of Solon, whom Philemon praised by writing: "You found a law for the use of all men, for you, they say, Solon, were the first to see this—a thing democratic, Zeus is my witness, and salutary; seeing our city full of young men, seeing, too, that they were under the compulsion of nature, and that they went in their erring ways in a direction that they should not, purchased and stationed women in various quarters, equipped and ready for all alike."

These *dicteria* under Solon's law were owned by the state, which derived a substantial revenue from them, and peopled by girls purchased by the state, either slave girls or freeborn youngsters who were sold to the state by their parents. The *dicteria* maintained schools which girls entered in their early or middle teens to be trained in the practice of their craft by more experienced harlots. The dramatist Alexis wrote an amusing description of how girls were prepared "who were making their first trial of the profession. They straightway remodel these girls, so that they retain neither their manners nor their looks as they were before. Suppose that one girl is too small; a cork sole is stitched into her dainty shoes. Another is too tall; she wears a thin slipper, and cocks her head on one side when she walks abroad. One has no hips; she sews together a bustle and puts it beneath her dress, so that all who catch sight of the fine curves of her back cry out in applause. One has a stomach that is too fat; such have bosoms made of the stuff that comic actors use, padding themselves straight out in such fashion. A part of one's body is beautiful; this part she displays bare."

Under Solon the *dicteriades* were confined to their brothels, which were so successful financially that the ruler erected a shrine to Venus Pandemos, the public Venus, opposite the principal *dicteria*. Solon's successor, Pisistratus, gave the *dicteriades* the freedom of the city and permitted his sons, on certain days, to take them to his beautiful gardens "and let loose upon them the whole petulance of Athenian youth."

Much Greek prostitution was associated with the worship of the gods and the gift of girls as votive offerings to Aphrodite was a common practice. When Xenophon was victorious at Olympia, Pindar wrote: "O Queen of Cyprus! Hither to thy sanctuary Xenophon hath brought a troupe of one hundred girls to browse, gladdened as he is by his vows now fulfilled." And to the girls he said: "Young girls, who welcome many strangers with your hospitality, ministers of persuasion in rich Corinth—who on the altar send up in smoke the auburn tears of fresh frankincense the many times that ye fly in thought up to the Mother of the Loves, heavenly Aphrodite; upon you, my children, free from reproach, she hath bestowed the right to cull the fruit of soft beauty in your desired embraces. When necessity requires, all things are fair."

It might be said that the younger *dicteriades*—although they were surely "wild kids"—cannot fairly be classified as juvenile delinquents. They were captured or purchased as slaves or sold by their parents. But it would seem that they had no objection to the life. Certainly the prostitutes who were the next step above the *dicteriades* were pleased and proud in their profession. These were the flute-players, whom Athenaeus described as "just beginning to be ripe."

The flute-players were young girls selected for their beauty and trained to excite the senses by singing and dancing at male banquets or in the rites of worship of certain deities. At banquets they were auctioned off for the night when their entrepreneur judged that their performance had aroused the audience to the highest point of excitement. Most of the flute-players were youngsters from the Ionic ports in Asia Minor, and the ability of these exotic young creatures to excite the senses is indicated by a story told by Persaeus.

"There was a philosopher drinking with us and when a flute-girl entered and desired to sit beside him, although there was plenty of room for the girl at his side, he refused to permit it and assumed an attitude of insensibility. But later, when the flute-girl was put up for the highest bidder, as is the custom in drinking bouts, he became very vehement during the bargaining and when the auctioneer too quickly assigned the girl to someone else, he expostulated with him, denying that he had completed the sale, and finally that insensible philosopher came to blows, although at the beginning he would not permit the flute-girl even to sit beside him."

Some of the most successful flute-girls became as affluent as present-day movie stars. They held an annual festival in honor of Venus, sometimes called the callipygian games, at which they drank and performed in competition, ending with a "Miss Flute-Girl" beauty pageant. Men were excluded from these rites. In this connection Dr. William Sanger, in a nineteenth-century study of Greek social mores, wrote: "It has been suggested that these festivals were originated by, or gave rise to, those enormous aberrations of the Greek female mind known as Lesbian love. There is, no doubt, grave reason to believe something of the kind. Indeed, Lucian affirms that, while avarice prompted common pleasures, taste and feeling inclined the flute-players toward their own sex."

Highest in the rank of the Greek prostitutes were the *hetaerae,* who, as a class, were the most influential women in Greece. These were courtesans or, in some cases, mistresses who were intellectual as well as physical companions to most men of note. Commenting on their physical charms and mental capabilities, Athenaeus wrote: "No wonder there is a shrine to the Companion everywhere, but nowhere in Greece is there one to the wife." Wrote Dr. Sanger: "They filled so large a place in society that virtuous females were entirely thrown in the shade, and it must have been quite possible for a chaste Athenian girl, endowed with ambition, to look up to them and covet their splendid infamy."

But the Athenian girl could covet in vain; the *hetaerae* were "foreign women," that is, non-citizens. It is unlikely that many girls reached this exalted rank while still in their teens, but most of them surely started young. One of the most famed, Lais, became the mistress of Aristippus, of Demosthenes the orator, and Diogenes the Cynic. Of her beginning Athenaeus wrote: "The painter Apellus caught sight of her when she was still a maid carrying water from the fountain of Peirene and, struck by her beauty, he took her to a symposium of his friends. When they jeered at him for bringing to the symposium not a professional courtesan, but a maid, he replied: 'Don't be surprised, for I want to show you her beauty is a promise of enjoyment to come in less, altogether, than three years.' "

Another famed *hetaera* was the Milesian girl Aspasia who, after she became successful, opened a house in Athens to which she imported young girls from the eastern Ionic cities. This seems to have been a practice of some *hetaerae,* for Demosthenes, when pleading in court against the courtesan Neaera, described her as having seven young girls in her house, "whom she knew well how to train for their calling, as was proved by the repeated sale of their virginity." While Aspasia's girls supplied the entertainment conventional in such establishments, the accomplished courtesan discussed philosophy and rhetoric with such prominent patrons as Socrates and Pericles; the latter subsequently divorced his wife and married her. Aristophanes claimed, perhaps in jest, that the capture of two of Aspasia's teen-agers by boys from Megara caused the Peloponnesian War. Wrote the witty dramatist: "Some young fellows, made drunk at too many games of cottabos, went to Megara and stole a whore named Simaetha; thereupon the Megarians, in agonies of excitement as though stuffed with garlic [fighting cocks were given garlic], stole in revenge two whores of Aspasia; and with that began the war that broke out all over Greece, caused by three strumpets."

Many male Athenian juveniles were "boy favorites" of more mature men. Homosexuality, involving older men with young boys, seems to have been common in Greece, although some hold that the relationship of the philosopher with his boy favorite was intellectual rather than physical. Grote, in his famous work on Plato, rather straddles the fence on this point by writing: "In the Hellenic point of view, upon which Plato builds, the attachment of man to woman was regarded as a natural impulse and as a domestic, social sentiment; yet as belonging to a *commonplace rather than to an exalted mind,* and seldom if ever rising to that pitch of enthusiasm which overpowers all other emotions, absorbs the whole man, and aims either at the joint performance of great exploits, or the joint prosecution of intellectual improvement by continued colloquy. . . . The beauty of women yielded satisfaction to the senses, but little beyond. It was the masculine beauty of youth that fired the Hellenic imagination with glowing and impassioned sentiment. The finest youths, and those, too, of the best families and education, were seen habitually uncovered in the Palaestra and at the public festival-matches. . . . The sight of the living form in such perfection, movement, and variety, awakened a powerful emotional sympathy, blended with aesthetic sentiment, which in the more susceptible natures was exalted into intense and passionate devotion. The terms in which this feeling is described, both by Plato and Xenophon, are among the strongest which the language affords—and are predicated even on Sokrates himself. . . . In their view it was an idealising passion, which tended to raise a man above the vulgar and selfish pursuits of life, and even above the fear of death."

Many writers who were contemporaries of the famous ancient Greeks do not take such a broad-minded view of their relationship with boys. Athenaeus wrote: "Now your philosopher-boy-lover is of the same breed that Alexis or Antiphanes brings on the stage in *Sleep;* 'For these reasons this male whore on all occasions at dinner with us never took any leeks either; this was because he did not want to offend his lover when he kissed him.' And Ephippus in *Sappho* put it well concerning such persons; 'For when one who is young furtively enters another man's house and lays upon the food a hand that does not pay its share, you may believe he pays the reckoning for the night.' The orator Aeschines says the same thing in his speech against Timarchus."

The poet Chios, in a work titled *Sojournings,* told a story of Sophocles in which he said: "I met Sophocles the poet at Chios when he was sailing as general to Lesbos; he was playful in his cups, and clever. A Chian friend of his, Hermesilaus, who was the proxenus of Athens, entertained him, when there appeared, standing beside the fire, the wine-pourer, a handsome, blushing boy; Sophocles was plainly stirred. . . . As the boy brought his face up to the cup, Sophocles drew the cup nearer to his own lips, that the two heads might come closer together. When he was very near the lad, he drew him close with his arm and kissed him. They all applauded, amid laughter and shouting, because he had put it over the boy so neatly."

Athenaeus summed up this aspect of sexual relations: "Altogether, many persons prefer liaisons with males to those with females, for they maintain that this practice is zealously pursued in those cities throughout Hellas which, compared with others, are ruled by good laws." Under the later tyrants homosexuality had a great political influence. The boys inspired their senior partners to take a stand against dictatorial government and were so effective that some of the tyrants "even went so far as to set fire to the wrestling-schools, regarding them as counterwalls to their own citadels, and so demolished them."

IN ROME THE BEHAVIOR OF JUVENILES, LIKE
that of adults, was undoubtedly very different in the virtuous early
republic from what it was in the later decadent empire. The
Romans of the republic have come down in history as the models
for fine family life. The Roman parents of the empire were pat-
terns of decadence. It is said that in the early days there was no
divorce in Rome for 500 years. Later, there is an account of one
man who married, as his twenty-third wife, a woman who had
had twenty previous husbands.

As in every other era, the delinquency of Roman youth was
blamed on the example set by Roman parents. The poet Juvenal
expounded on this at length, writing, in his sixth Satire:

> So nature prompts, so soon we go astray,
> When old experience puts us in the way:
> Our green youth copies what grey sinners act,
> When venerable age commands the fact.
> Some sons, indeed, some very few, we see
> Who keep themselves from this infection free,
> Whom gracious heaven for nobler ends designed,
> Their looks erected, their clay refined.
> The rest are all by bad examples led,
> And in their father's slimy track they tread.
> Is't not enough we should ourselves do,
> But that our children we must ruin too?

Today, much is written about "the affluent society" as a contributing factor in juvenile delinquency. Kids get too much too
easy; they do not, it is said, develop the moral stamina that comes
from struggle. This is diametrically opposed to most historical
evidence, in which juvenile delinquency and poverty went hand
in hand, but Juvenal, at least, made the same point about declining Rome when he wrote:

No crime, no lustful pastures are unknown,
Since poverty, our guardian angel, is gone.

One aspect that did not change as Rome declined morally was the relation of the child to the father. The male parent had absolute and complete authority over his children—*patria potestas*. He could mutilate them, sell them, kill them or throw them away. This last was a not uncommon practice, under which unwanted children were placed where they might be picked up by strangers, who could rear them to sell as slaves. Children were usually abandoned on a street on the western slope of the Aventine Hill or near the Forum Boarium, where there was a column around which abandoned babies were placed, called the *Lactaria*.

Because a crippled child is an object of sympathy, many of these foundlings were deliberately maimed by their foster parents so that they would be more successful as beggars. Seneca argued the morality of this heinous practice in his *Controversy:* "Look on the blind wandering about the streets leaning on their sticks, and on these with crushed feet, and still again look on those with broken limbs. This one is without arms. That one has had his shoulders pulled down out of shape in order that his grotesqueries may excite laughter. Let us view the entire miserable family shivering, trembling, blind, mutilated, perishing from hunger—in fact, already half dead. Let us go to the origin of all these ills—a laboratory for the manufacture of human wrecks—a cavern filled with the limbs torn from living children—each has a different profession, a different mutilation has given each a different occupation."

Seneca's conclusion was that the children so treated had no cause for complaint, for, he said: "Have not these children been done a service inasmuch as their parents had cast them out? Many individuals rid themselves of misformed children defective in some part of their body or because the children are born under evil auspices. Someone else picks them up out of commiseration and, in order to defray the expenses of bringing the child up, cuts off one of its limbs. Today, when they are demanding charity, that life that they owe to the pity of one, they are sustaining at the expense and through the pity of all." Whether or not they were deliberately maimed, juvenile beggars, who combined petty theft with their craft, loomed large on the Roman scene.

By the time of Augustus many well-born Romans, like Athenians, had come to the conclusion that children were more trouble than they were worth—so many that the emperor enacted laws to encourage larger families. Relief from all personal taxes was granted Roman citizens who had three or more children, and between two candidates for office, preference was given to the one with the most children. Still, wrote Tacitus: "Marriages and the rearing of children did not become more frequent, so powerful are the attractions of the childless state."

The Rome of "bread and circuses" was a climate in which juvenile delinquency flourished. The amphitheatre and the arena, which were open to children, presented indecent and obscene spectacles. The majority of the common people were wretchedly poor and these, as well as the vast number of slaves, reflected and exceeded the low standards of morality of the upper class. Youngsters, particularly of the upper class, were constantly exposed to lewd paintings and sculpture in their own homes of the type which, today, are kept from the view of even the adult public at the restoration at Pompeii. The Romans may have considered these sensual portrayals as works of art rather than pornography, but their effect on the juvenile mind was nonetheless degrading.

Contemporary Roman writers had nothing to say about most forms of juvenile delinquency. As in all eras before the nineteenth century, there was no distinction between juvenile and adult crime. But widespread sex delinquency among juveniles is attested by many writers. Livy tells of the Bacchanalian mysteries which were performed by societies of youths of both sexes that were established to "satisfy depraved instincts." This mania became so widespread that the Senate passed a decree ordering execution for participants in the mysteries.

Prostitution was rampant in Rome during its declining years. Roman prostitutes came in all sizes, shapes, colors and ages; the city was the melting pot of the world. But great preference was shown for young girls and many prostitutes were seduced into, sold into, or compelled into their trade shortly after puberty. In addition to full-time professionals, teen-aged girls who served in taverns and inns were available to the customer, as were bakers' girls who sold cakes for sacrifices to Venus. In the public baths, during the later years of the decadent empire, attendants were handsome young boys or pretty young girls, and a customer of either sex might have an attendant of either sex in a private cell that was supposedly devoted to massage.

Young virgins were in great demand as prostitutes and their panders could command premium prices. In a play, *Pericles, the Prince of Tyre,* is a description of a brothel that has secured a virgin: "The door of the house was adorned with twigs of laurel, a lamp of unusual size was hung out at night, and a tablet exhibited stating that a virgin had been received and enumerating her charms. When the purchaser had been found and a bargain struck, the girl, often a mere child, was surrendered to him and the wretch issued from the cell afterwards, himself to be crowned with laurel by the slaves of the establishment." Symposius, a Christian, describes a virgin named Tarsia for whom a sign was hung out inscribed: "He who deflowers Tarsia shall pay half a pound. Afterwards she shall be at the public service for a gold piece."

During the persecution of the Christians their religion was used as an excuse to secure virgins. If a Christian girl refused to sacrifice to the pagan gods she might be condemned by the prefect to serve in a brothel. Early Christian literature contains stories of girls who were saved from such a fate by miraculous intervention.

The later Romans accepted prostitution as a necessary part of their society and did not condemn the girls who engaged in this trade as juvenile delinquents, unless they were the daughters of citizens. But the virtue of even these Roman maidens was seriously questioned by several contemporary writers. Juvenal, whose sixth Satire castigated Roman women, thus cautioned eager husbands:

> That to wedlock, dotingly betrayed,
> Should hope, in this lewd town, to find a maid.

And again:

> But is none worthy to be made a wife
> In all this town? Suppose her free from strife,
> Grant her besides of noble blood that ran
> In ancient veins ere heraldry began:
> Suppose all these, and take a poet's word,
> A black swan is not half so rare a bird.

In his study of Roman society Dr. Sanger wrote: "A young Roman girl, with warm southern blood in her veins, who could gaze on the unveiled pictures of the loves of Venus, read the shameful epigrams of Martial, or the burning love-songs of Catullus, go to the baths and see the nudity of scores of men and women, be touched herself by a hundred lewd hands, as well as those of the bathers who rubbed her dry and kneaded her limbs—a young girl who could withstand such experiences and remain virtuous must, indeed, be a miracle of principle and strength. . . . Once a year, at the Lupercalia, she saw young men running naked through the streets, armed with thongs with which they struck every woman they saw; and she noticed that matrons courted this flagellation as a means of becoming prolific."

If the maiden did resist the erotic stimulants to which she was exposed, her virtue might be further endangered by a seducer who plied her with an aphrodisiac—a type of drug in which Greek and other Eastern physicians practicing in Rome did a thriving business. Even Ovid, who had nothing against illicit love, felt constrained to warn young girls against aphrodisiacs.

It is written that in later years it was necessary to take girls as young as six years to maintain the staff of virgin attendants at the temple of Vesta, the household goddess. For sexual misbehavior the Vestal Virgins were scourged and then buried alive. There is a record of but twelve who suffered this punishment, but it was generally believed that these were but the few who were caught or whose families did not have sufficient influence to save them.

Much of the sex delinquency of Roman girls was blamed on their decadent mothers, according to Juvenal:

> Who would expect the daughter should be other
> Than common punk if Larga be the mother?
> Whose lover's names in order to run over
> The girl took breath full thirty times, and more:
> She, when yet a tender minx, began
> To hold the door, but now sets up for man;
> And to her gallants, in her own hand-writing,
> Sends a billet-doux of the old bawd's inditing.

A feature of Roman sex mores was the male prostitute, available to both men and women. The latter favored young male dancers and athletes and, particularly, pantomime dancers who were described as, "very beautiful young men whose art lent them fresh grace." These were finally banished from Rome by a Senate decree because of the factions caused by their relations with noble women.

Most Roman authors allude to the relations between mature men and handsome boys, but do not, as in Greece, claim that there is anything intellectual about such companionships. Still, there was nothing in the mores that made homosexuality particularly immoral; the *aedile,* who supervised registered female prostitutes, paid no attention to homosexual activities unless a boy was violently treated by one of his patrons.

The Christian fathers of the first few centuries after Christ had little to say about children in their writings. The only extended reference to children by an early Christian writer was a letter from St. Jerome to the mother of a girl named Paula, in which he advised her: "Do not allow Paula to eat in public, that is, do not let her take part in family entertainments, for fear that she may desire the meats that may be served there. Let her learn not to use wine, for it is the source of all impurity. Let her food be vegetables, and only rarely fish; and let her eat so as always to be hungry.

"For myself, I entirely forbid a young girl to bathe.

"Never let Paula listen to musical instruments; let her even be ignorant of the uses served by the flute and the harp.

"Do not let Paula be found in the ways of the world [i.e. the streets] in the gatherings and in the company of her kindred; let her be found only in retirement.

"Do not allow Paula to feel more affection for one of her companions than for others; do not allow her to speak with such a one in an undertone.

"Let her be educated in a cloister, where she will not know the world, where she will live as an angel, having a body but not knowing it, and where, in a word, you will be spared the care of watching over her."

4

Wild Kids
of the Middle Ages

THROUGHOUT THE MIDDLE AGES LITTLE
attention was paid to the particular nature of children. It might
be said that childhood did not exist in medieval times; after infancy
there was no period at which a youngster would be considered a
juvenile delinquent. The extent to which the state of childhood
was ignored is evidenced by medieval art which, until the twelfth
century, made no attempt to portray children or young people.
When children were shown in paintings they were depicted as
half-sized adults.

Home discipline was strict in this era, but the child did not
remain long in the home. A boy of noble birth went to the castle
of some other noble to train as a page. In England it was a
custom in better families to board children out; baby farming
had started. The scholar stayed away from home, studying with
a master, almost around the calendar. The apprenticeship system
had started for poorer boys, who left home and lived with the
craftsmen to whom they were indentured. And the sale of children
was common among the poor. In an edict condemning the mis-

conduct of rustics at a fair the Anglo-Saxon King Athalaric made this point in listing the benefits of the fair: "There stand ready boys and girls, with the attractions that belong to their respective sexes and ages, whom not captivity but freedom sets a price upon. These are with good reason sold by their parents, since they themselves gain by their servitude. For one cannot doubt that they are benefited even as slaves by being transferred from the toil of the fields to the service of the cities."

Vagrant children and foundlings were a problem of the times in every European city. In France, "there was hardly a town in the kingdom where abandoned children were admitted freely and without information being requested. In the towns that were not too far from Paris they were carried thirty and forty leagues, at the risk of having them die on the way." By the fourteenth century thousands of children lived and died and practiced their delinquencies in the streets of London, Paris and Vienna—a condition which, in London particularly, would persist down to the nineteenth century.

That teen-agers of the period were, as always, creating problems for adult society is evidenced by an edict issued in 1398 by Richard Whittington, Lord Mayor of London, the Dick Whittington of cat fame. His Honor's ordinance was addressed to the *hurers,* a craft that had to do with treating hair and wool, and provided "that no one of the said trade shall scour a *cappe* or *hure,* or anything pertaining to scouryin, belonging to the said trade, in any open place; but they must do this in their own houses; seeing that some persons in the said trade have of late sent their apprentices and journeymen as well as children of tender age and others, down to the water of Thames and other exposed places . . . to the very great scandal, as well of the good folks of the said trade, as of the City aforesaid. And also, because of that divers persons, and pages belonging to lords, when they take their horses down to the Thames, are oftentimes wrangling with their said apprentices and journeymen; and they are then on the point of killing one another, to the very great peril that seems likely to ensue therefrom."

Juvenile sexual morality in Christian Europe from the tenth through the thirteenth century was almost as scandalous as in Rome in the later years. The great majority of girls were of the serf classes and their lord, or his sons, had the right to sexual intercourse with them at will. The state and the law had no concern for the person of a base-born girl. If she was seduced her father's only grounds for action was that she was his servant and the seducer had trespassed on his property and deprived him of the benefit of her labor. The era was one of constant warfare throughout Europe, and at that time rape was a natural and normal part of military operations. A girl was indeed lucky to get through her teens without having been the subject of attention by a member of some military band or marauding Vikings, if she had not already served the males of her own feudal fief.

A phenomenon of the period was the great number of girls, and some boys, who were seduced by demons. These were of two kinds: *incubi,* male demons who compelled virgin girls to have intercourse with them, and the less numerous *succubae,* who led young boys astray. Old chronicles are full of accounts of the misdeeds of these demons, whose existence was credited by many of the early Christian writers. So many girls claimed that they were forced to yield their virginity to these supernatural monsters that Pope Innocent VIII issued a bull against them, together with a formula of exorcism, but this did not seem to do much good. The number of reported cases of seduction by demons declined after the Inquisition started to burn damsels who confessed to having sexual relations with supernatural creatures, particularly if, as in most cases of such confessions, the girl had become pregnant.

Many of the customs of the Middle Ages were adverse to sound juvenile morals. The *Jours des Innocents* is one example. On this annual occasion, which took place on December 28, boys and men were allowed to invade the bedrooms of girls armed with birch switches. If they found a girl in bed they could raise her night-gown and whip her.

THE MOST NOTORIOUS DELINQUENTS OF the Middle Ages were the medieval equivalent of college boys. The college boy of that day might be of any age from ten to twenty, but most delinquents seem to have been thirteen and fourteen. Originally, the schools that they attended consisted only of a master and a group of pupils. Each master taught independently at a site of his own choosing. When several masters gathered in neighboring locations, a university was born.

Boys did not usually attend one master or university for a fixed period of time. Rather, they wandered from city to city, master to master, as the spirit moved them. On their travels the boys lived by begging and stealing. Usually they moved in groups in which younger boys were protected by older comrades and, in return, were required to do most of the illicit financing and provisioning for the group.

A description of the life of a wandering scholar in the fifteenth century was written by Thomas Platter. After he had become a schoolmaster and humanist in his later years, he looked back with apparent relish on the delinquencies of his youth. His wanderings started at about the age of ten when an older cousin, Paulus, who had already been on the road for several years, visited his home town of Valais and took him on an educational tour through Germany, Switzerland and much of France over a period of ten years. Thomas termed Paulus and the senior scholars "old hands" and himself and the younger boys "greenhorns."

"We set off," wrote Platter. "I had to start begging . . . and earned almost enough to support Paulus, for, when I went into a tavern, people enjoyed hearing me talk the Valais dialect and willingly gave me something." It must be remembered that taverns in those days were considered dens of iniquity, unsuitable haunts for a ten-year-old. Platter told of one occasion on which a tavern patron "offered me a six kreutzer piece if I would allow him to whip me on my bare skin. I finally agreed. He promptly seized me, threw me across a chair, and beat me horribly—and then took back his six kreutzers."

During their wanderings the cousins joined other old hands and greenhorns. The younger boys were sent out to steal geese, not only by the older scholars but also by some of the masters under whom they were supposedly studying. "At Dresden the schoolmaster and our old hands sent us goose hunting one day," Platter wrote. "We caught two geese which the old hands and the master ate at a farewell meal." From Dresden they moved toward Munich in two bands; one to steal geese and the other vegetables. When they rejoined, "the youngest of us were sent to Neumark, the nearest town, to beg for bread and salt. We had agreed to meet in the evening near the town gates where we intended to camp. But the inhabitants had no sooner seen the fire we had lit than they started firing at us. Luckily nobody was hit." At Munich the cousins left the band and obtained lodgings with a soap-maker, "whom I helped with his soap-making more than I studied." This lasted only until the soap-maker caught Paulus, who was then about seventeen, in bed with his maidservant and threw the cousins out.

The wandering students were a plague to both town and country, for vagrancy was the least of their delinquencies. Said a contemporary account: "The students of Paris attacked and slew passersby, carried off the women, ravished the virgins, committed robberies and broke into houses." Originally, the teaching was done in rooms hired by the masters, and the boys found lodgings where they could, living entirely without supervision. "Studies were

Wild Kids of the Middle Ages 67

in a jumble . . . the rooms on one side were leased to students and on the other side to whores, so that under the same roof there was a school of learning and a school of whoring," one commentator wrote.

In an effort to correct this chaotic condition, colleges came into existence, at first, merely as boarding houses for students in which there could be some kind of supervision and discipline. College authorities drew up statutes and rules which started by denouncing youths who considered the university as a "place of unbridled license, and who by bad example ruin others; who destroy quiet and studious industry, disobey the rector, do not attend church; wander about by day and night stirring up disturbances, breaking into houses, robbing gardens, committing thefts, and wantonly insulting and injuring others."

The rules were honored mainly in the breach and attempts to enforce them cost many masters and rectors their lives. A contemporary treatise on the subject says: "Never were youth so hostile to the laws; they are resolved to live according to their own decrees and not to regard the will of God." Virtually all of these teen-agers were armed, usually with a sword. As in the better-run saloons of the American West at a later day, weapons were supposed to be checked at the door, but, as with other rules, this was not enforceable with young rebels. Even without his sword the schoolboy could still be a dangerous character. After one master was soundly beaten by his pupils in the university at Djon, the High Court of that community forbade "all students to carry sticks, stakes and other offensive weapons in the classroom."

The most common delinquencies were fighting incidents—individual combat, general brawls and full-scale riots. Medieval teen-agers fought duels with their ever ready swords for any reason, or no reason. One study of the customs of German students states: "This impartial observer must accuse the student of fighting just because he likes to fight. It is a notorious fact that nine-tenths of the duels are fought without any real provocation." In Germany student duels later became tests of courage in university honor societies. Any boy that did not duel was considered cowardly, and the duelling scar became a status symbol for Prussian youth. An English student at a German university left this description of a college duel:

"Perhaps the closeness of the room, thick with the confined tobacco of yesterday's festivities, or the bathos of students eating sausages during the encounter, or the businesslike indifference of the waiters passing in and out, or the fumes of cigars before breakfast on a hot summer morning, or the grotesqueness of the iron spectacles and padding [protection for eyes and torso], were conditions unfavourable to the heroic. At any rate, insular or not, I must confess that when the blood began to ooze and spurt, every other feeling gave way to an invincible nausea and disgust. I certainly had not realized that there could be so much bloodshed with so little damage."

It was rather common practice for students, in protest against some rule or punishment, to barricade themselves in the college or the classrooms and hold their citadel by force of arms against the masters. Inter-college and inter-student riots were frequent, and usually resulted in bloodshed. Day students and college boarders were traditional enemies and frequently expressed their enmity with lethal weapons. There is one tale of a day student who entered a college at LaFleche disguised as a woman, presumably as a prank. The Jesuit brothers who staffed the institution captured the intruder and locked him up. Whereupon the day students "laid siege to all the doors of the college. . . . When morning came they entered the college under arms. . . . The rebels stood in the avenues, armed with swords, sticks, blackjacks and stones driving back the pupils who came out when the bell rang to go to the classrooms." The Jesuits then armed their servants with halberds and muskets and, before the affair was over, one master lay dead and several students on both sides were wounded.

Conflicts between town and gown—some of them pranks, others riots—were a regular part of medieval university life. A typical prank was the custom of the students at Jena to capture a town constable. At times they tied him to a tree with a sign stolen from an inn, picturing a bear or a monkey, suspended over him. On other occasions they paraded him through the streets, compelling him to blow his horn to arouse the citizens. Typical of the serious student riots of the era was one started by Oxford boys in 1345 when a party of students hurled pewter mugs at the head of an innkeeper. The boniface appealed for help to his fellow townsmen, the bells of the town were rung, and students and citizens poured out to riot through the streets of Oxford for the rest of the day. The results of the first day's fighting were inconclusive, but on the following day word was sent into the country and 2,000 rustics swarmed in to invade the university, burn the books and some of the buildings. Several students and masters were killed and many wounded before the military stopped the fray.

Town-and-gown riots and inter-college brawls come down to the present day. Compared to the riots of old, modern panty raids or student demonstrations at Berkeley for civil rights or free speech are Sunday School picnics. The only such affair in this century that might be compared to the medieval riots was that at the University of Mississippi a few years ago. This made banner headlines across the nation. Had newspapers been common 500 years ago, a student affray of this size would not have rated more than a paragraph on an inside page in other than a local paper.

Second to fighting as a delinquency of medieval schoolboys was drinking. It would seem that *all* students drank heavily. Every advance in their academic careers was marked by a drinking bout, as were meetings of secret societies, festivals and holidays, and some occasions were dedicated solely to drinking. Between times most boys drank moderately, but steadily. In the early days of the colleges, minor infractions of rules were punished by requiring the culprit to buy wine for the group. At Cornwall College in 1380 pupils who laughed, shouted or played immoderately at meals were fined "a mug of ordinary wine which shall be drunk among friends." At the Cistercian College in Paris pupils who spoke in any language other than Latin had to buy a pint of wine "which shall be distributed to those companions who are present." At the same institutions a pint of wine was the forfeit for wearing long, pointed shoes. The way teen-agers prefer to dress has been a problem since the dawn of civilization.

A serious drinking bout was described by a writer of the day as follows: "I saw a great chamber, a common lodging room or museum, or study, or beer-shop, or wine-shop, or ball-room, or harlot's establishment. In truth, I can not say what it was, for I saw all these things. It was swarming full of students. The most eminent of them sat at a table and drank to each other until their eyes turned in their heads like those of a stuck calf. One drank to another from a dish, out of a shoe, one ate glass, another dirt, a third drank from a dish where there was all sorts of food— enough to make one sick to see it. . . . Those with whom another refused to drink acted like a madman or a devil, sprang up as high as they could for anger, tore out their hair in their eagerness to avenge such an insult, threw glasses in each other's faces, out with their swords and at each other's heads, until here and there one fell down and lay there; and such quarrels I saw between close friends and blood relatives with devilish rage and anger. Others drank to each other off seats and benches, or off the table or the floor, under their arms, under their legs, with the cup under them, over them, behind them, or before them. Others lay on the floor and let it be poured into them as into a funnel." It must be remembered that these kids who were "pouring it in with a funnel" were the same age as our high school boys.

In Germany, student beer-drinking sessions became a tradition that lasted through the centuries. The students of Heidelberg held their *kommers,* or drinking bouts, in neighboring villages away from college authorities and the town watch. Here they played practical jokes on the peasants who "sometimes became enraged and assailed their guests in troops with heavy cudgels and often-times proved merciless antagonists, treading on and even stamping on the faces of the students who were thrown down." The same English student who commented on dueling later had this to say about beer-drinking: "The subject of student beer-drinking is not an inviting one. . . . It is a coarse and tedious proceeding. Its dullness is not even relieved by the deviltry of a big wine at Oxford. It is worse than sinful, it is vulgar." He saw nothing to deplore in excessive drinking, providing it was done in a mannerly fashion.

Sex played its part too. The french writer Montaigne tells us: "A hundred scholars have caught the pox [venereal disease] before getting to their Aristotle lesson." And students in those days got to Aristotle by their early teens. All of the statutes forbade boys to bring women or girls into the colleges, but the penalty was usually a mild one. In Narbonne college in 1379 it was a fine of five sous; in another institution a boy might be expelled for a third offense.

Today some eastern colleges have bowed to student demand and permitted juniors and seniors, who are not juveniles, to have girls in their rooms at certain hours, presumably for social or intellectual companionship. The Jesuits who ran many of the early colleges took a more cynical view and believed that if a boy and girl were alone together they were up to no good. They tried to further protect the morals of their young charges by prohibiting boys from lodging in taverns and ruling that prostitutes could not ply their trade within a certain distance from the school, but these, like other regulations, were defied by most students. The daughters of the citizens of university towns were considered fair game by the boys. One French writer commented: "It seems to me that Paris has been put in such a plight by these libertines and fairground hunters [students] that chickens have to be kept cooped up and even then they are none too safe."

Students have always been rebellious; indeed, today's teen-agers are far more restrained in their rebellion than their peer groups in former times. Professor Henry Sheldon in the preface to a volume on student life and customs through the ages accounted for student rebelliousness as follows: "It is marked in the entire history of the race that the cultural world, the world of self-estrangement, as organized in the school, the church, the state, and especially in the family, always assumed the attitude of authority and demands implicit obedience on the part of the child or the individual citizen. This obedience . . . has been insisted upon to such an extent as to threaten to produce the effacement of the individual. . . . Goaded by the contradiction between his growing individuality and his sense of the slight done to his likes and preferences by the requirements of the school, the student reacts against the established order in which he finds himself, and endeavors to recover his internal equilibrium by proving his personal ability to destroy the social might that manifests itself in his community, and more especially in the school of which he is a member."

PERHAPS THE GREATEST OUTBREAK OF juvenile delinquency in recorded history occurred in 1212, although anyone who so labeled the movement then would have found himself in a dungeon of the Inquisition charged with heresy. The delinquency was caused by the Children's Crusades, one of the biggest news stories of the thirteenth century, mentioned and recorded in no less than sixty chronicles and annals of the era.

The movement involved tens of thousands of children in France and Germany who spontaneously left home and took to the road— a modern social worker would label it "transiency." There were either two or three independent movements in the same year, one in France and one or two in Germany; it is not clear whether the German kids started as one group and then separated or were two independent groups. None of the accounts were written by a participant, and it is significant that none of the four chronicles of the French movement that were written by contemporaries label it a crusade. This idea and many of the details, are found only in accounts that were written in later years, based on hearsay.

Most of the earlier accounts ascribe the origin of the movement to divine inspiration, or to a message from an angel, or to a vision. Many later accounts, taking into consideration the disastrous outcome of the expedition, attribute the motivation to Satan. Wrote one chronicler: "It was done by the instinct of the devil, who, as it were, desired a cordial of children's blood to comfort his weak stomach long cloyed with murdering of men." At that time of religious mysticism any such pheonomena would be attributed to divine or supernatural inspiration. No commentator considered that it might have a more mundane or natural cause. Although religious hysteria may have been a factor with some of the children involved, it seems probable that the prime motivation with most of the many thousands of kids who left home was one of rebellion against discipline, chores and boredom.

Pieced together from all of the chronicles, the story of the Children's Crusades starts with twelve-year-old Stephen, the son of a shepherd, who lived in the village of Cloyes in the old French province of Orléanais. One day in the spring of 1212, while Stephen was tending his father's flock, he was approached by a stranger who asked for food, saying that he was a pilgrim from the Holy Land. While he ate he told Stephen stories of the miseries of the Christians who were enslaved by the infidels. Then the stranger announced that he was really the Savior and commissioned the boy to preach a crusade to children, promising that, with Stephen as their leader and prophet, they would gain the victory that soldiers in previous crusades had failed to achieve. He gave the boy a letter to the king of France demanding his support, and disappeared.

The account of the stranger and the letter appears only in chronicles written many years after the event. If there was a Stephen he was probably a precocious kid who may have been inspired by religious hysteria such as the annual Latinia Major, which was celebrated on April 25, about the time that Stephen decided to leave home. In this ceremony processions of priests and cowled monks marched along the roads and through the streets of the towns carrying crepe-shrouded crosses and chanting prayers to implore mercy for those who had been slain in the Crusades and the Christians still besieged in Africa. Such pageantry could have a stimulating effect on an imaginative youngster; or the boy might have had a less holy inspiration from tales of the fine fun and excitement of looting Constantinople told by veterans of the most recent crusade as they passed through his village.

In any event, Cloyes was obviously too narrow a field for Stephen's purpose. He shortly set out, with some young local followers, for St. Denis, five miles north of Paris, preaching along the way. This Parisian suburb contained a shrine which made it an ideal headquarters for an hysterical religious uprising. Pilgrims in great numbers came to St. Denis seeking physical relief and spiritual aid; here, in the spring of 1212 they heard young Stephen preach.

Stephen's call for a children's crusade spread like a plague throughout France, carried by returning pilgrims. He was proclaimed a prophet and tales were told of miracles of healing that he performed. Other minor prophets arose at several points; some of them, say the chronicles, were as young as eight and ten years. Soon the roads of France were thronged with processions of youngsters marching behind the oriflamme, the standard of the church, and bearing candles and crosses. It would seem that there must have been some adult hand in the organization of this, and there is reference to priests who accompanied the children; but, on the whole, the movement seems to have been a spontanous uprising of youth.

Many parents surely were not carried away by the hysteria and sought to restrain their children. "But," says an old account, "persuasions, threats, and punishments were all in vain. Bolts and bars could not hold the children. If shut up, they broke through the doors and windows, and rushed, deaf to appeals of mothers and fathers, to take their places in the processions, which they saw passing by, whose crosses and banners, whose censers, songs, and shouts, and paraphernalia seemed, like the winds of torrid climates, to bear resistless infection. If the children were forcibly held and confined, so that escape was impossible, they wept and mourned, and at last pined, as if the receding sounds carried away their hearts and their strength. It was necessary to release them, and saddened parents saw them exultingly depart, forgetting to say farewell. Regardless of the severance of tender ties, they ran to enlist in those deluded throngs that knew not whither they went."

The king of France, Philip Augustus, when urged by his ministers to stop the uprising, referred the matter to the newly organized University of Paris. Here the learned greybeards, after mature deliberation, decided that the movement was inspired by Satan and advised the king to stop it. Philip issued an edict ordering the children to return to their homes, but no effort was made to enforce it. The children marched to Vendôme, where Stephen had established a new headquarters.

From here Stephen and his followers, who had been joined by some "unworthy characters," started out for Marseilles on the Mediterranean coast 300 miles away. None of the chronicles give details of the pilgrimage except to say that it was a particularly hot, dry summer with food scarce and heat prostration frequent. According to one account: "These hardships and the influence of the unworthy characters soon resulted in more or less complete loss of discipline and of authority. Want produced dissensions and developed selfishness, each one being on the alert to outwit the others in the search for food and in endeavors to keep it concealed. They then straggled on, becoming more and more a loose, congregated horde, until at last Stephen's authority was entirely disregarded, and it was a race for the sea."

The children were welcomed at Marseilles, whose citizens were no strangers to Crusaders, and stayed there for several days, perhaps weeks, waiting for the sea to part miraculously and provide a path to the Holy Land. When the sea refused to open, they became discouraged, gave up the venture, and sadly started the long walk home.

Four chronicles, all written many years after the event and probably fictitious, contain a different ending to the story. According to these accounts two merchants of Marseilles, Ferreus and Procus, provided seven vessels to take the children to the Holy Land. Nothing was heard of the youngsters for eighteen years until, in 1230, a priest who had been with them returned from Africa and related the last chapter. He reported that two of the vessels had been wrecked on the little island of San Pietro, off the coast of Sardinia, and all their passengers lost. As the other five ships approached the coast of Algiers it became evident—the chronicles say not how—that the children "were victims of an infamous treachery." The merchants who had supposedly befriended them were in reality slave traders and the children were landed at Bujeiah and Alexandria, where they were dispersed and sold as slaves throughout the Saracen empire.

The chronicles that recount the German crusades tell of another twelve-year-old, Nicholas of Cologne, who claimed to have received divine guidance from angel voices and miraculous lights in the sky—medieval "Unidentified Flying Objects." Like St. Denis, Cologne was a shrine, with its cathedral built by Charlesmagne in which reposed the supposed bones of the Three Kings from the

East who had come to worship Christ. (Several centuries would pass before it was disclosed that one of the revered King's skulls was that of a child with milk teeth.) The scene in Germany paralleled that in France except that the movement seems to have embraced a much higher percentage of girls and had more support from the wrong kind of adults. One account states that many "men and women joined the armies from motives of a baser nature. All that were depraved in every sense found this a rare chance for profit. Abandoned women flocked in numbers in the expectation of fulfilling their infamous plans and of robbing as well as of ruining the youths. Thieves and sharpers never had such easy prey, and they did not neglect it. Everyone whose disposition would lead him to consider this an occasion for gain or plunder, hurried to the rendezvous." Another account says that "the number of depraved women that mingled with the armies was, it is told us, especially great, and to them is attributed the greater part of the evils which ensued."

Another chronicle reiterates the delinquency of the adults in the group: "There were women who came to profit in their baseness or suffer in their weakness, and girls who were destined to a bitter lot of shame, instead of a rest in Palestine. And priests and monks were there, some to rob, and some to pray. But the mass were boys of about twelve years of age." Descriptions of how they lived on the march are sadly lacking, but one account stresses that no city on the route could accommodate the horde: "Some slept in houses, where the kindhearted or the sympathizing invited them to rest; others reposed in the streets and market places; while they who could find no space within, lay down without the walls. But if, as was generally the case, the darkness found them in the open country, they passed the night in the barns and hovels, under the trees of the forest, or on the green bank of some stream. When morning came, they ate whatever they had in their wallets or what they begged or brought as they went."

All of the chronicles blamed any disorders on the adults; none criticized the youngsters—this would have involved the danger of heresy. But it is obvious that this vast band must have swarmed over the sparsely settled countryside in search of food, terrifying the peasants by their very numbers and pillaging orchards, barns and chicken coops. The walled domains of nobles were proof against them, but reference is made to numbers who were kidnapped by the minions of local lords. Others, discouraged, returned home or wandered off to find new homes. And many perished in crossing the Alps. This crossing, by two different passes, would be unbelievable were it not mentioned in the annals of the monasteries at both passes. When Nicholas' band reached the gates of Genoa on August 25, 1212, its 20,000 is said to have been reduced to 7,000.

If the children had given any thought to a means of crossing the Mediterranean, it is assumed that they expected the waters to part for them as the Red Sea had parted for Moses. While they awaited this miracle they requested permission to stay within the walls of the city for a single night. This was first given by the Genoan Senate and then rescinded because, it was said, "there was to be feared the effect upon the morals of the city that might be produced by seven thousand unrestrained boys. In a short time they might, relying on their numbers, give way to lawlessness, and introduce results which the jealous government well knew how to dread."

When the waters of the sea obstinately refused to part and the Senate of Genoa proved inhospitable, the children wandered southward. But, "their spirit was broken, and the disintegration, which had ceased for a while, was renewed. The people by the way induced many to remain, and compelled others. Many became daily more willing to secure homes in so fair a land, and to exchange weary marching for repose. And henceforth discipline seems to have been lost; they became an unregulated, headless band. Nicholas is not heard of again. It is not probable that his authority survived the disappointment of Genoa."

From Genoa they trudged to Pisa, whose new campanile did not yet lean. Here they seem to have broken into bands and continued to straggle southward. Mention is made of groups of children at Florence, Perugia, and Sienna; and some or all of them finally reached Rome. Here they were brought before the Pope, who rather callously told them to go home and hold themselves in readiness for a more martial crusade when they reached their majority.

There was a second band of German children who may have started with Nicholas and split off or been entirely independent of the first. In any event this group crossed the Alps through what is now Switzerland and, without approaching the coast, marched south the entire length of Italy. These youngsters fared worse than Nicholas' band. In wars between the German Emperor and the Pope much of the region they traversed had been ravaged by Germans and the populace "made these children of the hated race feel that they had been unfortunate in their choice of a route. Full of enmity, they made the young crusaders pay for the excesses of their countrymen, so that their journey was stained with tears and blood. Many were murdered; others were stolen to be carried away to misery, dishonor and slavery." Another record says that "liberated from all restraint, they fell a prey to vice in the various cities of Italy, while in their condition of exhaustion and of want they were ready to listen to any temptations. The result was that every city and town through which they passed retained numbers of them, especially of the girls. Years afterwards travellers found them still there, sunken in vice and lost to purity. It is stated that for a long time they formed a large element in the depraved classes of the land." They finally reached Brindisi, then an important seaport at the foot of Italy. Here the *Rhythmical Chronicle* tells of the sad plight of the remaining girls:

Foes hunt them, though, for gold.
The people of old Brindisi treat them with shame untold;
And in the lowest dens of vice, the girls as slaves are sold.

The moral state of southern Italy was low even by medieval standards, and it is understandable that blonde, blue-eyed girls, available for the taking, would have been considered fine prizes. Some children were supposedly enticed aboard ships by a promise of voyage to the Holy Land, and disappeared into oblivion. A few from this band (more from the Roman group) reached home, and it is said that the parents of Cologne avenged their loss by hanging the father of Nicholas, who had encouraged the boy in his fantasies.

The estimates of the number of French and German kids who became "transient juveniles" in 1212 are admittedly unreliable; some accounts place the total as high as 100,000. This would represent a sizeable portion of the total juvenile population in the area, who left home and became vagrants—for vagrants they were, whether inspired to wander because of religious motives or, as is much more probable, by youthful rebellion.

Today, one surprising aspect of the juvenile picture is the relatively small number of kids who run away from home. Juvenile vagrancy is probably less common now than at any time in history. In contrast to its prevalence in the thirteenth century, ours is a barely discernible ripple.

5

The Unmerry Children
of Merry England

IN 1851, THE *EDINBURGH REVIEW* BEMOANED the juvenile delinquency that was sweeping England in these words:

"What shall we do with our Juvenile Delinquents? is a question often asked, but as yet most unsatisfactorily and variously answered. 'Punish them more effectually,' says one class of philosophers, 'and so deter.' 'Educate them better,' says another class, 'and so prevent.' 'Open houses of refuge and asylums,' says a third party, 'and so reform.' But prisons multiply and are better regulated; Juvenile Offenders Acts are passed and boys whipped by the hundreds; the schoolmaster walks abroad enlightening our youth on geography, history, the steam engine and social sciences. . . . And still, in spite of all, the vexing fact of a large amount of juvenile delinquency remains and the young offender gains ground among us, the plague of the policeman, the difficulty of the magistrate, a problem to the statesman and a sorrow to the philanthropist."*

The journal disclosed that in the year 1849, 17,126 youths under seventeen had been incarcerated in British prisons, two-fifths of

83

them in London. The editor wondered, even as editors today, what was causing what he supposed was a phenomenon of the times and what could be done about it. Actually, the prevalence of juvenile delinquency in midnineteenth-century England was the crest of a tide that had been rising for three centuries and was receiving widespread attention for the first time under the relative social enlightenment of the Victorian era.

It might be said that many of the wild kids of this era were more sinned against than sinning. There was an appalling lack of concern for children, particularly those of the poor of the cities. Cruelty to children was everywhere common and generally ignored or accepted by society and the law. Intolerable social conditions bolstered the normal youthful urge to rebel, and this, combined with a fight for survival, led untold numbers of youngsters to depart from the moral code of the times, lax as it was, and to transgress the law.

The more than three hundred years between the rules of two queens, Elizabeth and Victoria, were the golden age of British history, during which the "tight little isle" became the focal point of the world's greatest empire. It compared, in many ways, with the last century in the United States in terms of economic, political, social and industrial progress. A middle class was born and throve. Those were the days of "Merrie England," but, for most of the kids, life was not so merry, and there probably has not been a time in modern history when kids ran so wild.

At the beginning of the era an increase in crime generally, including juvenile, can be traced to the decline of feudalism and the birth of capitalism shortly before the first Elizabeth came to the throne in 1558. As a social or political system, feudalism had many faults, but pauperism was not among them. The medieval serf led a sorry life, but he had a master to take care of him. With the breaking of the feudal bonds and, in England, the decline of the monasteries that had provided some charity, a great mass of dependent people were thrown on their own in an economy in which there was no provision for them.

Many gravitated to the cities, a trend that continued throughout the era. Elizabeth's London was a small community; Victoria's London was the world's leading metropolis. The cities and society made little or no attempts to provide for the influx of these indigent folk. A historian of the period wrote: "The sediment of the town population was a dense slough of stagnant misery, famine, squalor, loathsome disease and dull despair. . . . What added greatly to the dreary wretchedness of the lower order in the towns was that the ever-increasing throng of beggars, outlaws and ruffian runaways were simply left to shift for themselves."

It was the belief of most of the better class that the great impoverished mass should be kept not only poor, but ignorant. Under the title *Private Vices, Publick Benefits,* this opinion was defended in 1724 thusly: "From what has been said, it is manifest that in a Free Nation, where Slaves are not allowed of, the surest wealth consists in a Multitude of laborious Poor; for, besides that they are the never failing Nursery of Fleets and Armies; without them there could be no Enjoyment, and no Product of any Country could be valuable. To make the Society Happy, and People Easy under the meanest Circumstances, it is requisite, that great Numbers of them should be Ignorant as well as Poor. Knowledge inlarges and multiplies our Desires, and the fewer things a Man wishes for, the more easily his Necessities may be supplied."

Here was a magnification of the classic causes of juvenile delinquency: poverty, ignorance, and urban congestion. There were others. Although divorce was rare, broken homes were not. Death of husbands or wives at an early age left vast numbers of widows and widowers with small children. Desertion by the father was commonplace. When a man could be imprisoned for debt, he frequently chose to depart rather than languish in jail, leaving a destitute family to shift for itself. There was much illegitimacy among all classes, and many of these children who were not entirely deserted were brought up by the mother or, among the upper class, farmed out.

There is some reference to the strict discipline of the children of the upper classes, but this seems to have been more for the sake of manners than morality. An eighteenth-century parent deplored the lack of respect shown by children who no longer kneeled to ask their parents' blessing and used the familiar "father" or "mother" instead of the more respectful "sir" or "madam." There seems, however, to have been little affection or concern behind this façade of good breeding of an earlier era. A sixteenth-century mother wrote her older son to find his sister Anne a place away from home as follows: "I wull help to her fyndyig, for we be eyther of us werye of other. With me she shall but lese her time . . . and put me in great inquietenesse." When another teen-aged daughter, Elizabeth, objected to marrying the fifty-year-old husband selected by her mother, she was "betyn" and "hir hed broken in to or three places."

Children of all classes and ages were sent away from home to live. Infants were boarded out; baby farming was a thriving business. Older boys were sent away to school or apprenticed. Girls were placed in the houses of the wealthy or the nobility as servants or ladies-in-waiting, depending on the circumstances. The establishments of nobles seemed to throng with other people's children, many of them boys serving as pages. There were well-born "chyldrene of owir Lady chappell" in the establishment of the Duke of Norfolk and, of youngsters of lesser position, there were four "chylder" of the "stabylys" and four "chelderne of the Kechyn." Among the well-born, early marriage was another means of getting youngsters out of the home. The age of consent for marriage was twelve for girls and fourteen for boys, and there is a tale of a child bride who wept bitterly because she could not take her dolls to her husband's home.

Some parents were so anxious to rid-themselves of a daughter that they advertised, offering a substantial bonus to any man who would take the girl off their hands. A broadsheet distributed around London in 1691 was headed, "A CATALOGUE OF LADIES AND OTHER WOMEN FROM FOURTEEN YEARS OF AGE. THEIR FORTUNES FROM ONE HUNDRED TO A THOUSAND POUNDS. WILL BE DISPOSED OF BY AUCTION OR WHO BIDS THE MOST AT PINNER'S HALL ON THE TENTH OF AUGUST." In the lot was a tobacconist's daughter, "very pretty but wild, if taken with her faults her father gives £400." One hundred pounds was offered with a coffeeman's daughter who "squints a little," and a cook's daughter "well skilled in raising pasteries and making apple dumplings."

In addition to separation from home and broken homes, there were drunken homes. In those days drunkenness, for adolescents or adults, was hardly considered a vice. In fact, the consumption of strong beer and ale in great volume was practically held to be a British virtue. In 1702 Daniel Defoe wrote: "An honest drunken fellow is a character in a man's praise." When Benjamin Franklin worked in a large London print shop in 1725, he reported that he was the only worker, journeyman or apprentice, who did not drink beer copiously at breakfast, dinner, supper and after work.

All youngsters at least drank beer, which was a staple in the diet of all children's institutions. At a boy's school in England in the eighteenth century, "for breakfast they had two loaves of twelve ounces each, beer, broth, or water gruel." A visitor to the girl's reformatory at Bridewell described "about twenty young creatures, the eldest not exceeding sixteen. . . . Every day they were given three pints of beer. It was probably very small beer, but it was thought that even a reformatory could not insist on the inmates drinking only water." On a different level, a student at Rugby, whose boys were in their early and middle teens, writes in the eighteenth century: "The last days of the half-year were spent in all kinds of riotous excesses. What is called a feast or a supper was given at each boarding house and punch *ad libitum* was the order of the night."

Above and beyond this ordinary drinking, until the middle of the eighteenth century, there was a positive passion for gin, particularly among the poorer people. In some London parishes almost every shop sold gin, and some gave it away to secure trade. The young servant girl who came to a chandler's for candles or soap was treated to a dram of gin; the link boy was offered a drink when he came in for his nightly light. A justice wrote in 1736: "Not only the vicious and immoral give in to this practice [of gin drinking] but also those who are in other respects sober and regular; not only one person here and there in a family, but whole families shamefully and constantly indulge themselves in this pernicious practice, fathers and masters, children as well as servants."

When pressure from distillers caused Parliament to rescind an act to curb gin-drinking, one chief justice quipped:

> Riot and slaughter once again
>   Shall their career begin;
> And every parish babe
>   Again be nursed on gin.

SUPERIMPOSED ON ALL BASIC DELINQUENCY-promoting factors of the times was the widespread practice of apprenticeship, which was a leading cause of youthful misbehavior. This method of training started among the artisans' guilds during medieval days. Under it a boy was apprenticed to a master craftsman, usually for seven years, to learn his trade. The master received a fee from the boy's parents. The boy was not paid but lived with the master, who fed and clothed him, had complete authority over him including supposed responsibility for his manners and morals as well as his technical education. Some masters (but not many) diligently served as foster parents to their charges. By the eighteenth century apprenticeship had become the most general way of giving a child a start in life, and had developed into a complex institution, many aspects of which encouraged juvenile delinquency. In 1808 it was estimated that there were seldom fewer than 150,000 youths in London "bound to mechanical employments" and that, because of the bad examples set by their masters in frequenting public houses, this was "a bad and immoral education." In a classification of juvenile delinquents made in London, the worst class consisted of "boys who live with prostitutes and subsist by housebreaking, etc." These were found to be "mostly parish apprentices" with some "respectably connected and refractory apprentices."

The apprentice's indentures provided that "taverns and alehouses he shall not haunt, at cards, dice, tables, or any other unlawful game he shall not play, matrimony he shall not contract, nor from the service of his said master day or night absent himself." But these rules were disregarded by most boys and masters, particularly after "outdoor apprenticeship" came into being. Under this modification of the system the master boarded his apprentices out; consequently, the boys were completely on their own and without any supervision after they left the shop. A commentator of the time had this to say: "There is scarce an apprentice boy turned fifteen years of age who, contrary to the practice of our forefathers, is not suffered to go abroad almost as soon as the shop is shut. These boys and young men challenge it as a kind of right, and if the master is as dissipated as his servant, which is often the case, he takes no thought until he finds himself robbed; which I believe happens much more often then he discovers. . . . Many keep bad company, the society of each other is dangerous. . . . vice is costly, money must be supplied from what quarter it may."

Apprentices were traditionally a turbulent and troublesome lot, at best. One ex-apprentice who later wrote a biography told how he and his friends "used to go to Temple Bar in the evening, set up a shouting and clear the pavement between that and Fleet Market of all the persons there. The boys all knew boxing, and if anyone resisted one or two would fall upon him and thrash him on the spot, nobody interfered. . . . This was one of their tricks, they played all sorts of blackguard tricks." This delinquency was mild compared to the apprentice riots that were serious and frequent disturbances in London. Some groups organized gangs, either by trade or parish. It was usual for the boys of St. Anne's parish to fight those of St. Giles with clubs and stones for "a week or two before the holidays." In one such "gang rumble" the eighteen-year-old captain of St. Giles was killed by a sixteen-year-old.

The boys naturally sought amusement and not having the wherewithal to pay for it, they turned to thievery, most frequently stealing from their masters. Cutter clubs, in which groups of boys rented boats to go up the Thames and drink, were popular. Francis Place, the ex-apprentice who left a biography, wrote: "Our club was no better than many others; most of the members either robbed their masters or other persons to supply means for their extravagance." A Bow Street officer wrote that the cutter clubs were "a great source of crimes . . . there are more young men fall victims from that thing than any one thing I know. . . . These young men cannot support this expense and from that they commence thieves. It is this that hangs a number of young men." Place recalled that the "cox" of his club was later transported for robbery and the "stroke" hung for a murder that he did not commit; he could not prove an alibi, "being at the time committing a burglary with some of his associates."

Whether the boys earned or stole money, London offered few opportunities for them to spend it on wholesome recreation. There were "cock-and-hen" clubs in some public houses, where they could drink with girls whom they picked up, or found on the premises. Francis Place wrote that he made the acquaintance of the lowest class of prostitutes in the cock-and-hen clubs. "I went frequently among these girls, that is, I went with other lads . . . and at that time spent many evenings in the dirty public-houses frequented by them. We were all sons of master tradesmen, or of persons of some consideration, not sons of the meanest of the people, yet among us this bad conduct was suffered to exist unchecked, uncontrolled."

The association of apprentices with prostitutes who tempted them to steal from their masters became a London tradition, celebrated by a poem *The Poor Whore's Complaint to the Apprentices of London,* which read, in part:

> Something we know may now and then be made,
> By over-work or sleight of hand in trade,
> How e're you get it, so't be silver, we
> Without all niceness will contented be.
> But such of you who careless masters have,
> May most securely for expenses save.

Other haunts of teen-age apprentices were "chair clubs," all-male groups that were devoted to drinking, the singing of ribald songs and the telling of off-color stories. There were also two-penny theatres and concert halls which, according to contemporary descriptions, offered less than edifying entertainment. An observer reported:

"In company with a serjeant of police, in plain clothes, I visited fourteen of these concert saloons one Saturday night between the hours of nine and twelve. . . . In many of the rooms lads from about 13 to 18 years of age formed a considerable number of the audience; and in every instance I marked the presence of abandoned women. In one there were about 150 persons, a third of whom were boys. In another, a young woman, with a rouged face, dressed as a Swiss flower-girl, with a basket of flowers in her hand, was singing, while in a state of intoxication; and the extravagances occasioned by the excitement of the drink were the principal sources of amusement. This was a scene too disgusting, perhaps, to be dangerous; but in the better conducted rooms, where there is more attention to appearances and a thin gauze of propriety thrown over all the scenes, everything is calculated to deprave the taste, to intoxicate the senses, and to stimulate the passions."

Another observer noted: "The principal singing room is capable of holding from 800 to 1000 persons; one end is fitted up as a stage. The bar, where the liquors are served out, is placed in the middle. The place between the bar and the stage is appropriated to juveniles, or boys and girls from 10 to 14 years of age; of them there were not less than 100—they were by far the noisiest portion of the audience, and many of the boys were drinking and smoking. The lower gallery, which extends round three parts of the room, was occupied by the young of both sexes, from 14 years and upwards. There could not be less than 700 individuals present, and about one-seventh of them females. The pieces performed encourage resistance to parental control, and were full of gross innuendoes, 'double entendres,' cursing, emphatic swearing, and incitement to illicit passion. Three-fourths of the songs were wanton and immoral, and were accompanied by immodest gestures." This was a typical "Teen Canteen" of the day.

The most serious trouble caused by the large class of apprentices was attributed to the many runaways who, merely by deserting their masters, had committed an unlawful act. Some, perhaps most of them, were shiftless youths, prime subjects for law-breaking. In many cases, however, masters sought to induce apprentices, by one means or another, to break their indentures, often by brutality, in order to keep the apprenticeship fees without supporting the boys.

Most miserable and troublesome of the indentured youngsters—and most prone to run away—were the parish apprentices. These were homeless children, orphans, the children of paupers or of any who were so burdened with children that they could not take care of them. They were a charge on the parish, and the law provided that the authorities could bind out any child over the age of five as an apprentice, boys until they were twenty-four years of age and girls until they were twenty.

"A most unhappy practice prevails in most places, to apprentice poor children, no matter to what master, provided he lives out of the parish, if the child serves the first forty days we are rid of him for ever," a commentator on the Poor Laws in 1738 wrote. "The master may be a tiger in cruelty, he may beat, abuse, strip naked, starve or do what he will to the poor innocent lad, few people take much notice, and the officers who put him out the least of anybody. . . . It is the fate of many a poor child, not only to be half-starved and sometimes bred up in no trade, but to be forced to thieve and steal for his master, and so is brought up for the gallows into the bargain."

The records of London's Old Bailey are replete with evidence of brutality that led to news items such as this: "William Moles and Sarah his wife were tried at the Old Bailey for the willful murder of John Hewley, alias Hasely, a boy about six years of age, in the month of April last, by cruelly beating him. Under the direction of the learned judge they were acquitted of the crime of murder." The husband was retried for a misdemeanor and got two years.

A master named Jouveaux employed seventeen parish girls at embroidery and treated them so cruelly that five of them died "in a decline." Although Jouveaux had to move his establishment because neighbors complained about the crying and screaming of the children, and some threatened action when they discovered the girls rooting for food in a hog trough, he was never brought to trial.

Not so fortunate was an infamous midwife, Mrs. Brownrigg, who was hung for treating three little parish girls with such horrible brutality that one of them died. The most noted case of the era, which aroused the ire of even the callous London mob, was that of Mrs. Sarah Metyard and her teen-aged daughter. Mrs. Metyard and her daughter kept a haberdashery in which five apprentice girls were employed to make nets. The children were kept shut up in a room, "a little slip about two yards wide at one end and coming off like a pennyworth of cheese," and treated so cruelly that one of them ran away. When she was brought back by a milkman the fiendish Metyards literally beat her to death. They dismembered the body and tried to dispose of it in a sewer that led to the Thames. When they could not remove the grating, they left the grisly relics in the mud. The coroner assumed that it was a body on which somebody had been practicing dissection, and the matter was closed until Mrs. Metyard unwisely beat her own daughter. This lass, after running away with a lodger, informed on her mother. Although the daughter claimed that she had no part in the iniquities that were practiced on the children, the jury believed the other little apprentices, who branded her as equally guilty. Both Metyards were hung, to the satisfaction of the great crowd that witnessed the event.

The cases of brutality that came to court represented but an infinitesimal proportion of the little apprentices who were beaten, burned, starved and neglected. Many sought to escape by running away to become beggars, vagrants or thieves.

Girls apprenticed by the parish seem to have been particularly ill-used. Justice John Fielding, when proposing an orphanage instead of apprenticeship for little girls, said that "they are generally placed in the worst of families and seldom escape destruction." Another investigation found that "it appears that some of these girls have been seduced by their masters, that some have run away. In either of which cases, forlorn and unprotected, they generally become the victims of prostitution." On the whole, concluded the report, "their depravity is truly deplorable."

In the case of most parish apprentices there was little opportunity to learn a trade. The masters were itinerant workmen, if they worked at all. Girls were supposed to be taught "the art of housewifery," but more often they were employed as unpaid domestic drudges, or sent into the street to sell fish, flowers, vegetables or to peddle milk. Boys were apprenticed to tavern-keepers as pot boys, to rag pickers and old shoe collectors, and to any mean trade for which only parish children were available. Such apprentices, when in their teens, were very popular with watermen because in time of war the master could get the boys impressed into the navy and the boys' wages and prize money were legally the property of the master. Watermen, it was said, "have no settled abode and are idle and profligate persons. For the sake of small sums of money they take great numbers of apprentices who are suffered to idle about, which brings them to pilfer for their sustenance and, for the generality, they become vagrants and not seldom come to a fatal end."

At the very bottom of the heap of apprentices were chimney sweeps. A London guide book for 1747 said, "I think that this branch is chiefly occupied by unhappy parish children and may, for ought I know, be the greatest nursery for Tyburn of any trade in England." Chimney sweeps had to be small and, although a later law specified a minimum age of eight, this was regularly evaded. There are records of sweeps as young as four, and six was a common age at which to start. Some sweeps were kidnapped children, and a great many were purchased from poor parents for a few shillings. One reformer wrote that it was common practice "for parents to carry about their children to the master chimney sweepers and dispose of them to the best bidder as they cannot put them to apprentice to any other master at so early an age."

Master sweeps, most of whom were of the lowest order of society, frequently kept a stable of boys, sometimes as many as two dozen; life expectancy was not great. When there was no work for them they were put on the streets to beg or rented out to adult beggars for a few pence. The work of a sweep was dirty and hard on the clothes, so that the kids were constantly ragged and filthy. Strangely, these little ragamuffins were seldom viewed as objects of compassion; rather, they were considered as likely candidates for the gallows, and, in a great many cases, this view was borne out by events.

The usual custom was to send an experienced boy up the chimney behind a novice, so that when the lad slipped he fell on the shoulders of the boy beneath. This prevented severe falls, but not the painful scraping of skin against the sides of the flue. This assistance was given novice sweeps by the more kindly masters. Less considerate ones, it was reported, had the lower boy stick pins in the feet of the novice to force him to climb, or applied lighted straw to hasten his ascent. By the time he was sixteen, if not before, a boy was too big to go up most chimneys and was released. Having no trade, he often started on a career of crime. "Many through their skill in climbing [became] expert and enterprising burglars, breaking into places where few men would have cared to venture."

A means of disposing of parish children who were too young to apprentice was placing them on "baby farms," usually run by old harridans whose main concern was to keep as much as possible of the few pence allotted by the parish for the child's care. An appeal to establish a Foundling Hospital to replace baby farming referred to "barbarous nurses" who "do often suffer them [the children] to starve for want of due sustenance or care, or if permitted to live either turn them into the streets to beg or steal, or hire them out to loose persons by whom they are trained up in that infamous way of living and sometimes are blinded or maimed and distorted in their limbs in order to move pity or compassion."

The charge for hiring out children to beggars was generally four pence a day and preparing the child to make it a more compelling object of compassion was the responsibility of the lessee. The law frowned on maiming children, but that it was not considered a major crime is indicated by a trial in 1761 in which "The Court of Hick's Hall lately committed Anne Martin alias Chapbury to Newgate, where she is to be imprisoned for two years pursuant to her sentence. She is accused of putting out the eyes of children with whom she went begging about the country." Had Anne been convicted of larceny, she would have been hung.

In 1722 an "enlightened" move was made to protect children from the iniquities of the baby farm and to prepare them for apprenticeship, and parish workhouses were started where "all the poor children now kept at parish nurses, instead of being starved or misused by them will be duly taken care of and bred up to Labor and Industry, Virtue and Religion." The preparation for industry consisted of beating hemp and picking oakum. The religion consisted of learning a catechism. Further education was not considered desirable for children of the poor, for it was believed that "notwithstanding the innocence of the children, yet as they are exposed and abandoned by their parents, they ought to submit to the lowest stations, and should not be educated in such a manner as to put them upon a level with the children of parents who have the humanity to preserve them and the industry to support them."

The workhouses were not exclusively for children. Paupers of any age were herded together indiscriminately. In one such establishment, housing some 6,000 in a single year, approximately 40 per cent of the inmates were under twenty-one. These institutions were fine breeding grounds for juvenile delinquency, because a sizeable part of their population were vagrants, beggars, petty thieves, and prostitutes who, when times were too hard sought shelter in the workhouse for a short period, even though it meant working. These became the instructors of youth in many things other than catechism.

It was generally accepted by the upper classes that the offspring of the poor, whether in workhouse, under apprenticeship, or running loose, would be juvenile delinquents. Sir Josiah Child expressed this attitude when he wrote: "The children of the poor bred up in beggary and laziness, do by that means become not only of unhealthy bodies and more than ordinarily subject to many loathsome diseases . . . but they are, by their idle habits, rendered for ever after indisposed to labour, and serve only to stock the kingdom with thieves and beggars."

IN THE OPINION OF THE TIME THE MOST damning juvenile delinquency was vagrancy. Idle youths would rather wander than work, and supported their wanderings by petty crime. This large and troublesome class in England flourished from the sixteenth to well into the nineteenth century. They spent the winters in London or other cities. Then, with the coming of spring, they moved to more attractive climes. In all cities and most towns there were unions, or casual wards, in the workhouses where they could obtain a night's lodging. These wards were presumably for migratory labor, but most of their patrons despised labor of any kind. A member of the Board of Guardians of the Poor described such vagrant youth in an interview: "The largest number were seventeen years old—indeed, just that age when youth becomes disengaged from parental control. These lads had generally run away, either from their parents or masters, and many had been reared to a life of vagrancy. . . . They have nearly all been in prison more than once, and several a greater number of times then they are years old. . . . They are a most difficult class to govern, and are especially restive under the least restraint. . . . They often come down to the casual wards in large bodies of twenty or thirty, with sticks hidden down the leg of their trousers, and with these they rob and beat those who do not belong to their own gang. . . . Being repeatedly committed to prison for disorderly conduct and misdemeanour, the gaol soon loses all terrors for them. . . . Hence they soon become practiced and dexterous thieves . . . they form one of the most restless, discontented, vicious, and dangerous elements of society. At the period of any social commotion, they are sure to be drawn towards the scene of excitement in a vast concourse. . . . The youths of the vagrant class are particularly distinguished for their libidinous prospensities. They frequently come to the gate with a young prostitute, and with her they go off in the morning. With this girl, they will tramp through the whole of the country."

During an extensive study which culminated in a multivolume work, titled *London Labour and the London Poor,* an early sociologist, Henry Mayhew, interviewed scores of the juvenile vagrants. Excerpts from a few of their stories indicate the lives that they led and some of the varied types of delinquency that plagued England in the eighteenth and nineteenth centuries. One seventeen-year-old boy told Mayhew: "I thought I could make my fortune in London, I'd heard it was such a grand place. . . . I started without money, and begged my way from Manchester to London, saying I was going up to look for work. I wanted to see the place more than any thing else. I never tried for work in London. I slept in unions, I begged, I got acquainted with plenty of boys like myself. We met at the casual wards, both in London and the country.

"Once in Birmingham, we smashed all the windows, and did all the damage we could. I can't tell exactly why it was done, but we must all take part in it, or we should be marked. I believe some did it to get into prison, they were so badly off. They piled up the rugs; there was no straw; and some put their clothes on the rugs, and then the heap was set fire to. We were nearly suffocated before the people of the place could get to us. Seventeen of us had a month a-piece for it; I was one. The rugs were dirty and filthy, and not for any Christian to sleep under, and so I took part in the burning, as I thought it would cause something better. . . .

"There used to be great numbers of girls in the casual wards in London. Any young man travelling the country could get a mate among them, and can get mates—partners they're often called—

still. . . . Some of the boys of fifteen have their young women as partners, but with young boys older women are generally partners —women about twenty. They always pass as man and wife. All beggar-girls are bad, I believe. . . . The young women steal the most. I know, least, I did know, two that kept young men, their partners, going about the country with them, chiefly by their stealing. Some do so by their prostitution. Those that go as partners are all prostitutes."

Another youthful tramp was a farm boy who told Mayhew: "I'd heard people say, 'Go to Bath' and I went there; and I was only about eleven then. I tried to get work on the railway there, and I did. I next got into prison stealing three shovels. I was hard-up, having lost my work, and so I stole them. I was ten weeks in prison. I came out worse than I went in, for I mixed with the old hands, and they put me up to a few capers. When I got out I thought I could live as well that way as by hard work; so I took to the country. . . . I've had sprees at the country lodging-houses— larking, and drinking, and carrying on, and playing cards and dominoes all night for a farthing a game; sometimes fighting about it. . . . Sometimes we danced all night—Christmas time, and such times. Young women dance with us, and sometimes old women. We're all merry; some's lying on the floor drunk; some's jumping about, smoking; some's dancing; and so we enjoy ourselves. That's the best part of the life."

Another youthful vagrant was a mulatto girl of eighteen who had been on the road for four years. As a parish apprentice she had been a maid-of-all-work who ran away because "my mistress knocked me downstairs for being long on an errand to Pimlico." Hers was a story of wandering from Crotdon to Brighton to Mendicity to Lewes, begging and singing in the streets. She concluded her tale by saying: "I'm sorry to say that during this time I couldn't be virtuous. I know very well what it means, for I can read and write, but no girl can be, so circumstanced as I was. I seldom got money for being wicked; I hated being wicked, but I was tricked and cheated. I am truly sorry for it, but what could a poor girl do?"

The most colorful of the English delinquents were the street urchins, who never left London. Some of these had homes, some slept in archways, doorways, parks, or the warm ashes under a bottleworks. When she arrived in London in 1785 Abigail Adams was appalled at the situation of these children of the streets. "I have been creditably informed that hundreds of children of four years old and upwards sleep under the trees, fences, and hedges of Hyde Park nightly, having nowhere else to lay their heads; and they subsist by day upon the charity of the passengers."

Some of the street children were beggars, some thieves and pick-pockets, but most offered something for sale or offered to perform some service for a few coppers. There were sellers of matches, flowers, laces, radishes, fish, trinkets of many kinds and almost every conceivable small object which the child could offer for a few pence, usually depending on the compassion of the buyer to over-look the relative worthlessness of most of the merchandise. Some of these young street vendors have inspired song and story and found a place in history. The subject of "Cockles and Mussels Alive, Alive O" was a streetgirl, as was "The Poor Little Match Girl," whose hardships brought tears to the eyes of generations of youngsters. The most famous is surely *My Fair Lady,* the prototype Eliza Doolittle was much younger than Julie Andrews or Audrey Hep-burn. Historically, the most successful juvenile delinquent was an orange girl, Nell Gwynn, who was fourteen when she started to sell oranges around Covent Garden Theatre. At fifteen she was on the stage, at sixteen she was the mistress of Lord Buckhurst and at seventeen she had moved to the bed of Charles II. She was still a teen-ager when the opening of a play that Dryden had written for her was postponed while she bore the king a son.

Not all of the young street vendors were delinquents. In his study Mayhew interviewed a few who worked hard and took their mites home to a widowed mother, but he concluded that "perhaps the most remarkable characteristic of these wretched children is their extraordinary licentiousness. Nothing can well exceed the extreme fondness for the opposite sex which prevails among them." The conduct of the girls "cannot be powerfully swayed in favor of chastity, especially if the street-girl have the quickness to perceive that marraige is not much honored among the numerous body of street-folks. If she has not the quickness to understand this, then her ignorance is in itself most dangerous to her virtue."

The most engaging young rogues among the street children were the street sweepers. These youngsters provided themselves with brooms, swept the mud from the path of well-dressed pedestrians at street crossings, and then implored them for something for "poor little Jack, your honor," or "please remember honest hindustry." Most of the street sweepers belonged to gangs with older leaders whose fists protected the younger boys against encroachment on their territories. The most successful sweepers were also acrobats who finished their act with a cartwheel or a handstand. Some drew designs in the mud at their crossings; a "V. R." enclosed in a wreath above the words "God Save the Queen" was usually good for a few pence.

The police frowned on this "honest hindustry," and there was constant friction between the law and the boys. "We don't mind the police much at night-time because we jumps over the walls around the place at Trafalger Square and they don't like to follow us at that game and only stands and looks at you over the parrypit," said a boy. "There was one who tried to jump the wall but he split his trousers all to bits and now they're afraid."

Neither the hours nor the associations were conducive to good morals among street sweepers. The boys usually worked until about two in the morning, and the best locations were adjacent to public houses and theatres where drunks and theatregoers, as well as some prostitutes, were good prospects. One youngster explained,

"After the Opera we go to the Haymarket, where all the women are who walk the streets all night. They don't give us money, but they tell the gentlemen to. If they are crossing and we says to them as they go by, 'Good luck to you,' they always give us something either that night or the next. Sometimes a gentleman will tell us to go and get them a young lady, and then we goes and they usually give us six-pence for that. If the gents is dressed finely we gets them a handsome girl; if they're dressed middling, then we gets them a middling-dressed one; but we usually prefers giving a turn to girls that have been kind to us, and they are sure to give us something the next night. If we don't find any girls walking, we knows where to get them in the houses round about."

Begging was the vocation of many London street children. In a report to the House of Commons in 1815 it was stated that there were 15,000 beggars in London, of whom 9,288 were children. Many of the "lurks" of the street beggars were ingenious and imaginative. The "fits" lurk and the "paralytic" lurk were rather ordinary. Somewhat more advanced was the "shivering" lurk performed by a half-clad youngster in cold weather. There was one lad, called "shaking Jemmy" who did this so long that he could not stop; "he shivered like jelly, like a calf's foot with the ague, on the hottest day in summer." This lurk had to be performed by a loner, "for if one boy shivers less than another he shows that it isn't so cold as the good shiverer makes it out—and then it's no go."

The "clean family" lurk was a group affair, involving at least one adult. "We dressed to give the notion that, however humble, at least we were clean in all our poverty. On this lurk we stand on the pavement in silence, the kids with long, clean pinafores, white as the driven snow; they're only used in clean lurk and taken off directly they come home."

For little girls the "lucifer" lurk was usually effective. In this the child carried matches, not to sell but to drop in the mud when a likely prospect approached. The girl then fell to her knees and wept bitterly while trying to pick up her scatttered wares. Even more heart-rending was the "sugar and tea" lurk. In this a child sat crying on the curb. When questioned she explained that her mother had sent her out to buy a small amount of tea and sugar and a big boy had snatched the change from her and thrown the tea and sugar in the mud. The effect of this might be heightened by a shill who said: "And was that your poor mother's last shilling and daren't you go home, poor thing?"

Begging was frequently associated with crime. In 1731, among the delinquencies listed by the *London Journal* were "the multitude of beggars and the many villainies and robberies committed in this city, the threats of incendiaries, and those threats actually executed; boys of seven or eight years old taken in robbing a shop; and some of thirteen or fourteen robbing in the streets." Pickpockets and sneak thieves were also common offenders among children and youth. The light-fingered haunted every crowd and took pride in their accomplishments. "If you're in prison for begging you're laughed at," said one, "so a boy is partly forced to steal for his character." And another: "Picking pockets, when anyone comes to think on it is the daringest thing a boy can do." The proficiency of the young thieves was sometimes the result of careful training. Charles Dickens' description, in *Oliver Twist,* of Fagin making the Artful Dodger and Charley Bates practice endlessly, with himself as the victim, was based on fact; many fences maintained schools to teach the picking of pockets and other forms of thievery. Such a school was described in the *Annual Register* for 1765.

"At an examination of four boys before the Lord Mayor, one of them gave the following account: 'A man who kept a public house near Fleet Street, had a club of boys whom he instructed in picking pockets and other iniquitous practices. He began by teaching them to pick an handkerchief out of his own pocket, and next his watch, by which means the witness at last became so great an adept that he got the publican's watch four times in one evening, when his master swore that his scholar was as perfect as one of twenty years' practice.'"

Youthful pickpockets were wont to combine pleasure with business. Fairs where the crowds contained many unsophisticated countrymen were favorite places to ply their trade. Greenwich Fair, a three-day session of rollicking and junketing on the outskirts of London, was finally abolished because it became associated with all kinds of lawlessness. It was said that, considering its duration, more girls were debauched at Greenwich Fair than any other place in England. Race tracks, where gambling could be combined with pilfering, were also popular haunts for pickpockets, and it is safe to say that there were more young thieves in the crowd at Ascot than there were pearl-toppered toffs in the boxes.

Most of the juvenile pickpockets were boys, although some teen-age girls practiced the art of picking pockets. Telling about how she had been trained, a girl said: "My fancy-man always kept near to me whenever I went out of a night. I usen't to go out to take the men home; it was only to pick them up. My young man used to tell me how to rob the men. I'd get them up in a corner, and then I used to take out of their pockets whatever I could lay my hands on; and then I used to hand it over to him, and he used to take the things home and 'fence' them."

FEW HOMELESS STREET CHILDREN STAYED in the casual wards of the parish workhouses, where the sexes were separated and liquor hard to come by. When they had the necessary three- to sixpence for a night's stay, they much preferred the cheap lodging houses. There were several hundred of these in the outskirts of London that were notorious dens of delinquency, in which landlords doubled, ordinarily, as fences for thieves and pickpockets.

A lodging house typically consisted of one or more rooms in a dilapidated tenement. Threepence would buy a place on the floor and sixpence a share in a bed with from two to five companions of one or both sexes. The guests were required to leave in the morning, but they had the use of a communal kitchen in which to carouse and to prepare their dinner and breakfast.

In most lodging houses men, women, and children were mixed indiscriminately, although some houses were patronized almost exclusively by youth. Gangs of boys had favorite dens to which they returned every night, and some of the street sweepers maintained communal treasuries to pay for lodging. Mayhew's study is filled with accounts of delinquent fun described by youthful patrons of these houses. Sex and drinking led the list of activities, followed by gambling, lewd dancing, and the singing of ribald songs.

A youngster described his quarters thus: "There were forty men and women sleeping in one room. . . . There were plenty of girls there; some playing cards and dominoes. It was very dirty. . . . There was one tub among the lot of us. . . . Those who lived there were beggars, thieves, smashers, coiners, purchasers of begged and stolen goods, and prostitutes. The youngest prostitute was twelve. The beastliest language went on. It's done to outrival one another."

Another boy said: "After I'd worked by myself a bit, I got to live in a house where lads like me, big and little, were accommodated. We paid 3d [threepence] a night. It was always full; there was twenty or twenty-one of us. We enjoyed ourselves middling. I was happy enough."

A sixteen-year-old girl gave the following account of her life in the lodging houses: "There were a lot of girls like me at the same place. It was not a bad house, but they encouraged us like. No tramps used to come there, only young chaps and gals that used to go out thieving. No, my young man didn't thieve, not while he was with me, but I did afterwards. I've seen young chaps brought in there by the girls merely to pay their lodging-money. The landlady told us to do that; she said I could do better than knocking about with a man. If I hadn't had enough to pay for my lodging I couldn't have had a bed to lie on.

"We used to be all in the same room, chaps and girls, sometimes nine or ten couples in the same room—only little bits of girls and chaps. I have seen girls there 12 years of age. The boys was about 15 or 16. They used to swear dreadful. I fell out with the gal as first told me to go on the streets, and then I got with another at another house . . . I dare say there was upwards of twelve or thirteen gals; the kitchen used to be full. The mistress used to treat us well if we paid her; but she used to holler at us if we didn't. The chaps used to serve her out so. They used to take the sheets, and blankets, and everything away from her. She was deaf. They was mostly all prigs [thieves] that used to come to see us."

A somewhat sensationalized study of prostitution in London in the early nineteenth century had this to say about the lodging houses: "Here prostitution is habitual—a regular institution of the place . . . adults, youths, and children of both sexes are received, and herd promiscuously together; no questions are asked and the place is free to all. A new-comer is soon initiated, or rather forced into all the mysteries of iniquity. Obscenity and blasphemy are the staple conversation of the inmates; every indecency is openly performed; the girls recite aloud their experiences of life; ten or a dozen sleep in one bed, many in a state of nudity. Indeed, the details of these places are horrible beyond description. Unmitigated vice and lustful orgies reign, unchecked by precept or example, and the point of rivalry is as to who shall excel in filth and abomination." As the concert halls were in those days England's "Teen Canteens," so lodging houses were the "Youth Hostels".

Until well into the nineteenth century little effort was made to treat juvenile delinquency as such. Youngsters were sent to gaol, flogged, transported to the colonies, or hung according to laws governing adults. In eighteenth-century England there were 160 crimes for which the penalty might be death by hanging. "Hanging judges" frequently did not consider youth a mitigating factor in imposing a death sentence. The *Annual Register* and the press of the day contain many accounts of juvenile hangings. The most incredible is that of a six-year-old boy who cried for his mother on the scaffold while the noose was being adjusted.

As an aftermath of the Gordon Riots in 1780, in which a mob burned Newgate and other prisons and some private houses, three teen-agers were hung as ringleaders. Charles Dickens, a journalist before he was a novelist, reported that "two cripples—both were boys—one with a leg of wood, one who dragged his twisted body along with the help of a crutch, were hanged in Bloomsbury Square, where they had helped to sack Lord Mansfield's house." Another witness to this execution commented: "I never saw boys cry so much." The *Annual Register* of 1791 gives an account of the execution of two boys aged fourteen and fifteen who had been guilty of stealing. Joseph Wood and Thomas Underwood, aged twelve and fourteen, were hung for highway robbery, and a boy named Leary was sentenced to death at the age of thirteen for stealing a watch and chain. In 1735 a parish apprentice, a little girl of nine, stole twenty-seven guineas from her mistress's cabinet and went out to have fun at the Rag Fair. She was apprehended and hung.

Flogging was a favored punishment for vagrants, beggars and those who misbehaved in gaol, but hitting youngsters with whips, rods and switches was usual for any offense. Parents, school teachers, apprentices' masters and the mistresses of domestic servants wearied their arms applying corporal chastisement. Many adults justified a sadistic thrill by not "sparing the rod," or so it appears from this story in *The Diary of a Lady of Quality,* [1760]: "Dearlove, my maid, came to my room as I bade her. I bade her fetch the rod from what was my mother-in-law's rod-closet, and kneel and ask pardon, which she did with tears. I made her prepare, and I whipped her well. The girl's flesh is plump and firm, and she is a cleanly person, such a one, not excepting my own daughters who are thin, and one of them, Charlotte, rather sallow, as I have not whipped for a long time. She hath never been whipped before, she says, since she was a child (what can her mother and the late lady have been about I wonder?) and she cried out a great deal." The maid's offense, incidentally, was gossiping about the family in the servants' quarters.

Vicious flogging in the prisons seems to have been of little value as a deterrent to juvenile delinquency. Most boys took pride in absorbing the punishment stoically, and thus becoming a hero in the eyes of their peers. Typical of this attitude is that of a youthful offender who told Mayhew, "When I was first flogged there was inquiry among my fellow convicts as to 'How did D—— (meaning me) stand it? Did he sing?' the answer was 'He was a pebble'; that is, I never said 'Oh!' or gave out any expression of pain. I suffered. I took my flogging like a stone. I used to boast of it. I would say, 'I don't care, I can take it till they see my backbone.' After a flogging I've rubbed my back against a wall, just to show my bravery like, and squeezed the congealed blood out of it."

No provision was made for keeping children in separate custody in the prisons. They mixed with and learned from criminals of all types and ages. About London's infamous prison, Newgate, the statement was made that "the gaol was the government school for education in crime, and every form of judicial machinery was employed in sending the juvenile thither. The child was committed for almost every description of misconduct—the worst might be larceny, the least, trespass, ringing doorbells, or throwing stones. . . . Boys laughed at imprisonment; they were in and out of gaol perpetually. Lads of thirteen and fourteen might be found among the prisoners who had already been sentenced ten, twelve, sixteen or seventeen times. . . . old housebreakers expatiated upon their own deeds and found eager and willing listeners. . . . One with twenty previous convictions against him, who had been in Newgate as often, would have alongside him an infant of seven or eight, sent to gaol for the first time for stealing a hearth broom."

Juvenile delinquency was almost universal among the lower class throughout this period of English history, but there is much evidence that it was by no means limited to the poor, at least during the early Victorian era. By the mid-nineteenth century reformatories had come into being, and the records of one of these, Parkhurst, disclosed that of 957 inmates, 732 had attended day schools where tuition was charged. These were middle-class youths whose delinquency could not be attributed to extreme poverty.

Youths of the affluent upper class and the nobility had such great special privilege that their delinquencies, unless they involved major crime, were noted only by their parents. Many parents of this class looked on excessive drinking, gambling, and illicit sex on the part of teen-age sons as "sowing wild oats" and held that it was better for a boy to get such urges out of his system early so that he might settle down to a proper marriage and a worthy life. Lord Chesterfield was not among these indulgent parents. His famous letters to his illegitimate son disclose the type of life that many boys of this class were leading, and he exhorted Philip not to do likewise. When the lad was fifteen, and traveling with a tutor, his father wrote him:

"Many young people adopt pleasures, for which they have not the least taste, only because they are called by that name. They often mistake so totally, as to imagine that debauchery is pleasure. You must allow that drunkenness, which is equally destructive to the body and mind, is a fine pleasure. Gaming, that draws you into a thousand scrapes, leaves you penniless, and gives you the air and manners of an outrageous madmen, is another most exquisite pleasure; is it not? As to running after women, the consequences of that vice are only the loss of one's nose, the total destruction of health, and, not unfrequently, the being run through the body. These, you see, are all trifles; yet this is the catalogue of pleasures of most of those young people, who never reflecting themselves, adopt, indiscriminately."

But even the highly moral Lord Chesterfield apparently did not expect that a boy would remain celibate through his teens. A few years later he wrote: "Let the great books of the world be your principal study *Nocturna versate manu versate diurna*, which may be rendered thus: 'Turn over men by day and women by night: I mean only the best editions.'"

DELINQUENCY, OR WHAT WE WOULD TO-day call delinquency, was a fact of life in the British public schools, which were attended by the scions of the upper class and the nobility. Drinking was commonplace, and sex experience with girls of the town was not unknown. The major form of misbehavior, however, was forceful rebellion against school authority. The high-school-age student of that era was a far more aggressive rebel than any that we know today, and the histories of the schools are records of a long-drawn conflict between boys and masters.

That the masters and the teachers in public and grammar schools lived somewhat in dread of their charges is evident from the rules of conduct for students that were published by various schools as far back as the sixteenth and seventeenth centuries. In Manchester, "No scholar there being at School [shall] wear any dagger, hanger, or other weapon invasive, nor bring into the School, staff or bat, except their meat knife. That no scholar there make any affray within the same School upon the Master, or the Usher, upon pain of leaving off his said School by one month." At Hawkshead it was ruled that "they shall use no weapons in the School as sword, dagger, waster [wooden sword or cudgel], or other like, to fight or brawl withal, nor any unlawful gaming in the School. They shall not haunt taverns, alehouses, or playing at any unlawful game as cards, dice-tables or such like." In Wigan, "Any scholar bringing any weapon to school or making any affray is to be liable to severe correction. . . . and all stubborn and disobedient scholars that are pertinaciously and exemplarily bad, by resisting the Master or

Usher, or offering to struggle with, strike, spurn and abuse, the Master or Usher when he or they are orderly correcting them for their fault . . . shall the third time be expelled the school."

Modern parents may take some comfort from the fact that their children are not peculiar in their rebellion against adult-approved dress and grooming, for it is a tradition of youth that goes back to ancient times. At Harrow, the rules provided that "the schoolmaster shall have regard to the manners of his scholars, and see that they come not uncombed, unwashed, ragged, or slovenly." And the Heath Grammar School ruled: "If any scholar shall go undecently in his apparel . . . or use long hair on his head undecently or come with face and hands unwashed, he shall be severly punished, and upon the second admonition, if he do not reform, he shall be expelled the School."

Stern masters sought to cope with their rebellious and rambunctious charges with a strap or rod applied with a strong right arm for the slightest misbehavior. On one occasion at Eton the masters flogged more than eighty boys on a single night. At Winchester, with 198 boys in residence, 279 cases were reported for punishment on one day. If the boys considered that punishment had been carried too far, they frequently rebelled *en masse,* and the records of England's best schools are rife with accounts of student uprisings. The students of Eton threw their books in the river and marched to Maidenhead, where they spent £55 on a feast and drinking bout. When the headmaster of Rugby administered what the boys considered unjust punishment, they broke all the windows in the school, dragged out the furniture and the master's books and made a fire in the close. The insurrection was not suppressed until a party of constables arrived with drovers' whips and drove the rebels to an island in the moat, where they were finally subdued.

A riot by the boys of Winchester is described in a contemporary chronicle as follows: "They suddenly attacked the porters, forced from them the keys of the College, and locked out all the Masters. Having thus obtained full possession of the building, they proceeded to take up, with pickaxes, etc., the large stones with which the Court was paved, and soon conveyed upwards of a cart-load of them to the top of the building, threatening any one who approached the gates. In this barricaded state, they kept possession all the night, deaf to the remonstrances of their friends, and bidding defiance to their masters. On the following morning, after many admonitions were in vain given them to return to their duty, it was found necessary to call out a party of Military, some Constables, etc., who procured crowbars and other instruments to force the gates. . . . There were only six out of 230 who did not join in the revolt."

The mass rebellion of students became a tradition of British public schools, so much so that George III, meeting some Eton students at Windsor, joked with them about the floggings and mutinies in their school life and asked: "Have you had any good mutinies lately, heh, heh?"

At some schools it became the custom for the boys to take over the school by force near the end of the year. "It has been the custom from time out of mind to bar out the master . . . and keep him out for three days," relates a contemporary account. "During the period of this expulsion the doors of the citadel, the school, were strongly barricaded within; and the boys who defended it like a besieged city were armed. . . . The master made various efforts, by force and stratagem to regain his lost authority. If he succeeded, heavy tasks were imposed . . . but if, as more commonly happened, he was repulsed and defeated after three days' siege, terms of capitulation were proposed by the master and accepted by the boys." Most important of these terms were fewer floggings and more food.

Cruelty and brutality to younger boys was accepted as a matter of course in the British public schools. Fagging was practiced in all schools. Under this system the younger boys served the older as valets, bootblacks, errand boys and general servants. Seniors might make fags hold hot coals in their hands, to toughen them to carry hot dishes, they said, or they would hold youngsters before the fire until their legs were blistered. William Pitt declared that nearly every boy was cowed for life at Eton, and one story tells of a boy who was "taken from the Charterhouse because he was almost literally killed there by the develish cruelty of the boys. They used to lay him before the fire till he was scorched and shut him up in a trunk with sawdust till he had nearly expired with suffocation."

In 1835 "The London Society for the Protection of Young Females and Prevention of Juvenile Prostitution" had this to say about juvenile delinquency in London: "The committee cannot avoid referring to the present dreadfully immoral state of the British metropolis. No one can pass through the streets without being struck with the awfully depraved condition of a certain class of the youth of both sexes. Nor is it too much to say that in London crime has arrived at a frightful magnitude; nay, it is asserted that nowhere does it exist to such an extent as in this highly-favored city. Schools for the instruction of youth in every species of theft and immorality are here established. It has been proved that 400 individuals procure a livelihood by trepanning females from eleven to fifteen years of age for the purposes of prostitution."

It was taken for granted that the vagrant girls, the inmates of lodging houses and most female parish apprentices should be prostitutes. The *London Times* quoted the master of a workhouse to the effect that nine-tenths of the girls who were apprenticed "eventually got corrupted and took to the streets." But juvenile prostitution was not limited to the very poor. Most girls who had to make their own living were virtually forced to supplement their incomes by selling sex. Wages for waitresses, needleworkers, laundresses, milliners, and, in fact, almost every class of female workers, were so low that they did not provide subsistence. Unless a girl had help from parents or relatives she was faced with a choice of prostitution, starvation, or the workhouse, and there were tens of thousands of young girls in this situation who chose prostitution rather than picking oakum.

Girls who were employed as domestics did not have the excuse of necessity; at least they had shelter and food. Yet this class was notoriously immoral. There was a great oversupply of girls for domestic service; it provided the best opportunity for a country girl who wanted to come to the big city. In the mid-nineteenth century there were over 300,000 teen-aged domestics in England, and probably as many more wide-eyed rural lasses ready to take their places. In such a situation few girls resisted the advances of the master or, more frequently, the master's son. It is somewhat ironic that in the supposedly highly moral Victorian age the seduction of servant girls was rather a common practice. If the girl was caught, or became pregnant, she lost her situation without a reference and usually became a prostitute. Also maid servants seldom had a chance of marrying, so that it was not unusual for a lonely girl to give herself to the cop on the beat, a soldier in the park, or the shopmen whom they met in the course of their duties. Mayhew concluded: "Female servants are far from being a virtuous class."

Not all immoral girls were willing delinquents, at least initially. Girls were sold for prostitution or concubinage throughout the eighteenth century. One Cornwall pair of yokels who were picked up for offering their twelve-year-old daughter for sale to patrons of a tavern naively gave as their excuse that they had heard that "maidens were very scarce in London, and that they sold there for a good price."Another father put his daughter up as a stake in a card game. As part of a campaign against selling girls the *Spectator* published this letter from a prospective seller in the 1760's.

"My Lord,—I having a great esteem for your honor; and a better opinion of you than of any of the quality, makes me acquaint you of an affair that I hope will oblige you to know. I have a niece that came to town about a fortnight ago . . . She is not sixteen; as pretty a gentlewoman as ever you saw; a little woman; which I know your lordship likes; well-shaped, and as fair a complexion for red and white as ever I saw. I doubt not but your lordship will be of the same opinion. . . . If your lordship thinks fit to make an appointment, where I shall wait on you with my niece, by a line or two, I stay for your answer, for I have no place fitted up, since I left my house, fit to entertain your honor. I told her she should go with me to see a gentleman, a very good friend of mine; so I desire you to take no notice of my letter by reason she is ignorant of the ways of the town."

Procurers haunted the metropolis in droves, using their wiles to lure young girls into brothels or provide them to private patrons. Motherly women and kindly old men approached incoming country girls at coach depots or way stations to "help" the bewildered youngsters find lodging or a situation. Women met arriving coaches posing as potential mistresses in search of a servant. The more elite procuresses served only one or two wealthy patrons who had a taste for young girls. Some of these operated shops patronized by servant girls whom they invited into a back room for a friendly spot of gin and a proposition. One such testified that she had supplied ten girls to her two wealthy patrons over a period of four months. The Society for the Protection of Young Females told of women who attended church and Sunday School to decoy girls of eleven or twelve either for brothels or private patrons. In the brothel it was customary to give young virgins to preferred patrons at an inflated fee before making them publicly available. There are cases of girls whose virginity was sold half a dozen times—a procedure which must have involved the connivance of the child.

A high standard of sexual morality, particularly for females, was supposedly one of the most noted characteristics of the Victorian era. Actually, this standard applied inflexibly to girls of the upper class, for whom no departure from the rigid code was permissible, but did not govern the behavior of the great mass of juveniles. The attitude towards morality which prevailed down to the twentieth century was that the upper classes were an elite with special privileges and matching responsibilities. The delinquencies of the ordinary children and youth were considered part of the natural order of the society. After all, what else could one expect of the offspring of the poor and laboring classes? Not everyone subscribed to this view, of course. A reformer, for instance, campaigning for a bill to protect children, asked the Parliament: "Do you really know what takes place on the sands of the seashore at our resorts or in Epping Forest on Bank Holidays?" And, she declared: "You have in London couples, and very often young couples, or mere boys and girls, waiting in queues in order to gain entrance to disorderly houses on the South Side of London and pay a shilling for the use of these rooms."

The foregoing might give the impression that pretwentieth-century English kids terrorized the land by running wild. This is not true, of course. Even as today, the great majority of them were well brought up in loving homes and were guilty of nothing more serious than the pranks, mischief and minor rebellions that are normal to youth and which were, at that time, not considered delinquency. But the structure of the class society and the prevalence of abject poverty fostered juvenile delinquency on a scale which would make the current "wave" in America a minor disturbance.

6

Early American
Rebels

A CASE MIGHT BE MADE FOR THE PREMISE
that delinquent juveniles were a factor in triggering the American
Revolution. Admittedly, this is a rather far-fetched idea. Juveniles
had nothing to do with "taxation without representation," nor with
commercial objectives and the resentment of the "have nots" for the
"haves" which were less publicized causes of the upheaval. But
boys were involved in the *acts* of incitement to rebellion that helped
to develop the differences with the mother country into a shooting
war.

On March 5, 1770, a British sentry at King Street in Boston was
so plagued by a group which was taunting him and throwing snowballs that he became panicky and called out the main guard, a
captain and six or seven men. History does not tell the ages of those
who heckled the sentry by throwing snowballs—then, as now, primarily a juvenile practice. With the appearance of the guard, a
crowd gathered and "pressed on the soldiers." There were murmurs
and threats and at least one thrown rock, which laid low a private

named Montgomery. At this, either with or without orders, the guard fired, killing three Bostonians and wounding two others mortally. Some accounts of the Boston Massacre state that the stone which felled Montgomery was thrown by a boy. If so, this unknown juvenile delinquent may be credited with starting the shooting phase of the American Revolution.

The Colonial participants in the Boston Massacre were part of the "Boston Mob" which had already become a nuisance to the law-abiding inhabitants. This group of trouble makers was described as being made up of "vagrants, sailors, Irish and apprentices." How many were juvenile apprentices is not known, but they undoubtedly outnumbered the others, among whom were also many teen-agers. Thus it is reasonable to assume that a good portion of the so-called "mob" was adolescents. This was not mentioned in contemporary accounts because it had no special significance. Boys of fifteen and upward were considered adults.

Juveniles were involved in the actions of the Sons of Liberty, although the leaders of these groups, organized in each colony after the passage of the Stamp Act in 1765, were adults and sometimes men of stature and property. But one cannot imagine men of the stamp of Sam Adams and John Hancock, leaders of the Sons of Liberty in Massachusetts, participating in the acts of delinquency and vandalism perpetrated in the name of liberty during the ten years before the Revolution. Taunting of loyalists and the erection of Liberty Poles were minor manifestations of the unruly spirit. More serious were many cases of houseburning, bookburning, boatburning, and assaults on and indignities to customs officers and affluent citizens who showed little desire for rebellion. In American history the participants in these actions against law and order are labeled patriots. In British history, they are considered rebellious delinquents.

Aside from the pre-Revolutionary assault and vandalism in the name of liberty, the Colonial era in America was a bright spot in the world history of juvenile delinquency. The chronicles of the colonies contain few records of wild kids. The conditions that were causing such a high incidence of juvenile misbehavior in England were exactly reversed in her colonies in the New World. For most of the period, America was a frontier, and juvenile delinquency has always been rare under frontier conditions. Poverty was far less prevalent than in England. Although wages were miserably low, there was work for everybody and destitution was the fault of the individual rather than of the society.

The colonies were predominantly rural; there were few cities in which juvenile delinquency could breed. The first United States census, taken in 1790, disclosed that only 3.3 per cent of the people lived in towns and cities of more than 8,000 population. Education, while not completely universal, was available for most children. Masters were required to see to it that their apprentices learned to read and write, and most towns had schools conducted by ministers. There were few broken homes. Wives were in such demand that a widow seldom remained single for long. In an agrarian population desertion by the husband and father was rare. Everybody, or almost everybody, drank, but there was none of the gin-swilling that blighted the lives of the lower class in England.

Although better education, less poverty, more stable family life, and the absence of urban congestion all helped to keep colonial youth on the straight-and-narrow, the principal cause of their good behavior was work. From the time they were toddlers, most Colonial kids, except on the southern plantations, were required to work from dawn to dusk at lessons, chores, as apprentices, or in home industry.

In New England there were child labor laws, but they did not forbid the employment of children; rather, they compelled it. A Massachusetts edict in 1641 provided: "It is desired and expected that all masters of families should see that their children and servants should be industriously employed so that mornings and evenings and other seasons may not be lost as formerly they have been." In the same year Plymouth ruled that in regard to "those that have relief from the townes and have children and do not employ them . . . it shall be lawful for the towneship to take order that those children shall be put to worke in fitting employment according to their strength and abilities and placed out by the townes." The people of Rowley were praised when they "built a fulling mill and caused their little ones to be very diligent in spinning cotton wool."

The colonists brought most of the old-country customs and attitudes concerning children to the New World, but here they were shorn of their delinquency-breeding aspects. There were almshouses, but they were for honest paupers and sheltered none of the depraved class that corrupted the morals of children in English workhouses. The town authorities were responsible for orphans and deserted children and could take idle poor children away from their parents and put them with a more industrious family, but there was a much greater concern for the welfare of such children and supervision of their moral upbringing. The equivalent of English parish apprentices were placed with carefully selected families who were required to provide the child with both religious and secular education. Baby farming was limited and supervised, and cases of extreme brutality to children, with which the English chronicles abound, were rare in the colonies. Except for apprentices, children were seldom sent out of the home in the colonies. A greater concern by parents was probably a factor in this, although the economic value of the child's labor in the home or on the farm was a compelling reason for keeping it at home.

The apprentice system as practiced in the colonies was more akin to the original guild apprenticeship of medieval days. Children were placed with honest artisans to learn a trade as they earned their keep with long hours of labor. There was no outdoor apprenticeship and little evidence of masters who took apprentices solely for the fee. There were runaway apprentices, many of them, but they seldom ran away to a life of vagrancy and thievery. Rather, they answered the call of opportunity and excitement offered by the sea, the frontier, or the hopefully greener pastures of another colony, where they started a new career.

One such runaway, who by today's standards would be called a juvenile delinquent, was Benjamin Franklin. The man who became America's greatest early diplomat, philosopher, scientist, humorist and writer was apprenticed to his brother James, a printer in Boston, at the age of twelve. During the next five years he expressed his youthful rebellion against the adult code of the colony in some writing, of which he said, "I had already made myself a little obnoxious to the governing party." When he was seventeen, he wrote: "A fresh difference arising between my brother and me, I took upon me to assert my freedom. . . . The unfairness of it weighed little with me under the impressions of resentment for the blows his passion too often urged him to bestow upon me." The teen-aged Benjamin sold some books and had a friend book passage for him on a New York-bound sloop, telling the captain that the passenger was a "young acquaintance of his that had got a naughty girl with child, whose friends would compell me to marry her, and therefore I could not appear to come away publicly."

The most prevalent forms of juvenile delinquency in the old country did not exist in the colonies. Beggars were almost unknown in a society that made a fetish of work, and laws against begging were vigorously enforced. There was little opportunity to beg in a land with few large towns and those far from one another. Nor were there many large crowds such as pickpockets needed to ply their trade successfully. Some youthful apprentices and servants undoubtedly stole from their masters, but as there was no place for them to fence stolen goods, there was little temptation to steal.

In the northern colonies disturbing the peace was frowned on to an extent that has not been equalled until modern times. In New

England boys were constantly in trouble for misbehavior in church or otherwise profaning the Sabbath with worldly conduct. The Dutch in New York were plagued by boys who shouted "Indians" to stir up the night patrol, and sicked dogs on the watchman. The good burgesses of Albany did not mince matters in restraining youth from disturbing the peace of staid adults, as witness this 1713 regulation:

"Whereas ye children of ye sd city do very unorderly to ye shame and scandall of their parents ryde down ye hills in ye streets of the sd city with small and great slees on the Lord's day and in the week by which many accidents may come, now for preventing ye same it is hereby published and declard yt it shall and may be lawful for any constable in this city or any other person or persons to take any slee or slees from all and every such boys and girls rydeing or offering to ryde down any hill within ye sd city and breake any slee or slees in pieces."

All Colonial kids were drinkers, but this was not then considered delinquency. Everybody drank, including the children, in quantities that would today affect the steadiest head. Northern youngsters drank beer and watered rum; southerners of the better class favored wine or brandy. A seventeenth-century description of the funeral of a six-year-old child who was borne to his grave by six of his age group tells of the infant pallbearers being given glasses of sweetened gin and water to fortify them for their melancholy task.

THE RECORD FOR GOOD BEHAVIOR ESTABlished by Colonial kids seems to indicate that "spare the rod and spoil the child" is a more effective philosophy in bringing up children than our modern reliance on child psychology. The rod was applied freely in Colonial days. But it is probable that the Puritan ethic had more to do with juvenile behavior than corporal punishment. We are inclined to believe that Puritanism was confined to

New England. Actually, a large percentage of the people of the middle colonies also followed the Puritan tradition, as did, in most essentials, the Quakers and Moravians of Pennsylvania and the Scotch-Irish immigrants who formed a sizeable group in the south.

The Puritans had a stern and uncompromising attitude towards juvenile delinquency because they interpreted most aspects of youthful misbehavior as sins against God. There was little difference between sin and secular offense, because the New England colonies were theocracies in which all of the sins of the Old Testament were the basis for the secular legal code. For instance, it was a capital crime for a child to strike a parent in defiance of the edict of "Honour thy father and thy mother." The all-powerful leaders of the church held parents accountable for raising children in strict observance of the Puritan moral code. One ordinance provided that neglect of parental duty "whereby children and servants become rude, stubborn and unruly" should be penalized by the removal of such children into better hands until their conduct was mended. It seems that this ordinance was unenforced for a time and "sin and prophaneness" increased as the result of "the ensnaring of many children and servants by the dissolute lives and practices of such as do live from under family government." Selectmen were ordered to see that the law was enforced, for "many parents and masters are too indulgent and negligent of their duty."

In a preface to a children's book on morality, *The Token for Children,* Cotton Mather spelled out the responsibility of parents by asking: "Are the souls of your children of no value? Are you willing that they should be brands of hell? Are you indifferent whether they be damned or saved? Shall the devil run away with them without control? Will not you use your utmost endeavor to deliver them from the wrath to come? You see that they are not subjects uncapable of the grace of God; whatever you think of them, Christ doth not slight them; they are not too little to die, they are not too little to go to hell."

Puritan kids had more than parental discipline to contend with. In the opinion of the Puritan ministers, all children were born "depraved." They were "children of wrath," preached the Reverend Philemon Robbins, who were "as odious in the sight of God as snakes or vipers are to us." Jonathan Edwards also liked the viper simile and said that children "are young vipers and are even more hateful than vipers and are in a most miserable condition, as well as grown persons." Cotton Mather prayed for guidance to "see whether there bee nothing further that I can do to save the children of my flock from falling into the unquenchable Fire of the Wrath of God." The Reverend Alvan Hyde said that "infants are by nature sinners," as was proved by the words of the psalmist who wrote that "the wicked are estranged from the womb; they go astray as soon as they are born, speaking lies."

The first thing a child was taught when learning the alphabet from the *New England Primer* was: "In Adam's Fall, / We sinned All." Sermons, such as this addressed to children by Jonathan Edwards, were reminders that youngsters were born delinquent: "You are all naturally in a miserable state and condition. In a little time you will be in Eternity, some sooner and some later. Therefore were you here told of the anger of God at the sins of children. . . . God is angry with you every day. How dreadful to have God angry with you. How dreadful will it be to be in Hell among the devils and know that you must be there to all Eternity. . . . How dreadful it will be, to be all together in misery. Then you won't play together any more but will be damned together, will cry out with weeping and wailing and gnashing of teeth together."

It is not surprising that Puritan children did not enjoy the Sabbath and that church officers had to prowl the aisles to keep the "wretched boys" in line. John Pike of Dedham received sixteen shillings in 1723 for "keeping the boys in subjection six months," and demanded twice as much when his contract was renewed. In

Harwich it was voted that "the same course be pursued with the girls." Cotton Mather speaks of the "Unruly children on the Lord's Day in our congregation," and one Connecticut justice left this record of a small boy's wrongdoings in 1750: "Smiling and larfing and intiseing others to the same evil. . . . Pulling the hair of his nayber Veroni Simkins in the time of public worship. . . . Throwing Sister Penticost Perkins on the ice on the Sabbath day between the meeting hows and his place of abode."

Although there is little record of more serious offenses than "larfing" in church or whittling on the Sabbath, some seemed to believe that a wave of juvenile delinquency was sweeping the colonies in the seventeenth century. Governor Bradford wrote that "many of their children, by licentiousness of youth in ye countrie, and ye manifold temptations of the place, were drawn away by evil examples into extravagante and dangerous courses, getting ye raines off their necks and departing from their parents. Some became soldiers, other took upon them for viages by sea, and other some worse courses, tending to disoluteness and the danger of their soules, to ye great greef of their parents and dishonor of God."

The Reverend Ezekiel Rogers lamented: "I find great trouble and grief about the rising generation. Young people . . . strengthen one another in evil by example and by counsel. Much ado have I with my own family." That sounds familiar in the twentieth century as well as a comment by Jonathan Edwards' biographer. Edwards, he stated, was "utterly opposed to everything like unreasonable hours on the part of young people, in their visiting and amusements, which he regarded as a dangerous step toward corruption and bringing them to ruin. And he thought the excuse offered by many parents for tolerating this practice in their children—that it was the custom, and that children of other people are allowed thus to practice, and therefore it is difficult and even impossible to restrain them—was insufficient and frivolous and manifested a great degree of stupidity."

A paradox in Puritan morality was the apparently high level of sex delinquency. Colonial records, which report little youthful crime, are full of instances of illicit sexual relations. In Rhode Island in 1655 "the Lord Protector hath lately received complaints that we abound with whoredom." Of that colony it was also written that "illegitimacy was a not uncommon offence . . . at any time in the first century of our colonial history. . . . A young woman's prospects of marrying respectably and of moving thereafter in respectable society, do not seem to have been seriously impaired by her already having shown herself qualified to discharge the functions of a wife and mother." Another student of colonial folkways writes: "Sexual sins were common. It must be remembered that the Puritan was the inheritor of a fund of coarse sensualism from his middle-class Elizabethan and Stuart English origins. His religion permitted no class of recognized prostitutes. . . . A vast amount of sexual license was the result."

The Marquis de Castelleux, whose journal of a long stay in America during the closing years of the eighteenth century gives valuable insight into customs of that time, records a visit to a Connecticut family in which a girl was confined to her room because of improper sexual behavior, although she was treated kindly and the family had no hesitation in telling her story to a traveler. "It was the custom of the country to regard such accidents not as irretrievable ruin, but as misfortunes which could be remedied." The Marquis added that when girls strayed from the path of virtue, "their mistake was lamented rather than condemned, and they could afterwards marry and take as good a position as ever, although their story was neither unknown nor attempted to be concealed."

Sexual intercourse between courting couples was not unusual. In one case of a couple who were convicted of fornication before marriage, the parents were brought into court and fined because they had opposed an early marriage of the young couple "so long after they were in order thereto."

The church ruled that any couple who had a baby within seven months after they were married had to make public confession of their premarital misconduct, and newspapers published such items as this from the *Braintree Record* of March 2, 1683: "Temperance, the daughter of brother F——, now the wife of John B——, having been guilty of the sin of fornication with him that is now her husband, was called forth in open congregation, and presented a paper containing a full acknowledgement of her great sin and wickedness, publickly bewailed her disobedience to parents. . . . She was solemnly admonished of her great sin." The church records of Groton show that of 200 couples who had babies baptised during the fourteen years before the Revolution, sixty-six—one third—confessed to fornication before marriage. In another instance of sixteen couples who were admitted to communion during a two-year period, nine confessed to premarital sexual relations.

Much of this sexual delinquency can possibly be attributed to the Colonial practice of bundling. In this seventeenth- and eighteenth-century Old World custom, boys and girls shared a bed to do their courting, for the very practical reason that the girl's family could not afford to burn fuel to warm even a one- or two-room house on cold winter nights. And they had no other private place to go. There was little criticism of bundling until after the French and Indian War, when the clergy blamed "the loose camp vices, recklessness, which soon flooded the land with immorality and infidelity," on the boys who came back from the war. Ministers thundered against the old tradition. Their sermons were answered with poems and essays by pro-bundlers, most querying: "How else can a girl get a husband?" The bundlers were supposed to remain fully clothed, but there is ample evidence that many did not. Even that staunch Puritan Abigail Adams acknowledged this when, writing of a sea voyage, she said: "We only in part undress—about as much as the Yankee bundlers."

In his facetious *Knickerbocker's History of New York,* Washington Irving made tongue-in-cheek charges against his Connecticut neighbors by describing "the curious device among these sturdy barbarians [the Connecticut colonists], to keep up a harmony of interests, and promote population. . . . They multiplied to a degree which would be incredible to any man unacquainted with the marvellous fecundity of this growing country. This amazing increase may, indeed, be partly ascribed to a singular custom prevalent among them, commonly known by the name of *bundling*—a superstitious rite observed by the young people of both sexes, with which they usually terminated their festivities. . . . This ceremony was likewise, in those primitive times, considered as an indispensable preliminary to matrimony; their courtships commencing where ours usually finished, by which means they acquired that intimate acquaintance with each other's good qualities before marriage, which has been pronounced by philosophers the sure basis of a happy union. . . . To this sagacious custom, therefore, do I chiefly attribute the unparalleled increase of the Yanokie or Yankee tribe; for it is a certain fact, well authenticated by court records and parish registers, that wherever the practice of bundling prevailed, there was an amazing number of sturdy brats annually born into the state, without the license of the law, or the benefit of clergy. Neither did the irregularity of their birth operate in the least of their disparagement."

In 1790 the beginning of a change in the American economy offered many children what was then considered a great opportunity. When Samuel Slater started the first true factory in America, for spinning and weaving cotton, all of the operatives in the small establishment were children aged seven to twelve. Child labor in factories was heartily endorsed not only for its economic, but also for its moral value. An early treatise on the subject pointed out the great value to the economy of the labor of girls from ten to sixteen, "most of whom are too young or delicate for agriculture," and added that their work in industry would prevent the "vice and immorality to which children are exposed by a career of idleness."

This employment of children for twelve hours tending spindles meshed nicely with the Puritan tradition that industry was a virtue, idleness a sin. There could be little opportunity for juvenile delinquency in this system under which it was said that "when the child is through at the mill it is tired enough to go to bed." Actually the conditions under which juveniles were employed in American factories did not, in the early days, contribute to delinquency as they did in England. There it was the custom to ship parish apprentices by scores and hundreds to the northern cotton mills where they lived under the most appalling conditions. When a factory failed, as many did, the children were often turned loose to shift for themselves by begging or stealing.

This did not happen in the early American factories. In some places, such as Rhode Island, it became the custom to hire large families, the parents and all their children over the age of five or six, for factory work. Here the kids lived and worked under parental supervision. In other northern states, particularly Massachusetts, mill owners hired principally the young daughters of farmers. These girls came to such mill towns as Lowell and Waltham and lived in dormitories maintained by the factory owners. Factory work was considered as second only to school teaching as a desirable career for young girls. They were carefully supervised by matrons who were concerned with their religious and moral training, and the mill owners provided lecturers on cultural subjects and instruction in domestic arts. This idealistic pattern was brought to an end by the depression of 1830, which changed the relationship of the mill owners to their girls. The dormitories were given up and the girls left to live as they liked, or as they could on less than a subsistence wage. Later, child labor in factories became a contributing factor to delinquency, but the first child labor laws that sought to alleviate the situation did not appear until some years after the Civil War.

MOST ILL-FAMED OF PURITAN JUVENILE DElinquents are the numerous children who became accusers in some of the witchcraft cases in the latter half of the seventeenth century, whose mischievous bids for attention led to the execution of several supposed witches. The kids did not start the great witch hunts in New England, which had their genesis in customs and beliefs in the old countries. But many precocious Puritan youngsters saw in the witch-hunt hysteria an opportunity to confound their parents and ministers, to stir up some excitement, and to get even with adults whom they disliked.

In the year of 1688 the family of John Goodwin, of Boston, employed the teen-aged daughter of a woman named Glover as a laundress. The Goodwins' six children included a daughter Martha, thirteen; a son John, eleven; a daughter Mercy, seven; and a son Benjamin, five. Martha accused the young laundress of stealing some linen which was missing; whereat, in the words of Cotton Mather, the accused girl's mother "in her daughter's defense bestowed very bad language upon the girl that put her to the question; immediately upon which the poor child became variously indisposed in her health, and visited with strange fits. . . . It was not long before one of her sisters and two of her brothers were seized, in order one after another with affects like those that molested her. Within a few weeks they were all four tortured everywhere in a manner so grievous that it would have broken a heart of stone to have seen their agonies."

The children's "symptoms" were many and varied. They laid their heads on their shoulders and could not straighten them up; they opened their mouths and could not close them; they stuck out their tongues; they were deaf; they were dumb; they were blind, and sometimes all three at once; "they would make most pitteous outcries that they were cut with knives and struck with blows that they could not bear." Mather and the children's parents saw no inconsistency in the fact that the children were afflicted only during the day. "About nine or ten at night they always had a release from their miseries, and ate and slept all night for the most part indifferently well," according to Mather. It apparently never occurred to him that the children could have been pretending. They were model children who "had enjoyed a religious education," and had "an observable affection unto Divine Sacred things . . . their parents also kept them in continual employment which did more than deliver them from temptations of idleness." Of course, their "afflictions" interrupted the children's religious education and continual employment, but nobody considered this as a possible motivation.

The children were examined by skillful physicians, "particularly our worthy and prudent friend Dr. Thomas Oakes," who found himself so "affronted by the distempers of the children" that he concluded that nothing but "a hellish witchcraft could be the original of these maladies." Goodwin laid the charge of witchcraft against Mrs. Glover, "an ignorant and scandalous old woman," who, it is said, had been accused of being a witch by her "miserable husband" before he died.

The woman was hauled before the magistrates for trial. The Goodwin children were brought into court and promptly had fits when the accused looked at them. Another child, a boy named Hughes, "was taken ill in the same woeful and surprising manner of the Goodwin children. One night, particularly, the boy said he saw a black thing with a blue cap in the room tormenting him and he complained most bitterly of a hand put into the bed to pull out his bowels." This happened immediately before his mother was to testify against the Glover woman and to relate how another neighbor had accused her of witchcraft on her death-bed six years before.

Obviously the "black thing with a blue cap" was a demon sent by Glover in retaliation. All of this was conclusive proof. The poor woman was condemned and hung.

The death of the witch should have released the Goodwin kids from her spell, but they had a good thing going and had no intention of relinquishing it. At first it was thought that they were still being persecuted by Glover from the grave, but they later said that there were other witches, whom they could not name, who were revenging the old woman. Their fits now occurred when they were required to do anything that they did not want to do. "Upon the least reproof of their parents for any unfit thing they said or did, most grievous, woeful, heart-breaking agonies would they fall into. If any useful thing were to be done to them, or by them, they would have all sorts of troubles fall unto them. It would sometimes cost one of them an hour or two to be undrest in the evening, or drest in the morning . . . nor could they go to wash their hands without having them clasped so odly together, there was no doing it. But when their friends were near tired with waiting, anon they might do what they would do unto them. Whatever work they were bid to do, they would be so snapped in the member which was to do it, that they with grief still desisted from it."

Things improved somewhat when Mather took the oldest girl, Martha, into his home and another minister took John. Thereafter the afflictions of the two youngest ceased; they obviously did not have sufficient imagination to continue the game alone. John, too, improved greatly. But Martha was made of sterner stuff and carried the devil and his demons into the Mather household. Since infancy the child had been required to listen to four hours of preaching and prayer every Sunday. Now when Mather prayed over her she became deaf. When asked to read the Bible she was blinded, although she could read joke books with ease. Martha's spirits sent her an invisible horse on which she trotted and galloped around the Mather home while conversing with the demons. She told the minister that they were planning to afflict his wife, but the holy Mrs. Mather was apparently beyond their reach.

The whole group of Goodwin children had a final mass seizure when Martha and John went home, "at the time they call Christmas." [Good Puritans like Mather did not celebrate Christmas.] Led by Martha, the children "were by the demons made very drunk, though they had no strong drink (as we are fully sure) to make them so. . . . Immediately the ridiculous behaviors of one drunk were with a wonderful exactness represented." The children reeled, staggered, fell down, and spoke in a drunken manner. They finally slept off the imaginary binge.

Far more serious and inflammatory were the delinquencies of a group of teen-aged girls in Salem, of whom a twelve-year-old, Abigail Williams, was the ringleader. Abigail lived with her uncle, the Reverend Samuel Parris, and started her career as a witch detector by having a fit in which she first flew around the room with arms flapping and crying, "Whish, Whish, Whish." She then cried that a seventy-one-year-old woman, Rebecca Nurse, was in the room. "Do you not see her? There she stands." She insisted that Goodwife Nurse was trying to make her sign the devil's book.

Next day in church Abigail had another fit, which set off fits in several other girls. At one time or another, Anne Putnam, aged twelve; Elizabeth Hubbard, seventeen; Elizabeth Parris, eleven; Mary Walcut and Mercy Lewis had fits in a group or independently of one another. Of the first church incident, Reverend Deodat Lawson, the Salem minister, related: "In sermon time when Goodwife Corey was present in the meeting house Abigail Williams called out, "Look where Goodwife C sits on the beam suckling her yellow bird betwixt her fingers.' Anne Putnam, another girl afflicted, said there was a yellow bird sat on my hat as it hung on the pin in the pulpit."

On the following day Goodwife Corey was hailed before the magistrates and the girls, backed by a few hysterical women, "did vehemently accuse her of afflicting them of biting, pinching, and strangling, etc." They all told of seeing her likeness in their fits and of the book that she tried to compel them to sign. It was noted that when the accused bit her lower lip the afflicted youngsters were "bitten on their arms and wrists and produced the marks before the magistrates, ministers and others." One girl said that the devil in the shape of a black man was whispering in Goodwife Corey's ear. Another saw the little yellow bird again, suckling between the fingers of the accused. Mrs. Corey was "that afternoon committed to Salem Prison and after she was in custody she did not appear to them or afflict them as before."

Goodwife Nurse was tried two days later, and again the youngsters, abetted by a few women, put on their act. The Williams and Putnam girls "accused her that she appeared to them and afflicted them in their fits. Some of the others said that they had seen her but knew not that ever she had hurt them; amongst which was Mary Walcut who was presently after she had so declared bitten and cried out in the meeting house and produced the marks of teeth on her wrist." Reverend Lawson wrote: "Others also were grievously afflicted, so that there was once such a hideous screech and noise (which I heard as I walked some little distance from the meeting house) as did amaze me, and some that were within told me the whole assembly was struck with consternation, and that they were afraid that those that sat next to them were under the influence of witchcraft. This woman also was committed to Salem Prison."

The afflicted children now accelerated their vicious game. The extent of their mischief is indicated by this order, one of several, issued by the Salem magistrates: "To their Majesties Gaol-keeper in Salem. You are in Their Majesties Name hereby required to take into your care, and safe custody, the Bodies of William Hobs, and Deborah his Wife, Mary Easty, the Wife of Isaac Easty, and Sarah Wild, the Wife of John Wild, all of Topsfield; and Edward Bishop of Salem-Village, Husbandman, and Sarah his Wife, and Mary Black, a Negro of Lieutenant Nathaniel Putmans of Salem-Village; also Mary English the Wife of Philip English, Merchant in Salem; who stand charged with High Suspicion of Sundry Acts of Witchcraft, done or committed by them lately upon the Bodies of Anne Putnam, Mercey Lewes and Abigail Williams, of Salem-Village, whereby great Hurt and Damage hath been done to the Bodies of the said Persons."

The most appalling act of the Salem delinquents was the accusation of a four-year-old child, Dorcas Good, whose mother Sarah was already in prison. The girls went into their fits when this toddler looked at them, produced marks of her small teeth on their arms, and told of the snake that the little one suckled with her finger. Dorcas was confined in the Salem gaol for eight months, and "being chained in the dungeon was so hardly used and terrified that she has ever since been very changeable, having little or no reason to govern herself," or so her father said in an appeal for damages eighteen years later. He was awarded £30.

The witch hunt spread outside Salem when Joseph Ballard of Andover, whose wife was ill, "sent to Salem for some of those accusers, to tell him who afflicted his wife; others did like. Horse and man were sent from several places to fetch those accusers who had the spectral sight, that they might tell who afflicted those that were in any ways ill." As a result of the girls' fits, complaints of afflicting their neighbors were lodged against more than fifty people in Andover. Also, "at Andover the afflicted complained of a dog as afflicting of them and would fall into their fits at the dog looking upon them. The dog was put to death."

The hunt moved on to Gloucester "and occasioned four women to be sent to prison." The girls were then sent for by Ipswich. "In their way passing over Ipswich Bridge, they met with an old woman and instantly fell into their fits. But by this time the validity of such accusations being much questioned, they found not that encouragement they had done elsewhere and soon withdrew."

It was high time for the girls to end their reign of terror. One contemporary account listed "Nineteen persons having been hang'd, and one prest to death, and Eight more condemned, in all Twenty and Eight. . . . above an Hundred and Fifty in Prison, and above Two Hundred more accused." There is no doubt that juvenile delinquents contributed largely to the Salem witch hunts. Thomas Brattle, a contemporary observer who was more objective than most, put it this way: "That when I call these afflicted 'the afflicted children' I would not be understood as though I meant that all that are afflicted are *children*: there are several young men and women who are afflicted, as well as children. But this term has most prevailed among us, because of the younger sort that were first afflicted, and therefore I make use of it."

A CLASS OF JUVENILES WHO OFTEN BECAME delinquent in the colonies were bonded or indentured youngsters. Indentured servants came to the colonies in one of four ways. Redemptioners agreed to come voluntarily. Felons were transported by court order. Many young girls and strong lads were kidnapped in the old countries for transport as servants. And parish children were shipped from English cities by the boatload, starting with a group of 100 who were sent to Virginia in 1619. A record of 1627 reads: "There are many ships going to Virginia, and with them 1,400 or 1,500 children which they have gathered up in divers places."

A fair percentage of the felons, variously estimated at anywhere from 50,000 to 100,000, transported to the colonies were children, since many kindly judges were reluctant to expose them to the depravity of the prisons and believed that transportation might give them a new start in life. A London law permitted merchants to finance the shipment to the colonies of "Idle Persons who are under the Age of One-and-Twenty Years, lurking about in divers parts of London and elsewhere, who want Employment and may be tempted to become Thieves if not provided for. . . ." Usually the youngsters expressed a desire to go. These shipments paid off the original investment, plus a profit, from the sale of the indentures, "not exceeding the term of eight years."

Kidnapping for the colonies became a very profitable racket in England during the early eighteenth century. There was an organized ring of "spiriters" operating throughout the country, with headquarters in London and Bristol. Of them it was said that "all manner of pretenses were used to decoy victims aboard ships lying in the Thames or to places where they could be assaulted and forcibly conveyed on board, to be disposed of to the ship's company or to merchants." One ship's captain called regularly at the Clerkwell House of Correction, plied the girls there with gin, and induced them to sign an agreement to emigrate if he would foot the bill.

The Privy Council called the spiriters "so barbarous and inhuman that nature itself, much more Christians, cannot but abhorr," and ordered the London customs authorities to take action, saying that they had been informed "that, at this time, there is a ship called the *Seven Brothers* lately fallen down toward Graves-End, and two other ships in the River Thames in good forwardness to follow after in which there are sundry such Children and Servants of several Parents and Masters, so deceived and inticed away Cryinge and Mourninge for Redemption from their Slavery."

Most of the indentured youngsters who came to America, willingly or otherwise, tended to become delinquents. When they reached the New World, their indentures were purchased by masters from the ships' captains or agents acting for merchants or others who had advanced the passage money. The length of service was usually from four to eight years during which period the bond servant was, for all practical purposes, a slave.

The boys who thus emigrated to the colonies were employed as unskilled laborers, principally in agriculture. The girls worked for the most part as domestic servants, although in the South "some wenches that are nasty, beastly and not fit to be so imployed are put into the ground, for reason tells us they must not at charge be transported and then maintained for nothing." The northern colonies would not accept transported criminals, and here the moral level of the young emigrants was somewhat higher than in the South; yet the most frequent complaints of New Englanders had to do with the laziness, shiftlessness, thieving and lying of bondservants.

The living conditions of young people who were "bound out" depended largely on the character of the master. In some cases they were treated as members of the family; indeed, girls sometimes became one of the family by marrying into it. More frequently bond or indentured servants were viewed with suspicion and treated with severity. There were a few rather vague laws for their protection, dealing mainly with prevention of extreme brutality, such as maiming or inflicting injuries causing death. The youngsters could be beaten and, in some colonies, branded or have their ears cropped or their noses slit for relatively minor offenses.

Boys often ran away, thus depriving the master of the fruits of his investment in their indentures. If a boy could make his way to a city in another colony, he usually could get work with no questions asked, for labor was scarce everywhere. Or he could escape to the West if he was willing to face the perils and rigors of the frontier. Many of these runaways helped to pioneer the West.

Unless a girl was bought for the purpose of marriage, as sometimes happened, it would be rather unusual for her to get through her period of indentures without becoming involved in illicit sex. One social historian makes the point that these girls "generally belonged to the lowest class of the home country and not all were trained in virtue. In Virginia as contract servants it was not easy for them to marry. Masters did not want this species of cattle laid by for pregnancy and childbirth with the risk of death. Licentious masters were in a position to utilize the sex services of such as they chose. Moreover, the unfortunate women were thrown in contact with the lowest class of men and immorality was practically inevitable, especially as kinship ties and responsibility had been broken by the migration."

Bastardy involving female bond-servants was a problem in the southern colonies, which repeatedly passed laws designed to curb it. Most of those provided that the mother be whipped and serve an extra year of time; if the master was the father, this time was served for the parish. The most iniquitous law was passed in Maryland where, fearful of miscegenation, it was ruled that a white female bond-servant who had a child by a Negro must serve several years of additional time and the child would be a slave for life. Some utterly conscienceless masters thereupon forcibly bred their bond-girls with Negro slaves, thus getting several years of extra service from the mother and acquiring an infant mulatto slave.

Illicit sex was not entirely confined to young females. One account of Colonial Maryland tells of virile young male bondsmen who "injected themselves in the time of their servitude into the private and reserved favor of their mistress, if age speak their master deficient." An Episcopal minister of Maryland declared that in that colony "all notorious vices are committed; so that it is become a Sodom of uncleanliness and a pest house of iniquity."

The French colonists in Louisiana had something of a special problem because of the scarcity of marriageable girls. Bienville wrote plaintively: "Send me wives for my Canadians, they are running in the woods after Indian girls." The French government started to send girls over in 1703, a few years after the first settlement was established. Some were of good character and appearance; most were not. In 1713 a consignment of twelve girls were so "ugly and badly formed" that only two could find husbands. The governor "thought fit to suggest that in future those that sent girls should attach more importance to beauty than to virtue as the Canadians were not particular about what sort of lives their spouses had formerly led." The French government responded by sending twenty-five young prostitutes from Salpetriere, a house of correction in Paris.

It would seem that the better-class young men in the colony were hard to please as to their women's virtue, for, when one shipment of girls arrived, it was complained that the sea captain had seduced more than half of them on the voyage over and that they therefore had to be given to common soldiers. Even the boys in the ranks created difficulties. Antoine de la Mothe Cadillac, an early governor, complained that they were "a mass of rapscallions from Canada . . . abandoned in vice with Indian girls, whom they prefer to French girls."

Cadillac continued to have trouble with delinquent girls during his three-year term as governor. The French deportees, refuse of Paris slums and prisons, did not make good housewives. There are numerous accounts of girls of bad conduct who were "severely punished by putting them upon wooden horses and having them whipped by the regiment of soldiers who guarded the town." It was necessary to build a house of detention and reform for immoral females, under the supervision of the Ursuline nuns. The situation apparently improved when the first generation of French-American girls reached the marriageable age of twelve or fourteen, most of them, it was said, "not even knowing how many gods there are and you can imagine the rest."

Until the Civil War, the institution of slavery created in the South conditions in which children, like those of England in the previous era, were inevitably corrupted by adults. The Negro youths, at least, were more sinned against than sinning. Most Negro children grew up without much instruction in right and wrong other than that the property of the white man must not be touched on pain of serious punishment.

Other than thievery, the young slave had little opportunity for juvenile delinquency. He could not travel with gangs, for he would be whipped even if found walking on a public road away from his plantation. Fighting was rare. Striking a white would mean horrible consequences for the black transgressor, and fighting among blacks was severely punished because it might result in damage to the master's property, the combatants.

Sex delinquency among slave girls was commonplace from the time of puberty. In most cases she could not look forward to marriage, a home, and raising children, since any alliance she formed could be terminated at the will of the master. She was available to the whites who owned or supervised her. One commentator wrote that a slave girl "apart from mere natural bashfullness, has no inducement to remain chaste; she has many inducements the other way. Her person is her only means of purchasing favors, indulgences, presents. To be the favorite of the master or one of his sons, of the overseer, or even a driver is an object of desire and a position of dignity." The Lexington, Kentucky, *Luminary* observed that "chastity is no virtue among them; its violation neither injures female characters in their own estimation, nor in that of their master and mistress." Fanny Kemble, an English actress and author married to a southern planter, flatly stated: "It seems to me that there is not a girl of sixteen on the plantation but has children."

Many Negro girls preferred to be breeding wenches rather than strictly fieldhands, and many more had no choice in the matter. Breeding slaves was part of the system and was big business in the northern slave states after the Louisianna Purchase created a greatly increased demand for slaves by opening millions of acres of cotton land in the West. Negro girls of fourteen and up were bred for the property value of their offspring. A slave owner had this to say: "In Maryland, Virginia, North Carolina, Kentucky, Tennessee, and Missouri as much attention is paid to the breeding and growth of Negroes as to that of horses and mules. Planters command their girls (married or unmarried) to have children and I have known a great many Negro girls to be sold off because they did not have children. A breeding wench is worth one-sixth or one-fourth more than one who does not breed."

A more depraved aspect of this system was the deliberate breeding of a Negro girl with a white to produce more valuable mulatto offspring. Many masters fathered such halfbreeds and used them either as house servants or sold them. In the early days white male bond-servants were bred with Negro girls. There is a case on record of a Virginia planter who paid a white man twenty dollars for every girl whom he impregnated.

The slave system had a pernicious effect on the morals and characters of Southern white children. In his *Notes on Virginia,* Thomas Jefferson pointed out: "There must doubtless be an unhappy influence on the manners of our people produced by the existence of slavery among us. The whole commerce between master and slave is a perpetual exercise of the most boisterous passions, the most unremitting despotism on the one part, and degrading submissions on the other. Our children see this, and learn to imitate it; for man is an imitative animal. . . . The parent storms, the child looks on, catches the lineaments of wrath, puts on the same airs in the circle of smaller slaves, gives a loose to the worst of passions, and thus nursed, educated and daily exercised in tyranny, cannot but be stamped by it with odious peculiarities. The man must be a prodigy who can retain his manners and morals undepraved by such circumstances."

Almost every northern and foreign observer during the early and middle nineteenth century commented on the effect of slavery on white children. Among them was Charles Dickens, who wrote: "The delicate mamma . . . quiets her youngest child by promising the boy 'a whip to beat the little niggers with.'" Fanny Kemble exclaimed, "Think of learning to rule despotically your fellow creatures before the first lesson of self-government has been well spelt over!" Another foreign visitor, Miss Martineau, commented that "the generality of slaves are as gross as the total absence of domestic sanctity might be expected to render them. They do not dream of any reserve with children. The consequences are inevitable. The woes of mothers from this cause are such that, if this 'peculiar domestic institution' were confided to their charge, I believe they would accomplish its overthrow. . . . Among the incalculable forces in nature is the grief of mothers weeping for the corruption of their children." Frederick Olmsted in *Cotton Kingdom* wrote: "I never conversed with a cultivated Southerner on the effects of slavery, that he did not express a wish or intention to have his own children educated where they should be free from demoralizing association with slaves. That the association is almost inevitably corrupting and dangerous, is very generally . . . admitted."

One delinquent aspect of this corruption was the almost universal use of black girls by white teen-age boys. Willing or not, the girls were available, and their use for sexual purposes was part of the education of most southern boys. The unwilling girl had no recourse unless a white witness would testify that she had been raped. With chastity of little value—and unprotectable—most girls were willing.

If we believe many who were part of the scene, the extent of interracial sexual delinquency was appalling. According to a Tennessee slaveholder, "In slaveholding settlements of middle and southern Mississippi, where I lived for several years, there is not a virtuous young male of twenty years of age. . . . To send a lad to a male academy in Mississippi is moral murder." The mayor of Huntsville, Alabama, remarked: "As a general rule, every young man in this state becomes addicted to fornication at an early age." A minister who left the South said that he "believed that there was scarcely a young man in the South but what was more or less contaminated with this sin." Younger boys who witnessed slave auctions were prepared for later licentiousness by the indecent and lascivious remarks and jests that always accompanied the sale of pretty Negro girls.

A special class of juvenile delinquents were the quadroon girls of New Orleans, who were raised by their mulatto mothers to be concubines. The beauty of these quarter-Negro girls is legendary and most were carefully trained in feminine graces and arts. The girls were first exposed to prospective white patrons in their mid-teens at a quadroon ball. Here white men inspected the available young concubines and made financial arrangements with the mothers. One traveller to New Orleans wrote: "In some instances I was informed that various families of daughters by the same father appear at the quadroon ball on the very evenings when their legitimate brother is present for the purpose of following the example of his worthy papa."

THE EARLY NINTEENTH CENTURY SAW the beginning in America of a revolutionary change in society's attitude towards the child. In a work titled *The Social History of the American Family,* Dr. Arthur Calhoun calls a chapter on this period, "The Emancipation of Childhood." Children became much more important. They demanded and were accorded much more freedom. The patriarchal family system of the Old World and Colonial days declined; the father was no longer the source of all authority and more of the responsibility for the supervision of youngsters was transferred to the mother. De Tocqueville asserted that "in America the family, in the Roman and aristocratic significance of the word, does not exist." Ralph Waldo Emerson quoted a man who bemoaned the fact that he was born in an age when children were nothing and raised his own offspring in an age when children were everything.

Political, social and economic factors in the early nineteenth century all combined to elevate the position of the child and give him new freedom. The very essence of democracy is respect for the individual rather than the family and, in America, this respect was early accorded to juveniles. In the city, on the farm and on the frontier the child was important as labor and he could, at an early age, strike out for himself if home conditions displeased him.

The result was a lessening of parental authority that most foreign visitors viewed with alarm. In 1807 an English observer asserted: "One of the greatest evils of a republican form of government is a loss of . . . subordination in society. . . . Boys assume the airs of full-grown coxcombs. This is not to be wondered at, when most parents make it a principle never to check those ungovernable passions which are born with us, or to correct the growing vices of their children. . . . Often have I with horror, seen boys, whose dress indicated wealthy parents, intoxicated, shouting and swearing in the public streets."

A German visitor was dismayed by "the indulgence shown by parents toward the excesses of children in earliest youth. Often I saw children in quarrel with old people pick up stones and threaten to fling them at the head of the old man who wanted to punish him."

In a social study written in 1818, John Bristed declared: "Strictly speaking there is no such thing as social subordination in the United States. Parents have no command over their children. . . . Owing perhaps to the very popular nature of our institutions, the American children are seldom taught that profound reverence for, and strict obedience to their parents, which are at once the basis of domestic comfort and of the welfare of the children themselves."

A French visitor in the 1830's thought that "the Americans are too anxious to make money and too apt to spoil their children. . . . The boys are much more spoiled than the girls." An English woman wrote in the 1840's: "The indulgence which parents in the United States permit to their children is not seen in England, the child is too early his own master." A labor newspaper, *Man,* published a sarcastic "modern catechism adapted to the times" in which these questions and answers appeared: "Who is the oldest man? The lad of fourteen who struts and swaggers and smokes his cigar, and drinks rum; treads on the toes of his grandfather, swears at his mother and sister, and vows that he will run away and leave 'the old man' if he will not let him have more cash. In what families is there the best government? Those in which the children govern the parents. . . . Who brings up his children in the way they should go? He that teaches them to spend money without earning it; mixes *sling* whenever he thinks it will do him good, and always saves the bottom of the glass for little Frank."

Although the term "juvenile delinquency" was seldom used, many conservative observers surely believed that an epidemic of it was engufing midnineteenth-century America. The *Presbyterian Magazine* was alarmed by the manner in which "the signs of want of family discipline appear in the waywardness of the children while yet they are young. Given up to idleness, knowing no restraint but such as they are wont to defy, having no domestic exercise for entertainment and profit, and nothing to keep them at home but their bed and board, and dreading their home for their leisure hours as a place of confinement; familiar with drunkeness, profaneness, and all the captivating forms of youthful dissipation, what have the parents or the community to hope from such children?"

7

The City
Streets

DURING THE LAST THREE-QUARTERS OF
the nineteenth century America earned the title of "the melting
pot of the world." From New York's harbor the world's largest
statue proclaimed, "Give me your tired, your poor, your huddled
masses. . . . The wretched refuse of your teeming shore." Europe
obliged, and the poor and "wretched refuse" flocked to the land
of opportunity. For the most part these impoverished immigrants
stayed in the cities and vast slums developed in which juvenile
delinquency proliferated for well over half a century.

By the eve of the Civil War, New York, whose population had
been about 25,000 at the time of the Revolution, reached 800,000,
almost half foreign-born. The percentage would increase before
the end of the century. The East Side of the city, which then
embraced only Manhattan Island, became the most densely popu-
lated district in the world, with 290,000 people per square mile.
In the most crowded days of old London, concentration did not
exceed 175,000 per square mile.

The teeming city slums were ideal cultures for the growth of delinquency. Life in these crowded areas contributed to the under-mining of youthful morality. Parents were, for the most part, ignorant and illiterate. Many of the immigrants were law-abiding, hard-working peasants, but their children lost respect for parents who could not, in many cases, speak the language which became native to their offspring. Under the "free and easy" attitude of the New World toward the young, the sons and daughters of foreigners had little regard for Old World family customs, and family and home life virtually ceased to exist for many of them.

Education for children was compulsory, but this meant little when school facilities were inadequate. At one time it was estimated that there was no room in the schools for 50,000 New York children. Laws and organizations to protect children did not begin to come into existence until the last half of the nineteenth century, and they lagged far behind the need until well into the twentieth century. Drunkenness was a way of life for many of the slum dwellers, and homes that were not broken by desertion or death were often without parents because both father and mother worked outside the home. The "home" of thousands of slum children was the city streets. Shortly after the Civil War the *New York Times* estimated "at least 10,000 young boys roam the streets of New York by day and take shelter by night in any place that seems to afford a safe retreat."

The children who had homes lived in almost unbelievable squalor and congestion in the tenements that, by the 1890's, housed three-quarters of New York's population. These tenements started as private houses which were let out by the room to immigrants after the owners moved uptown. Sometimes several families lived in a room. Then structures were built in the backyards to house the ever swelling influx—first two stories, then additional stories were added, up to five. Finally, blocks of barracks were built that were divided into rooms, for the most part windowless.

Each room rented for from five to ten dollars a month to a family, and in it all ages and sexes cooked, ate and slept—and frequently took in boarders!

One of the earliest and most infamous tenements was the Old Brewery in New York's Five Points district, the city's first slum. The five-story brewery was converted to a tenement in 1837 when it became too dilapidated for its original purpose. It was described by a contemporary writer: "The cellars of the Old Brewery were divided into some twenty rooms . . . and there were about seventy-five other chambers above-ground arranged in double rows along Murderers' Alley and the passage leading to the Den of Thieves— a great room in which more than seventy-five men, women and children made their homes, without furniture or conveniences. During the period of its greatest renown, the building housed more than 1,000 men, women and children, almost equally divided between Irish and Negroes. In one basement room about fifteen feet square, twenty-six people lived in the most frightful misery and squalor.

"Throughout the building the most frightful living conditions prevailed. Miscegenation was an accepted fact, incest was not uncommon, and there was much sexual promiscuity; the house swarmed with thieves, murderers, pickpockets, beggars, harlots, and degenerates of every type. Fights were of almost constant occurrence, and there was scarcely an hour of the day or night when drunken orgies were not in progress; through the flimsy, clapboarded walls could be heard the crashing thud of brickbat or iron bar, the shrieks of the unhappy victims, the wailing of starving children, and the frenzied cries of men and women and sometimes boys and girls, writhing in the anguish of delirium tremens. Murders were frequent; it has been estimated that for almost fifteen years the Old Brewery averaged a murder a night, and the Cow Bay tenements almost as many."

Not all tenement conditions were as bad as those in the Five

Points and Cow Bay sections, but if these areas were not typical, they were indicative of the generally low living standards that prevailed. There was no room for children in such "homes" except to eat and sleep. At other times they were driven out on the street to play, or do whatever else occurred to them. These slum children were described by Jacob Riis, a crusading reformer of the 1890's, as follows:

"I counted the other day the little ones, up to ten years or so, in a Bayard Street tenement. . . . I gave up my self-imposed task in despair when I had counted one hundred and twenty-eight in forty families. Thirteen I missed, or not found in. Applying the average for the forty to the whole fifty-three, the house contained one hundred and seventy children [under ten or eleven years old]. It is not the only time I have had to give up such census work. I have in mind an alley. . . . I tried to count the children that swarmed there, but could not. Sometimes I have doubted that anybody knows just how many there are about. Bodies of drowned children turn up in the rivers right along in summer whom no one seems to know anything about. . . . The truant officer assuredly does not know, though he spends his life trying to find out, somewhat illogically, perhaps, since the department that employs him admits that thousands of poor children are crowded out of the schools year by year for want of room. There was a big tenement in the Sixth Ward. . . . I do not know how many children there were in it, but an inspector reported that he found only seven in the whole house who owned that they went to school. The rest gathered all the instruction they received running for beer for their elders. Some of them claimed the 'flat' as their home as a mere matter of form. They slept in the streets at night. The official came upon a little party of four drinking beer out of the cover of a milk-can in the hallway. They were of the seven good boys and proved their claim to the title by offering him some."

MOST COLORFUL URBAN KIDS WERE THE
street Arabs, who could be found in all big cities in any quarters
where they might make a dime, a nickel or a penny by ingenious,
industrious or illicit means. "The Street Arab has all the faults and
virtues of the lawless life he leads," commented Jacob Riis. "Vaga-
bond that he is, acknowledgeing no authority and owing no
allegiance to anybody or anything, with his grimy fist raised
against society whenever it tries to coerce him, he is as bright and
sharp as a weasel, which, among all the predatory beasts, he most
resembles."

Most of the thousands of street Arabs would steal anything
they could lay their hands on. Junking was a favorite form of
theft, encouraged by many adult junk peddlers who purchased
from the boys. Lead pipe and plumbing fixtures were popular
junk items, which boys obtained by breaking into empty buildings
and ripping them out. Some of the street children, both boys and
girls, became adroit pickpockets, sneak thieves and burglars under
adult criminal guidance.

Street girls specialized in selling matches or flowers and some of
these improved their lot by peddling in residential districts where
they could gain access to homes and steal whatever they could lay
their hands on quickly. These little peddlers soon learned, as had
their predecessors in London, that drunks and prostitutes were
usually generous, and girls of twelve and younger haunted saloons
late at night and canvassed brothels, with their wilted flowers.
Jane Addams tells of a not untypical instance in which a seven-
year-old news girl built up a clientele in brothels and disreputable
hotels because customers in such places seldom asked for change.
She was not a street girl. She had a home, but her mother thought
that she was too young to realize what was going on. At the age
of fourteen she became an inmate of one of the houses.

The elite of the street girls were the "hot corn" girls, who cried
this comestible on the streets at night. They wore gay calico dresses

and plaid shawls, were usually barefoot and often pretty. After their hot corn was sold, many offered their favors to particular patrons. The first man to be hung in New York's city prison, the Tombs, was a young Five Points tough who first married and then murdered a hot corn girl because her earnings did not come up to his expectations.

Many among the young street vendors were prostitutes, and there were several places of assignation in New York that catered solely to them. The owner of one of these bragged that her place was frequented by girls under sixteen exclusively. Another kept nine small girls, ranging in age from nine to fifteen, in the back room of an oyster saloon. These youngsters approached a man on the street and, instead of asking him to buy their flowers, matches or newspapers, said, "Give me a penny, mister?" The initiated knew that this meant that the girl was available but, if the child approached the wrong man, he could not claim that he had been accosted for immoral purposes.

A small class of juvenile delinquents in New York consisted of girls who had wandered into Chinatown from the adjacent slums and had become opium addicts. Few Chinese brought wives from China, but some had so-called "wives" who were teen-aged white girls whom they had introduced to the pipe. Of these girls, Riis wrote: "Easily tempted from homes that have no claim upon the name, they rarely or never return. . . . Of the depths of their fall no one is more thoroughly aware than themselves; no one less concerned about it." The police insisted that these girls were at least sixteen, and therefore of an age to choose their way of life. "But this," said Riis, "is disproved by the observation of those who go frequently among these dens, though the smallest girl will invariably, and usually without being asked, insist that she is sixteen. Such assertions are not to be taken seriously."

Some of the children of the city streets sold newspapers at all hours of the day and night on street corners, in saloons and on street cars. They thronged the newspaper rows of cities at edition time, and many slept in the distributing room between editions. The newsboy has been immortalized in legend as an industrious little paragon who usually supported a widowed mother, if he was not saving for his education. Surprisingly, this seems to have some basis in fact. The few statistics for the period indicate that delinquency was relatively rare among newsboys, perhaps because they worked such long hours and made enough money. Consequently they had neither the time nor the need to steal. An industrious newsboy could make at least as much as a woman employed in the unskilled or semiskilled occupations open to women.

Another factor in newsboy morality, in New York, was undoubtedly the Newsboys' Lodging Houses which were established by the Children's Aid Society. Here, a homeless boy could get a bed and washing facilities for six cents a night, a hearty breakfast for another six cents, and all the beans and bread that he could eat for dinner for a like amount. The lodging houses maintained a savings bank and many boys laid up sizeable sums. These institutions were not restricted to newsboys, but were open to any homeless youngster who could pay the small cost. Although they were subsidized, they were not charities and they were not for out-and-out vagrants. They were operated as necessary institutions for thousands of self-supporting kids, from the age of six or seven years up to seventeen or eighteen, who had no place else to live.

Street boys without the price of a lodging house, or who were too defiant for even the mild discipline of such places, slept in every nook and cranny of the slums and waterfront. In warm weather they "turned in" at night anywhere that offered a modicum of shelter and security from surprise. They slept with one eye open, ever alert for the cop who would move them on, or for an agent of the Children's Aid Society, who, if he could catch them, would take them to a shelter and try to find them a home. Wagons, outhouses, dugouts in hay barges, old boilers, iron pipes, spaces below wharfs, all made cozy nests. One group of thirty or forty boarded up the shore end under one of the East River banana docks to make a nocturnal retreat which they shared with thousands of rats.

In winter homeless boys covered themselves with newspapers and huddled in small groups in hallways. If they could get into a cellar near a boiler they considered themselves very lucky. Otherwise, preference was about evenly divided between steam gratings and sand piles. The former provided more warmth, but the latter were softer and one could "curl all up" in them.

One group of New York street Arabs had a fine den in the subcellar of a post office. After prying off a man-hole cover, they had discovered a coal chute leading from the street, which they used as a slide to their lair. The last boy down pulled the cover back into place and the youngsters snuggled comfortably on the coal around the boiler. The ideal arrangement was spoiled when an agent of the Society found it and, after the boys were asleep, slid down the chute and captured several of them.

A certain amount of petty larceny was common among *all* tenement children. In wintertime their parents expected them to scrounge around for coal or wood, and this fuel had to be stolen from the railroad yards, docks, or construction sites. "The line of least resistance has worn smooth in this neighborhood," said a social worker, "and it is easy and natural to fall in with the parental fiction that the fuel which reaches the tenement has miraculously dropped from heaven. From stealing for his family the boy naturally proceeds to steal for himself." Many of the slum kids obviously did not realize that there was anything wrong about stealing except getting caught. Jane Addams tells the story of a youngster who was paroled from the detention home of the Juvenile Court in Chicago and promptly returned to the home on a Saturday night to give the matron five chickens that he had stolen, telling her that he knew that she was "having a hard time to fill up so many kids and these chickens might help out for Sunday dinner."

The really wild kids among the slum children were like those that the Society for the Prevention of Cruelty to Children reported as a "few typical cases." One case involved "four professional cracksmen between the ages of nine and fifteen who had been caught with burglar's tools or in the act of robbery." Among the other cases, four had held up a man in the street and robbed him of $73. One, aged sixteen, was "the leader of a noted gang of young robbers in Forty-ninth Street. He committed murder, for which he is now serving a term in State's Prison." Four were "little girl consorts of the boys, who participated in their robberies."

By the dawn of the twentieth century there were laws forbidding children under sixteen from going into saloons, gambling houses and brothels. (This last prohibition was an amusing paradox. One statute outlawed brothels, another specifically prohibited children under sixteen from entering such supposedly non-existent establishments.) But the statute stated that it did not apply to children delivering messages or merchandise to such places. A social worker observed that "a boy fourteen or fifteen years old does not stop at the door of the house to which he is sent, but must not enter. The very prohibition stimulates his curiosity and makes it quite sure that he will go in. I do not know how any messenger boys, even in exceptional cases, succeed in remaining honest, with the wholly insufficient supervision which they have and the never-ending temptation to collect money at both ends, to suppress telegrams and to steal carfare. The temptations which beset them are so cruel and pitiless, so shocking, that they can neither be printed nor told."

Most of the teen-aged and subteen boys who haunted the city streets drank, when they could get anything to drink. The law forbidding saloons to serve patrons under sixteen (which was seldom enforced) said nothing about selling liquor to children for off-premises consumption. A minister touring the slums commented on a line of small fry waiting to buy ten-cent pint bottles of whiskey, presumably to take home to their parents. Small groups of boys chipped in pennies to get a two-quart tin can, a "growler," filled with beer which they took to their lair to drink.

"Rushing the growler" was a regular chore for most children, not only in the slums, but in middle-class neighborhoods. As soon as a child was old enough to carry the container without spilling the contents, he was sent to the corner saloon, with a can or a pitcher, a dime clinking in the bottom, to have the vessel filled with beer. In the better neighborhoods little girls went to the side or family entrance of the saloon, knocked and waited for someone to come take the containers and fill them. Boys brazenly knelt down and peering under the swinging doors at the front of the saloon, called to the bartender, "Hey mister! Fill my can." The bartender returned the foaming vessel, usually with a piece of bologna from the free lunch as a treat for the boy, who might—and most often did—wash it down with a surreptitious sip of beer on the way home.

There was nothing delinquent about kids buying beer for their parents in those days. Most families drank beer and, unless they were sufficiently affluent to have a servant, they naturally sent a child to get it. This is an interesting example of the changed attitude towards what is proper for a juvenile to do. Today, in some states, if a teen-ager is found with beer in his possession he may be referred to the juvenile court.

The years around the turn of the century were the great era of the saloon. There were 7,500 licensed saloons in New York and nobody knows how many unlicensed blind pigs. Most of these were perfectly reputable family saloons where sixteen-year-olds could legally bend elbows with their elders. In less desirable sections of cities, saloons frequently had back rooms for gambling and upstairs rooms for sex, and their proprietors asked no questions about age if a youngster had the wherewithal.

Even when such saloons were not patronized by juveniles, they could be an evil influence. The Chicago Vice Commission reported that "there are a number of saloons in the city frequented by dissolute and vicious men and immoral women in close proximity to school houses. One school property in particular on the North Side adjoins the lot on which a disorderly saloon building is located. The rooms over the saloon are used for immoral purposes, and the school authorities testify that the children may see into these rooms from the school windows and from the playgrounds."

Narcotics played their part in urban delinquency in the early years of this century. Accusations against modern youth in this respect are nothing new. As is true today, none in those days could say with assurance how extensive juvenile dope taking was, but Jane Addams wrote: "For several years the residents of Hull House struggled with the difficulty of prohibiting the sale of cocaine to minors. . . . The long effort brought us into contact with dozens of boys who had become victims of the cocaine habit." Miss Addams cited instances that parallel stories in today's press. One group of eight boys between thirteen and seventeen was approached by a pusher, "an agent of a drugstore, who had given them samples and urged them to try it. In three or four months they had become hopelessly addicted to its use. . . . They stole from their parents, 'swiped junk,' pawned their clothes and shoes, did any desperate thing to 'get the dope'." Another group had a hut. "They washed dishes in a neighboring restaurant and as soon as they had earned a few cents, they invested in cocaine which they kept pinned underneath their suspenders. When they accumulated enough for a real debauch they went to their hut and for days were dead to the outside world."

The concert saloon, of which there were some 300 in New York and a relative number in other cities, offered careers of delinquency to thousands of teen-aged girls. These establishments sold liquor and provided entertainment, but the main attraction was girls.

"Gentlemen" were charged a small admission, "ladies" were admitted free, and there were always far more gentlemen than ladies, because the big attraction was the corps of waiter girls who served drinks, and usually performed other services. These girls, "on whose cheeks the blushes of modesty seem to be set with the enduring pencil of the painter—these girls were not slaves, servants even—they were companions." Traditionally the girls wore dresses with low-cut bodices and short skirts. On their bare legs they wore high boots with tinkling bells. The Gaiety Saloon on Broadway advertised that it had "the prettiest waiter girls to be found in the world," maintaining "agents in all parts of the United States, England and France to engage the most accomplished young ladies. . . . Gentlemen will please call and prove our assertion. No Boys Admitted." This last prohibition was not based on a concern for the morals of the boys. The management did not want its girls being attracted to youths without the means to buy sufficient liquor.

Not all waiter girls were juveniles, but it is safe to say that a large majority of them were. There was a premium on youth and the ideal waiter girl was the youngest girl who had the shape of a woman. In the better-class concert halls the girls served the men, joshed with them, encouraged them to drink, and, perhaps, made a date for later. In the less reputable places there were curtained booths on a balcony in which girls, for a price, would put on a show for the drinkers. Allens on Water Street in New York had a staff of twenty waiter girls and, it was said, "every evening several hundred partake of the fun, among whom are boys and girls below twelve years of age. The atmosphere reeks with blasphemy."

American children of tender years had worked since Colonial days, but in the later nineteenth and early twentieth century their labor took on a new aspect in relation to their morality. Among the average working class families that comprised the great majority of the population of cities, few children went to school after the age of fourteen and many children of the poor dropped out to take their places in the work force at the age of ten or twelve. Sixty per cent of city girls worked. Writing of social conditions at the turn of the century, Jane Addams said, "Industrialism has gathered together multitudes of eager young creatures from all quarters of the earth as a labor supply for the countless factories and workshops upon which the present industrial city is based. Never before in civilization have such numbers of young girls been suddenly released from the protection of the home and permitted to walk unattended upon city streets and to work under alien roofs; for the first time they are being prized more for their labor power than for their innocence. . . . Never before have such numbers of young boys earned money independently of the family life, and felt themselves free to spend it as they choose in the midst of vice deliberately disguised as pleasure."

FOR WORKING KIDS WITH A FEW CENTS TO spend on pleasure—or, for that matter, for any kids—the cities offered virtually no wholesome recreation or entertainment. The YMCA opened its first building in New York in 1869, but growth was slow and the early emphasis was on prayer and Bible study rather than gymnasiums, pool tables and swimming pools. The first Boys Club was opened in 1878, but this could serve only forty or fifty boys and, again, growth was slow. The Boy Scouts did not come to America until 1910.

For the nineteenth-century city kids who sought adventure, excitement and fun there were nickel theatres offering very questionable fare, peep projectors in penny arcades with scarcely decent pictures, amusement parks, and dance halls by the hundreds. These, according to Miss Addams, were places that offered "vice deliberately disguised as pleasure." She described the entertainment provided by slide shows that preceded motion pictures in Chicago's nickelodeons: "A poor woman is wearily bending over some sewing, a baby is crying in the cradle, and two little boys nine and ten are asking for food. In despair the mother sends them out into the street to beg, but instead they steal a revolver from a pawn shop and with it kill a Chinese laundryman, robbing him of $200. They rush home with the treasure which is found by the mother in the baby's cradle, whereupon she and her sons fall upon their knees and send up a prayer of thankfulness for this timely and heaven-sent assistance." In most such shows thieves and murderers were held up to children as heroes, and crime, rather than virtue, was its own reward. Compared to the fare of those days, modern television and movies are akin to Sunday School.

Little girls who did not have a nickel hung around the nickel theatre, hoping that an older boy or a man would take them in. In view of his generosity they could not object when their "host" fondled them in the dark theatre. Girls of twelve to fourteen, starved for pleasure, haunted the amusement parks adjacent to cities, although unable to pay for the exciting rides on the roller coaster and other concessions. "These children," wrote Miss Addams, "easily accept favors from the young men who are standing near the entrances for the express purpose of ruining them. . . . This cruel exploitation of the childish eagerness for pleasure is, of course, possibly only among a certain type of forlorn city children who are totally without standards and into whose colorless lives a visit to an amusement park brings the acme of delirious excitement." An official of the New York Society for the Prevention of Cruelty to Children commented: "It is horribly pathetic to learn how far a nickel or a quarter will go towards purchasing the virtue of these children."

Another breeding place for juvenile immorality in the guise of recreation, in Chicago at least, was the excursion boats that plied the lake, most of whose patrons were teen-agers. The Vice Commission of Chicago investigated them in 1910 and reported that "practically all the boats are equipped with bars. . . . Liquor is openly sold to both young men and young women who are evidently minors. . . . These boats also have a large number of easily acquired state rooms. During the summer the excursion boats are often floating assignation houses. The state rooms are rented many times in the course of three or four hours; boys and girls lie in these berths together in an undressed condition."

A list of "typical instances" aboard the boats contained these: "Saturday, July 2nd, 1910, investigator left Chicago for South Haven at 2:00 P.M. on the steamer (X1050). The passengers consisted principally of boys and girls between the ages of twelve to twenty-one. The boat was loaded to its full capacity. . . . The bar room was filled with boys and girls. Two girls in particular who could not have been over sixteen years old were singing in drunken discord, lying in the arms of two men. . . . about twenty young girls were drinking beer, five of them not over twelve years of age. One child, eight years old, was drinking beer with older people.

"In state room No. 50 there were two boys in bathing suits, and two girls in kimonos, lying in each other's arms. . . . Room No. 64 was occupied by two boys and two girls; all appeared under the age of twenty. . . . In state room No. 28, two boys and two girls were lying in the berths and all under the influence of liquor. In room No. 56 were found two men and two girls; one of the girls appeared to be very drunk. . . . State room No. 74 was occupied by two girls and two young men; one of the girls was standing in front of the dressing table with nothing on except a dress skirt. . . . For a while investigator stood in front of state room No. 71 and watched a young girl who was in the room with four young boys. One of the boys was very much intoxicated and every time his companions tried to make him stand on his feet he would throw himself back in the berth."

Prime dens of delinquency in all cities, from the mid-nineteenth century until the advent of prohibition, were dance halls, patronized by teen-agers and older males who were interested in young girls.

The City Streets 163

Of 328 in Chicago, 190 had saloons attached and liquor was sold openly in most of the others. The Juvenile Protective Association reported that 86,000 people went to the dance halls on a Saturday night, "of whom the majority were boys between the ages of sixteen and eighteen and girls between the ages of fourteen and sixteen. . . . By twelve o'clock practically all the boys, who in many cases out-numbered the girls, showed signs of intoxication."

Not all of these 86,000 Chicage youngsters were delinquents. Many were nice kids who went to the dance hall hoping to meet one of the opposite sex for the primary purpose of dancing and talking and having a decorous good time. In that era the city offered little other opportunity for teen-agers of opposite sexes to meet. But if the kids were interested in dancing, the management was not. Profit came from the sale of liquor. Dances usually lasted five minutes, drinking intermissions fifteen or twenty. The halls were hot and poorly ventilated, and no water was available. The girl who did not "take a drink" was shunned by the boys, or men, as an uncongenial prude. The purpose of the liquor was, in most cases, to break down inhibitions as a prelude to illicit sex.

The Juvenile Protective Association was particularly distressed by the rental of dance halls for stag parties. At these gatherings many of the guests and some of the performers were juveniles. "An investigation of a dozen so-called entertainments has invariably revealed the presence of minors. At one affair the names of twenty-two boys from fifteen years of age and up were secured. At another 'smoker' attended by many minors, a girl of ten years and a nine-year-old boy were exhibited in a pugilistic contest. . . . Immediately following the bout a nude woman danced.

"It is impossible to describe in this bulletin the immoral practices permitted at some of these parties. . . . Stories of the most obscene character are related by a woman to a crowd of men and boys. Degrading dancing—vile beyond description—is indulged in by girls. . . . After these demoralizing exhibitions girls circulate through the audience taking up a collection and assuring the patrons that, 'the more you put in the more the girls will take off.' Then follows the climax of the evening. Dancers appear, first singly and later in groups, entirely nude and proceed to participate in a licentious debauchery in which the men nearby join. The scene finally culminates in a raffle of one of the girl performers, the man holding the winning ticket being awarded the girl for the balance of the night."

Dance halls were haunted by procurers seeking young girls for prostitution. Juvenile prostitution, which is quite rare today in terms of younger teen-agers, was widespread during the late 1800's and early 1900's. In the dance halls working girls of fourteen to sixteen were frequently approached by a sympathetic older man who commiserated with the "down-trodden working girl" and averred that "a pretty girl like you should have pretty clothes." He made glowing promises that he could get a better job for her if she would trust him. The better job was in a brothel or a house of assignation with a patron for whom the procurer was working.

Or the initial step might be engineered by an older boy who worked as a cadet, a professional seducer. The Committee of Fourteen in New York, organized to curb the rampant prostitution of the day, described the making of a cadet. "Usually he is a boy who first became acquainted with immoral women as he played about the steps or in the street in front of his tenement house. As the acquaintance grew the women engaged him to run errands, in return for which they gave him presents of candy, fruit or pennies. As the boy grew older he found that these women were sought by different men who gave him dimes and quarters to carry messages to them or take them to apartments where they lived." When the boy reached his late teens he went to work for a madam or an older procurer as a cadet. He might ply his trade at a dance hall where he pretended to become enamored of a younger girl while buying her drinks. In a muddled condition and excited by the handsome boy of whom she had seemingly made a conquest, she went out to eat with him and have another couple of drinks, the last of which might contain a few drops of chloral hydrate. She went with him later either willingly or too confused to know what she was doing, and woke up next morning in bed with the boy in a cheap lodging house. Unable to go home, she agreed to stay with the boy, who made fine promises to support or marry her. After a few days, the affair would conclude as follows: "The companion disappears and she finds herself an inmate of a house of prostitution. She is forced to receive visitors to the house. For each visitor the girl receives a brass or pasteboard check from the cashier of the house entitling her to twenty-five cents."

In 1908 a reformer in Chicago successfully prosecuted 150 boys who were working as cadets. Of these lads, Jane Addams wrote that "many of them begin a vicious career when they are but fifteen or sixteen years old. Because the trade demands very young girls, the procurers require the assistance of immature boys, for in this game above all others 'youth calls to youth.' Such a boy is often incited by the professional procurer to ruin a young girl, because the latter's position is much safer if the character of a girl is blackened before he sells her, and if he himself cannot be implicated in her downfall."

Brothels were recognized institutions well into the twentieth century. Originally, every city had its "red light" district in which they were concentrated, although more refined houses operated in better neighborhoods. The demand for young girls for these houses was insatiable. Said the Chicago Vice Commission, "Prostitution demands *youth* for its perpetration." A study in depth of thirty prostitutes made by the Commission revealed that sixteen, more than half, had started their careers in their teens, one at the age of twelve. Jane Addams averred that the average age of the recruits for prostitution was between sixteen and eighteen, and added, "We allow a minor to determine for herself whether or not she will live this most abominable life . . . in some states a girl as young as ten years of age may make this irrevocable decision for herself."

Many of the young prostitutes drifted into their way of life because they were seduced or were victims of a white slaver. Immigrant families usually took boarders; single men who came from the old country. These accounted for the initial seduction of a great many girls. A study of 130 girls living in a slum district in Chicago disclosed that the majority had been seduced by male members of their own households before puberty.

For most girls the choice of prostitution was a matter of simple necessity or an irresistible urge for life on something other than a bare subsistence level. The customary wage for a working girl in a factory, laundry, or department store was six dollars a week. Many earned less; a fifteen-year-old wrapping packages in a department store might receive four dollars a week, and domestics earned from six to ten dollars a month. These figures are for the first decade of the twentieth century. Tweny years earlier, according to the Working Women's Society, the wage of a girl working in a department store was $2.00-$4.50 a week. Jacob Riis wrote: "The girls are sent to the store before they have fairly entered their teens, because the money they can earn there is needed for the support of the family. If the boys will not work, if the street tempts them from home, among the girls at least there must be no drones. To keep their places they are told to lie about their age and to say that they are over fourteen. The precaution is usually superfluous. The Women's Investigating Committee found the majority of the children employed in the stores to be under age, but heard only in a single instance of the truant officers calling. In that case they came once a year and sent the youngest children home; but in a month's time they were all back in their places, and were not again disturbed." By this time there were child labor laws forbidding the employment of children under fourteen, but there was little effort to enforce them. There was *one* inspector in New York to see that the city's 12,000 factories, plus all retail establishments, conformed to the child labor law.

The Vice Commission reported: "From the testimony of the investigators employed by the Commission a fairly large number of girls employed in department stores supplement their income by a certain amount of prostitution, and with such girls the economic question is probably the main one." Added the Working Women's Society: "It is simply impossible for any woman to live without assistance on the low salary a sales woman earns, without depriving herself of real necessities. . . . It is inevitable that they must in many instances resort to evil." The theme was echoed in *"The Song of the Shirt."*

> Oh God! that bread should be so dear
> And flesh and blood so cheap.

In contrast to department store or factory wages, a waitress girl in a concert saloon could make about twenty dollars a week in commissions on drinks, if she hustled and was agreeable to her patrons. A prostitute in the cheapest house, where the fee was fifty cents, could make over twenty-five dollars a week. The Chicago Vice Commission got access to the books of one such house, which disclosed that the six regular inmates averaged twenty-eight dollars a week. But they had to work hard to do it, servicing an average of thirteen men per day. The biggest earner in the house, a sixteen-year-old named "Florince," served 130 men in a five-day period— forty-five on one particular day—and made $45.50. In the better houses where the fee was three or four dollars the girls made from fifty to one hundred dollars a week.

It is a small wonder that teen-agers were attracted to prostitution for purely economic reasons. The Vice Commission became lyrical in its condemnation of the industrial system that virtually compelled delinquency. "Are flesh and blood so cheap, mental qualifications so common and honesty of so little value, that the manager of one of our big department stores feels justified in paying a high school girl, who has served nearly one year as an inspector of sales, the beggarly wage of $4.00 per week? What is the natural result of such industrial condition? Dishonesty and immorality, not from choice, but necessity—in order to *live*. We can forgive the human frailty which yields to temptation under such conditions—but we cannot forgive the soulless corporation, which arrests and prosecuted this girl—a first offender—when she takes some little articles for personal adornment."

Not all juvenile prostitutes were full-time professionals. Houses of assignation in flats, hotels and lodging houses received young girls who occasionally came to the city from nearby towns, after making some pretext to their parents, to earn pocket money or enough to buy a pretty dress. "They usually tell other girls in their neighborhoods of this easy graft and these in turn come to the city." The keepers of the houses were dependent on a constant flow of young and fresh girls to supply men who frequented their establishments; or the girls might find their own men by spending the early hours of the evening in soliciting on the streets or leaving their cards in saloons.

The profits to be made from young prostitutes were so great that girls were approached by procurers with many and diverse lures. The most vicious was the practice of some madams to acquire "little girls who are too young to have received adequate instruction of any sort and whose natural safeguard of modesty and reserve has been broken down by the overcrowding of tenement house life." These conscienceless women operated through one or more amoral children whom they induced to invite other children to parties. After the guests had become acclimated to the place and looked forward eagerly to the treats provided, men were introduced who offered the children larger rewards. One madam, who was successfully prosecuted by the Juvenile Protective Association,

The City Streets 169

"founded her large and successful business upon the activities of three or four girls who, although they had gradually come to understand her purpose, were apparently so chained to her by the goodies and favors that they received, that they were quite indifferent to the fate of their little friends."

The tender age of many of these girls is indicated in an account given by Jane Addams. "Quite recently I visited a home for semi-delinquent girls against each one of whom stood a charge involving the loss of her chastity. Upon each of the little white beds or on one of the stiff chairs standing by its side was a doll belonging to a delinquent owner still young enough to love and cherish this supreme toy of childhood. I had come to the home prepared to 'lecture to the inmates.' I remained to dress dolls with a handful of girls who eagerly asked questions about the dolls I had once possessed in a childhood that seemed to them so remote."

The excursion boats were favored haunts of procurers seeking girls in their teens, for the mere presence of a young girl on a boat without her parents was an indication that she might be a good prospect. Cheap vaudeville theatres that held amateur nights were another lucrative source for the procurer, who lauded the talent of female performers and offered to introduce them to theatrical agents who would get them professional bookings. There were also some theatrical agents in league with disorderly houses or disreputable concert saloons who blatantly advertised for pretty girls, promising large salaries. The salaries were available—at least four or five times as much as they could make elsewhere—for girls who were willing to work as waitresses serving men in curtained booths or in a brothel.

Easiest access to groups of potential victims for the procurer were department store waiting rooms where girls came to apply for employment or to pick up a paper and read the want ads. Fifty girls might be found in the waiting rooms of a big department store. Such girls were likelier candidates for prostitution than girls employed even at a pittance. Procurers, male and female, frequented such places, striking up conservations with the girls, extending their sympathy and offering to buy the girls lunch or dinner. Two representatives of the Juvenile Protective Association, during a period of three weeks, secured convictions of seventeen men and three women carrying on their trade in nine department stores.

The procurer induced girls to adopt a "life of shame." The cadet seduced girls so that they had little choice. More deadly than those was the white slaver who tricked and coerced girls into prostitution. Today the very expression "white slavery" conjures up thoughts of tawdry novels set in some distant place or of sensationalized newspaper exposés. But white slavery was a very real business in America from post-Civil War days until the early twentieth century. The White Slave Act was not passed by Congress until 1910.

The most complex type of operation by the white slaver was the actual importation of girls. Typical is the case of fifteen-year-old Marie who had worked as a servant girl in Paris for three years. She met a man in a *pâtisserie* who bought her some sweets and told her of his friend, Monsieur Paret, who was gathering a theatrical troupe to go to America. Her new friend took her to Paret, who showed her pictures of young girls in gorgeous costumes and announcements of the coming tour. Marie joyously joined the company.

Paret sailed for America with four French girls between the ages of fifteen and seventeen. They passed immigration easily as the "Kinsella Troupe" and went directly to Chicago. Here the girls were taken to a brothel run by a man named Lair who had financed the trip, locked up, and told that they would have to receive men to pay the expenses of the trip. When Marie objected, she was raped and later beaten and forced to do household scrubbing until she became more amenable. The other girls apparently did not make so much fuss, but none was ever permitted to leave the house. Marie wrote a letter, in French to the police, which she induced a customer to mail. A detective visited the house and was easily convinced by Lair that the girl was there of her own accord. The facts finally came to light when Marie contracted typhoid fever and was sent to a hospital.

A great deal cheaper to acquire than foreign imports were non-English-speaking girls who came to this country alone, usually to join relatives. The slavers had several tricks to intercept such girls before they could establish contact with friends or relatives. Although great care was taken at Ellis Island to mark each girl's ticket with her destination, as soon as she left the point of entry she had no protection and was often an easy subject for the wiles of the white slaver.

A typical operation involved a fifteen-year-old girl coming from Poland to join her mother in Chicago. The mother went to meet the train, but her daughter was not on it. Some time later the girl was found in a brothel. Two men had boarded the train at South Chicago; one was a young Pole who told the girl that they had been sent by her mother. The girl confidently went with them to a disorderly house where she was locked up and forced to serve the patrons.

Less complicated was the white slaver's practice of employing cab drivers who picked up foreign girls at railway stations and openly delivered them to a brothel. The girls had the address where they were supposed to go written on a piece of paper which they gave the driver, but a girl had no way of knowing that the place to which he took her was not the right address, until too late.

Some foreign males of various nationalities exploited girls from the old country by starting a pen-pal relationship which led to a proposal of marriage if the girl would come to America. When the girl arrived the boy met her and either took her directly to a brothel or went through a fake marriage ceremony and then induced or compelled her to receive other men.

In 1909 the Commissioner of Immigration reported to the Congress that there was an active white slave traffic in New York, Chicago, Boston, Buffalo, New Orleans, Denver, Portland, Salt Lake City, Ogden and Butte. Its extent is indicated by the 328 cases that were investigated in Chicago during that single year by the State's Attorney and the ninety-one convictions that he secured for pandering, the only offense of which the white slavers were then legally guilty. The attorney estimated that his vigorous campaign had driven 1,000 white slavers from that city.

BY FAR THE GREATEST DELINQUENCIES OF the children of the city streets were the exploits of gangs. Never in history, perhaps, were there such universal gang membership, such large gangs, such delinquent gangs, as in America's cities from the mid-nineteenth to the early twentieth century. Even staid Boston, which in the 1890's bragged of its low incidence of delinquency, admitted that "almost every boy in the tenement house quarters of the district is a member of a gang. The boy who does not belong to one is not only the exception, but the very rare exception." During the early part of this era New York reputedly had the most gangs, the biggest gangs, and the most vicious gangs. Then, in the twentieth century, Chicago wrested that dubious honor from the eastern city. Professor of Sociology Frederic Thrasher, who became the leading authority on gangs of that time, made a study of 1,313 gangs in Chicago.

Most of the famous gangsters started their delinquent careers as juveniles and worked their way up. One who achieved leadership while still in his teens was Owen Victor Madden who, by the age of seventeen, had earned the nickname of Owney the Killer and, in the following year, assumed leadership of the Gophers in New York's Hell's Kitchen. Owney was twice indicted for murder before he was nineteen. In each case, by the time he was brought to trial, terrorized witnesses swore that they had never in their lives seen Owney and he was released.

Madden was a sociable youngster who liked a good time; he was also called the Duke of the West Side. He started a club for his boys where they could drink, gamble, and play with girls. These pursuits led to so many ferocious brawls that the police finally arrived in force. The gangsters barricaded the door and the first cop who tried to enter was met by a bullet that grazed his ear. The law broke in through the back, clubbed the boys into submission, and hauled them into court. Owney's lawyer pointed out that he was still a juvenile, "a misunderstood waif of the slums." After a lecture the judge released him under a $500 peace bond. Madden later served an eight-year term for the murder of another gangster and, after he came out, became one of the gangster overlords of prohibition.

The famous New York gangs of the last century, such as the Hudson Dusters, the Bowery Boys, the Gas House Gang, the Dead Rabbits and the Plug Uglies, were not strictly juvenile gangs. The leadership was usually more mature, but the bulk of the rank and file were from fourteen or fifteen up. And the bulk of the membership in the leading gangs represented small armies. For example, the Hudson Dusters, at their peak, had 1,500 members.

Small fry were often organized by lieutenants of big gang leaders to act as thieves of various kinds. In New York, Crazy Butch, one of Monk Eastman's henchmen, had a group of twenty to thirty little pickpockets called the East Side Gang. Butch himself had become a shoeshine street boy at the age of eight. Two years later he gave this up for the more lucrative career of picking pockets. At thirteen he stole a dog, named it Rabbi, and trained it to snatch handbags from women. The animal would grab the bag and race through the streets to meet Butch and, with a wagging tail, deliver his loot. Butch was still in his teens when he organized the East Side Gang. Daily they went abroad, Butch riding a bicycle and the little kids flanking him on each sidewalk. The leader would crash his cycle into a pedestrian, preferably an old woman, and then start to upbraid her. This quickly drew a crowd. Butch's light-fingered assistants flitted about lifting wallets while the people were intent on what was going on. If a policeman appeared, the boys melted away while Butch apologized to the old lady and pedalled off.

Ding Dong, a lieutenant in the Hudson Dusters, had a group of a dozen little thieves who climbed on express wagons and threw packages to the street. While the driver and the police were pursuing the elusive children, Ding Dong calmly picked up the loot and melted into the crooked alleys of Greenwich Village.

Below the great gangs, supporting them and serving as vast recruiting pools, were hundreds of strictly juvenile gangs. Some of these were as vicious and dangerous as the men's gangs. The Daybreak Boys were a group of river pirates who were all in their teens, a few as young as ten or twelve. Their most famous leaders, Nicholas Saul and William Howlett, were hung for murder when they were nineteen and twenty respectively, after working their way up to leadership over a period of five years. The Daybreak Boys gained their name because they preferred to operate at that time of day. Usually working from rowboats, they would board a moored ship at dawn and rifle it, cracking the skull or cutting the throat of the watchman without hesitation if necessary. It was said that "frequently they murdered for the sheer love of killing, without provocation or hope of gain." The police reported that, during the years when Saul and Howlett led the group, the gang committed twenty murders—and those were only the ones that the police knew about. A day rarely passed on which a corpse of a murdered man was not found floating in the river or stretched on a dock. None knows how many of these were the work of the Daybreak Boys.

An unusual all teen-age gang in New York was the Baxter Street Dudes, led by an angelic-looking little delinquent named Baby-Face Willy. The Dudes opened the Grand Duke Theatre in the basement of a stale beer dive where they performed plays and musicals of their own composition. The shows were always well mounted because the boys stole scenery and properties from the legitimate theatres of the Bowery or from merchants. At a ten-cent admission the playhouse became popular with street boys and a slumming attraction for adults until rival gangs, jealous of the Dudes' prosperity, took to bombarding the place with stones whenever a performance was started. This did not daunt the Dudes, who boiled out of the playhouse and fought back. The theatre was finally closed by the police because the boys refused to pay the city amusement tax.

In the Five Points and on the Bowery and adjacent streets there were several saloons that catered to these younger gang members, selling them vile whiskey at three cents a glass and providing little girls for their amusement. For the favor of one of these small vixens two boys of the Mackerelville Gang once fought a duel with knives in City Hall Park in which one of the boys was killed. The affair ended in a free-for-all battle in which more than fifty young supporters of the original duelists engaged.

The one gang activity that was common to all groups was fighting. It was said that a gang could not exist unless there was another gang for it to fight with. They fought to protect their territories from invasion by rival groups, they fought the police for their right to existence, and they fought simply for the sheer fun of fighting. Fights between boys' gangs which did not result in serious casualties took place almost daily, and occurred in every section of the city. The middle-class outlying districts were divided into adjacent neighborhoods inhabited largely by people of a single national origin, and here the Irish fought the Italians, the Italians fought the Germans, and they all fought the Jews and Negroes.

These fights were with rocks and fists and casualties were usually limited to black eyes, bloody noses and cut lips. Such gang disagreements between the "good boys" were not considered delinquency.

Typical of a more or less minor gang fight in a slum area in the early twentieth century was one described by the *New York Times*: "Down crowded, stifling Eleventh Avenue advanced a close crowd of a half-a-hundred boys. It is the Fiftieth Street bunch, and their object is to reclaim a store of election night barrels [for a celebration bonfire] that the Thirtieth Street gang have stolen. The whispered word has spread downtown along the furtive river dives. As far north as Thirty-eighth Street apparently purposeless loungers note the approaching mob. Without warning a raking crossfire of bottles from nowhere sweeps the invaders, and a second later they are charging down the startled street. At Thirty-sixth Street stands a compact blockade, the Thirtieth Street gang. They halt a hundred feet apart, howling insults. One gang advances. The air darkens with missiles and screaming women rush their babies into doorways as window-glass shatters overhead. At that moment scouts sound the familiar warning; 'Cheese it!' The Avenue clears; a policeman sauntering down notes a few broken windows, a littered sidewalk, and a street electrically hushed."

Such minor affrays were as nothing compared to the great gang fights that terrorized New York from pre-Civil War days until the opening years of the twentieth century. One of these pitched battles took place July 4-5, 1857. At this time the gangs virtually controlled New York. The Municipal Police were so corrupt that the State Legislature had passed a bill abolishing them and creating the Metropolitan Police, under a board appointed by the Governor. The Municipals refused to disband and for a short period New York had two police forces which spent more time battling each other than combating crime. "In consequence of this situation the gangsters and other criminals ran wild throughout the city, revelling in an orgy of loot, murder and disorder. Respectable citizens were held up and robbed in broad daylight on Broadway and other principal streets, while the Municipal and Metropolitan policemen belabored each other with clubs, trying to decide which had the right to interfere. Gangs of thieves and rowdies invaded and plundered stores and other business houses, and stopped the stage coaches and compelled passengers to surrender their money and jewelry, while private residences had no protection save stout locks and the valor of the householders."

Against this background the rival gangs of Five Points and the Bowery undertook to settle old grievances. It started on the Fourth when all the gangs of the Five Points, led by the Dead Rabbits and the Plug Uglies, raided the headquarters of the Bowery Boys and the Atlantic Guards. After furious fighting the Bowery Boys drove the attackers back to their dens in the Five Points. Incidental rioting spread around the perimeter of the fight and, when a few Metropolitan policemen sought to interfere, they were badly beaten. The Municipals said that it was not their fight and remained aloof.

Next morning the Five Points gangs, now reinforced by the Roach Guards, attacked again, wrecking a saloon and dance hall before the Bowery gangs could rally. The fight continued throughout the day as the most ferocious free-for-all in the city's history. When a squad of Metropolitans was dispatched to the scene to restore order, the gangs made common cause against them and they were forced to retreat. There was a lull at this point and the fight might have subsided had not a howling mob of wild-eyed, screaming Five Points girls rushed into the melee, calling their boy friends cowards. Reinforcements arrived from other sections of the city, some to fight and some to loot. It was estimated that there were 800-1,000 combatants, armed with clubs, paving stones, brickbats, axes, pitchforks, pistols and knives. The *New York*

Times reported: "Brickbats, stones and clubs were flying thickly around and from the windows in all directions, and men ran wildly about brandishing weapons. Wounded lay on the sidewalk and were trampled upon."

In the afternoon the police appeared in greater force and briefly drove the rioters off the street, pursuing them to the roofs of buildings. One Five Points thug was knocked off a roof by the police and promptly trampled to death in the street. The police captured two leaders of the Dead Rabbits and retreated after this minor accomplishment. Then both sides built barricades and continued the fight from behind these defenses with stones and pistols. The hero of this phase of the engagement was a young junior auxiliary of the Bowery Boys. A leader of the Dead Rabbits was parading before his own barricade, firing a pistol so accurately that he killed two Bowery Boys and wounded two others. The little Bowery fighter crept along the top of the barricade, lifted a rock almost as heavy as himself, and brought it down to crush the opposing leader's skull.

By evening the gang members had started to set fire to buildings in the neighborhood, and several were burning brightly when two regiments of militia, supported by 150 Metropolitan Police, finally drove the rowdies from the battlefield and restored order. The official casualty toll was eight dead and over 100 injured, but it is believed that the actual count was much greater. Several new graves were later reported in the cellars of Five Points tenements, and some of the best sluggers on both sides were seen no more.

THE GREATEST VIOLENCE THAT NEW YORK has ever known—the greatest riots in the history of the nation— were the Draft Riots which raged through the city for a week during July, 1863. History does not classify the Draft Riots as juvenile delinquency, yet in the opinion of the press of the time most of the actual fighting was done by juveniles. On the second day of the riots the *New York Times* reported: "This mob is not the people, nor does it belong to the people. It is for the most part made up of the vilest elements in the city. It has not even the poor merit of being what mobs usually are—the product of mere ignorance and passion. They talk, or rather they did talk at first, of the oppressiveness of the conscription law; but three-fourths of those who have been actively engaged in violence have been boys and young men under twenty years of age, and not at all subject to conscription." The *New York Herald* first described the rioters as "the people" and the *World* called them "the laboring men of the city," but both these papers soon came around to the viewpoint of the *Times*.

The total number of rioters was estimated at 50,000 to 70,000, with individual mobs ranging up to 10,000. It is obvious that these could not all have been juveniles. It would seem likely that most members of the mobs, as with all mobs, did much milling, marching, shouting, and screaming, and that the hard core of actual fighters were organized gangs, mostly juveniles, who poured from the slum areas of the city. These wild kids were the action arm which battled the police and military, burned and looted buildings, and hung Negroes to lamp posts.

The supposed cause of the fighting was the Conscription Act which had been passed in April, 1863. Under this Act names of draftees were drawn from a wheel. A man whose name was drawn need not serve, however, if he could pay $300 as a bonus for a substitute. This provision of the Act was unpopular everywhere, for under it the poor would fight the war.

The first day of the drawing, Saturday, July 11, passed quietly, with nothing more ominous than a muttering crowd in front of the Provost Marshal's office. On Sunday detectives reported unusual activity among the gangs. Messages were going back and forth among the different leaders, and quantities of clubs, paving stones and other weapons were collected at various headquarters. Before the drawing was resumed on Monday, groups started to assemble at several points in the slum areas on the West Side, and these marched, early in the morning, to a vacant lot east of Central Park. Obviously this was not a disorganized mob; these tactics were planned by gang leaders.

The assembled mob, variously estimated from 5,000 to 15,000, marched on the Third Avenue Draft Office, which was guarded by about seventy police and fifty members of the Invalid Corps, wounded soldiers who were on guard duty in the city. At first the rioters contented themselves with stopping carriages and horse cars, stealing the horses and driving the passengers from the vehicles. Then, as they pressed against the Draft Office, a pistol shot rang out and, on this signal, they rushed the building, overpowering the police. They promptly applied the torch and refused to permit fire companies to extinguish the flames. Meanwhile another mob had gathered around the Broadway Draft Office, but this group was held in check by the police.

The morning passed with both milling mobs surging through the center of the city, battling police who sought to control them. In the afternoon imaginative members of one mob realized that they might actually capture the city if they had firearms. They marched to attack the Second Avenue Armory, drove out fifty police who were stationed there, and swarmed up to the drill room on the third floor where the guns and ammunition were stored. To prevent police interference while they sacked the armory, they barricaded the door. Meanwhile the police were reinforced; they rallied and gained control of the ground floor of the building. Before they were driven from the lower floor the rioters fired the structure at half a dozen points. In ten minutes the old building was a mass of flames which trapped the looters in the drill room, since they were unable to remove their own barricade. A score jumped out windows before the floor collapsed, but the number burned to death was never known. When the mess was cleaned up, more than fifty barrels and baskets of human bones were carted away to Potter's Field.

While the battle was raging at the armory, the main mob had dispersed in small groups which ranged through the city looting pawnshops and hardware stores to obtain arms, pillaging and burning residences, and hanging Negroes. One group attacked and burned the Negro Orphan Asylum, from which the children had previously been taken to safety except for one little girl who was killed by the mob. An attack on Horace Greeley's *Tribune* was beaten off by editorial and mechanical workers of the paper who had been armed by the police. A second attack, the next day, was repulsed with a howitzer supplied by the military.

On Tuesday the rioters erected barricades in the streets and fought off the police and military successfully, except in one instance in which four pieces of artillery were brought against them. Six rounds of grape dispersed the defenders, who took to the roofs. Here fifty police cornered them, clubbing down some and forcing others to leap to the street. New York's Governor Seymour proclaimed the city in a state of insurrection on Tuesday afternoon and wired Secretary of War Stanton for troops. The Secretary replied that forces were being rushed from Pennsylvania where they had participated in the battle at Gettysburg a few days before.

The first of the regiments arrived Wednesday. By the end of Thursday all or parts of thirteen regiments of infantry and cavalry, plus a dozen batteries of artillery, faced the rioters. Fighting was sporadic throughout the day and flared up intermittently on Friday, but, by that evening, the 10,000 troops had the city under control.

The exact number of casualties in the Draft Riots was never known, but they exceeded those of most of the battles of the Civil War. Conservative estimates placed the dead at 2,000 killed and the wounded at 8,000, most of whom were rioters. The mobs hung eighteen Negroes and drowned five; seventy Negroes were listed as missing. Over 100 buildings were burned and about 200 others damaged and looted. This was the toll of an insurrection that, according to the press, principally represented wild kids on a rampage.

Throughout the nineteenth century the police were largely impotent against the gangs, which were all protected by corrupt politicians. In the heyday of Tammany Hall, ward bosses found hoodlums useful to get out the vote "early and often," and to terrorize voters in non-Tammany districts. Shortly after the turn of the century a reform administration permitted the police force to organize squads that used the gang's own strong-arm tactics to fight them. The police did not bother to bring delinquents in; they clubbed down known gang members where they found them.

In Chicago in the early twentieth century there were few large gangs with mature leadership such as those in nineteenth-century New York, but there were many more smaller, strictly juvenile gangs which terrorized a large section of the city. In his survey of more than 1,300 such groups, published in 1927, Thrasher described their influence on the community. "The broad expanse of gangland with its intricate tribal and intertribal relationships is medieval and feudal in its organization rather than modern and urban. . . . Gang leaders hold sway like barons of old, watchful of invaders and ready to swoop down upon the lands of rivals and carry off booty or prisoners or to inflict punishment upon their enemies. Sometimes their followers become roving, lawless bands, prowling over a large territory and victimizing the community. The feudal warfare of youthful gangs is carried on more or less continuously. Their disorder and violence, escaping the ordinary controls of the police and other social agencies of the community, are so pronounced as to give the impression that they are almost beyond the pale of civil society. In some respects these regions of conflict are like a frontier; in others, like a 'no man's land,' lawless, godless, wild."

In addition to fighting, which was universal, the typical delinquencies of these groups of boys ranged from robbery to rape, with
much vandalism, some mugging and an occasional murder. Their
various activities are indicated by a few instances from the hundreds of interviews reported by Thrasher.

Olaf's crowd consisted of "about twenty members, ranging from
twelve to sixteen years of age. . . . Not only the main but apparently
the sole bond that held these boys together has been the recounting
and committing of delinquencies. . . . Thieving in stores was carried on extensively, at one time by a system—groups of three or
four going into a store and getting away with anything they could.
The articles were distributed or sold to the other boys; there was
never any systematic sharing of booty. . . . Satisfaction was clearly
obtained not only in the committing of the delinquency and
through the enjoyment of the booty but also in the recounting of
their adventures of delinquency."

The Murderers were a group of about thirty Polish boys, most
of whom were "bumming away from home, sleeping under side-
walks or in the prairies. They had little difficulty in swiping their
food; the milk and bread wagons were a source of abundant pro-
visions. They broke into box cars and 'robbed' bacon and other
merchandise. They cut out wire cables to sell as junk. They broke
open telephone boxes. They took autos for joy-riding. They purloined several quarts of whiskey from a brewery to drink in their
shack."

Of the very common practice of stealing, Thrasher had this to
say: "Stealing, the leading predatory activity of the adolescent gang,
is as much a result of the sport motive as of a desire for revenue.
It is regarded as perfectly natural and entails no more moral oppro-
brium for the ordinary gang boy than smoking a cigarette. 'C'mon,
let's go robbin','' is the common invitation. The response might be
'Naw, too tired,' or 'Too busy,' but never, 'T'aint right.' Unless

under conventional pressure, these boys do not regard such delinquencies as misconduct."

Vandalism—breaking things merely for the fun of destruction—ranked second to thieving. Said one young gang member: "We did all kinds of dirty tricks for fun. We'd see a sign, 'Please keep the street clean,' but we'd tear it down and say, 'We don't feel like keeping it clean.' One day we put a can of glue in the engine of a man's car. We would always tear things down. That would make us laugh and feel good, to have so many jokes." The Mudlakers, a group of forty sixteen- to eighteen-year-old Bohemians, "used to cause trouble by setting the wooden bridge on fire at Lawndale Avenue. They would also break windows and break into school buildings. In one case they stole pencils, ink, story-books, and light bulbs, and ripped the telephone off the wall trying to get the nickels out. They also broke up the furniture."

Most of the gangs consisted entirely of boys, although the older teen-aged gang members were frequent patrons of the dance halls and were involved in stag parties. In his study, Thrasher reported a few mixed gangs in which the girls justified their membership by serving the boys. An observer of one group in the eighth grade of a school said: "The main purpose of this gang was sexual, and the indications are that not only normal but many unnatural or degenerate methods of sex gratification were in vogue. . . . On the whole, they made no effort to conceal the nature of their activities and seemed to take pride in flaunting them before the rest of us. They possessed certain signals by which one of the boys could 'ask' one of the girls while in class. These signals soon became known to the rest of us, and it is probable that even the teacher was not entirely unaware of what was going on."

Gang fighting has been headlined as part of today's "wave" of juvenile delinquency. Until recently much was heard about "rumbles" between Negro and Puerto Rican gangs in New York. According to the *New York Times,* this aspect of juvenile delinquency is subsiding, except for the participation of juvenile gangs in racial rioting. In mid-1966 the paper carried an article under the headline "Fighting Gangs Vanish from the City's Ghettos," in which it was claimed that there is only one gang left in New York dedicated to perpetual violence, a group of twenty-five Negro youths who call themselves the Five Percenters—a far cry from the dozens of fighting gangs which numbered their memberships in the hundreds during the last century.

The *Times* article smugly continued, "In Chicago and Los Angeles, however, the gangs number 200 or more and fights are frequent." There may still be frequent gang fights in some cities, although it seems that in this respect today's youth is definitely not the wildest generation. Much boyish energy is now being directed along more wholesome lines. Chicago, although it is now twice the size it was fifty years ago can muster only the paltry boy-power of 200 gangs against the 1,300 plus that formerly roamed the city's streets, and gang violence in other cities, as a regular part of juvenile activity, has decreased in like proportion.

8

Flaming
Youth

IN THE EARLY 1920s A CARTOON WAS PUB-
lished in the *New Yorker* which symbolized the revolt of youth.
The picture showed a mother and her five- or six-year-old daughter
seated at a dinner table with plates before them. Said the mother,
"But darling, that's broccoli." Said the moppet, "I say it's spinach,
and I say to hell with it."

Here was Flaming Youth in embryo. The child was utterly defiant of authority. It had its own standards as to what it would eat
and expressed itself frankly, forcefully and rudely in defense of
them. On matters of much more significance than diet, the cartoon
youngster's real-life older brothers and sisters had a new set of
behavior standards which they defended with equal defiance, force-
fulness, frankness and rudeness to the great distress of parents, educators, the clergy and a new group of child experts. In the view of
these oldsters, youth was running wild and would come to no good
end. The entire generation was going to hell in a handbasket.

What was considered a rash of juvenile delinquency in the 1920's was the first to receive wide publicity and universal attention. Articles and pronouncements on the subject were even more prolific than they are today. Almost every issue of every magazine—from *Good Housekeeping* and *The Ladies Home Journal* through the *New Republic* to the *Elementary School Journal* and the *Bulletin of the National Conference on Social Welfare*—had something to say about wayward youth. "The Revolt of Youth" was a favorite title, as was "Flaming Youth." Other headings which might be dusted off and used today included, "Sin with a Capital S," "The Great American Scandal," "Is Modern Youth Going to the Devil?", "On Our Way to the Dogs," "They Are Hell Bent," and countless more.

It was alleged, even as today, that there was a mounting crime wave which had gotten out of hand and for which juveniles were largely responsible. This headline appeared in *World's Work:* "80% of Crimes Committed by Boys." The story afforded no support for this contention. It was stated as a fact, take it or leave it. A researcher for *Good Housekeeping* went further, citing the New York District Attorney's office as authority for the statement that 80 per cent of the criminal cases in New York's courts in 1925 involved defendants under twenty, and then went on to interview several judges, all of whom said in effect: "My experience in this court leads me to believe that most of the serious crime in our country is being carried on by young people."

Aroused by popular clamor, the Children's Bureau of the Department of Labor in 1926 began a study of the records of juvenile crime in fourteen cities from 1913 until the mid-twenties. Accurate statistics on the subject were even harder to come by then they are now, and cities could not be compared with each other because their methods of record-keeping varied so widely. But, as a result of this research, the Children's Bureau came to the conclusion that "although juvenile delinquency increased slightly during the war years, available figures for the period between 1913 and 1923 and in some cases for 1924 and 1925 indicate a reduction of the delinquency rate." Only four of the fourteen cities reported a slight increase, and in each case there seemed to be a special reason, as in Detroit, where it was attributed to "the vast increase in population, including many foreign-born parents who always find it difficult to control their English-speaking offspring."

It would seem that, so far as criminal delinquency was concerned, youngsters in the Roaring Twenties behaved very much as they had in the Gay Nineties, or in any other decade back to Colonial days, but with more moderation. Large numbers of them played hookey, snitched fruit, stole junk, and indulged in other minor misconduct. A much smaller number, and seemingly fewer proportionately than in previous eras, were involved in major crime. Neighborhood gangs still existed and still fought each other and defied the police, but most of the great juvenile-based gangs were gone and fighting was less bloody. On the whole it would seem that the social and recreational agencies for youth, which by this time were approaching full flower, had successfully deflected much youthful energy from delinquent to non-delinquent pursuits. Still, the popular press, various police and legal agencies, and a wide variety of experts declaimed at length on the amount of juevnile crime that was sweeping the country.

There were some new forms of criminal juvenile delinquency brought on by prohibition in the 1920's. Teen-agers were seldom bootleggers or large-scale makers of illegal liquor. But boys of sixteen could and did "ride shotgun" on liquor trucks, ready to shoot it out with "revenoors" or hijackers. Jane Addams observed that "city boys in bootlegging neighborhoods have many opportunities to participate and even to collect hush money or, at least, to help by guarding secrets as to location of bootlegging outfits. They are quite often used as outposts, and are expected to give an alarm if a policeman or a hijacker appears to 'be wise' as to the location of the hidden activity. . . . While much of the amateur city banditry developed previous to bootlegging days, the liquor situation has given it a tremendous impetus and a certain warfare between the constituted authorities and the outlaw has become a recognized factor in the situation."

Car theft became prevalent in the 1920's. In a study of a typical midwest city, Muncie, Indiana—which they called Middletown—sociologists Robert and Helen Lynd reported that 154 of the 6,221 cars in the community were stolen in 1924, or about 2½ per cent. The local paper had this to say: "The desire of youth to step on the gas when it has no machine of its own is considered responsible for the theft of the greater part of the automobiles stolen from [Middletown] during the past year." Most of these cars were not really stolen; they were "borrowed" from their owners without permission and abandoned, undamaged, after a joy-ride.

These and other youthful misdemeanors did not add up to a wave of juvenile delinquency, declared the Children's Bureau, in spite of the popular cry that a mounting wave was engulfing the country. The explanation seems to be that for the first time in the 1920's, youngsters who were expected to be "good" boys and girls started to be "bad" boys and girls in greater numbers. Juvenile delinquency among slum children had always been taken for granted. "What can one expect?" asked the righteous, middle-class, white, Anglo-Saxon, Protestant American, "from these children of the foreign-born or from Catholics, Jews and Negroes?" But now the kids in the suburbs, which were mushrooming with the spread of the automobile, were misbehaving, as were kids in country seats and smaller cities that did not have a slum problem. This delinquency hit home among those who considered themselves "better class," and these people were very vocal when their own children misbehaved.

The big-city slums no longer ranked so large, proportionately, in relation to urban life. Immigration curbs that started in the 1890's had led to the extreme restriction of immigration through the

Quota Act of 1921. For over a generation the flood of destitute foreigners that had previously poured into the slums had been reduced to a trickle. Also, increased wages and job opportunities of the war years had made it possible for many slum dwellers to improve their lot, moving into the better neighborhoods that the group just above were leaving for the spreading suburbs.

In many ways, the foundation for the juvenile social pattern that exists today was being laid. Because more people were better off economically, more children were going to school longer. A child could still get a job at fourteen in a case of extreme economic hardship, but the general rule was that a kid did not work before sixteen. High school attendance nationally increased from 10 per cent of the age group in 1900 to 50 per cent in 1930. The child who left school at or before the eighth grade had become the equivalent of today's high school dropout, who is currently the cause of so much concern. There was a sharp contrast with previous decades when most youngsters aged sixteen or over had been working for two or three years and were not considered juveniles. By the 1920's, a good percentage of youths of that age were still in school, and were expected to act like school kids.

ALTHOUGH THERE WAS MUCH TALK OF A great increase in juvenile crime, most of the parental and other distress about wild kids in the twenties had to do with immorality and defiance of authority rather than crime. High school students, particularly, were castigated as Flaming Youth for their lack of morals and respect for authority. These juveniles, it was said, had adopted a horrifying moral code of their own based on promiscuous sex and excessive drinking and including such minor but shocking delinquencies as indecent dress for the girls and dancing that would have been considered lewd and lascivious in grandmother's day. The little hussies also painted their faces and puffed daringly on cigarettes, and it seemed as though *all* youth was united in defying adult authority.

The general tenor of the hundreds of articles condemning Flaming Youth is expressed in these words from *Century* magazine in 1921: "It seems that the young people have taken the bit between their teeth and are running wild. They are wholly contemptuous of the traditional controls and show no disposition to impose a speed limit upon themselves. Fond parents, maiden aunts, all the amateur censors of morals, are at their wit's ends. They are shouting voluminous warnings after the runaways, but the pace only gets hotter. And the end is not in sight." Another comment in the same volume: "The elders of today are convinced that never before have the established and responsible members of society had to remonstrate against so many anarchic notions and such alarming behavior. No age, they say, has had on its hands such a problem of reckless and rebellious youth."

Looking back at the 1920's from the vantage point of 1931, Frederick Lewis Allen in *Only Yesterday,* after commenting on the Russian Revolution, considered the internal upheaval in America: "A first-class revolt against the accepted American order was certainly taking place during those early years of the Post-War Decade, but it was one with which Nikolai Lenin had nothing whatever to do. The shock troop of the rebellion was not alien agitators, but the sons and daughters of well-to-do American families, who knew little about Bolshevism and cared distinctly less, and their defiance was expressed not in obscure radical publications or in soap-box speeches, but right across the family breakfast table into the horrified ears of conservative fathers and mothers. Men and women were still shivering at the Red Menace when they awoke to the no less alarming Problem of the Younger Generation, and realized that if the Constitution were not in danger, the moral code of the country certainly was."

A contemporary who became a very controversial figure because he defended the rebellious youngsters was Denver's Juvenile Court judge, Ben Lindsey. He admitted youth was in revolt and praised the underlying motivation. In a book entitled, *"The Revolt of Modern Youth,"* written with Wainwright Evans, he said, "Not only is this revolt from old standards of conduct taking place, but it is unlike any revolt that has ever taken place before. Youth has always been rebellious; youth has always shocked the older generation. That's traditional. The 'modern girl' wearing skirts that reached only to her shoe tops, was a 'problem' in mid-Victorian England. But this is different. It has the whole weight and momentum of a new scientific and economic order behind it. It has come in an age of speed and science. . . . an age in which the fear of Hell Fire has lost its hold. In the past, the revolt of youth always turned out to be a futile gesture. It never brought much change. But now the gun's loaded. These boys and girls can do what boys and girls never were able to do in the past. They can live up to their manifesto, and nothing can prevent them. The external restraints, economic restraints that were once so potent, have gone never to return; *and the sole question now is how soon and how effectively will the internal restraints of a voluntarily accepted code, which alone can keep people going straight, take their place."*

There were experts of many hues during the twenties who advanced theories galore as to the causes of youth's revolt—theories that ranged from the influence of Darwin and Freud at one extreme to "sparing the rod" at the other. One summary enumerated the following causes: "Give the motor-car its due share of responsibility. Give the movie more blame, please, than it has hitherto received. Give the war some—but not too much; for all this antedates the war. Give the radical intellectuals a little for their tendency to howl down everything that has ever, anywhere, been of good repute. Give a lot of it to the luxury of the *nouveaux riches:* a luxury which inevitably, at first, finds expression in pampering

Flaming Youth   193

the body. Give 'prohibition' a little, if only as an earnest of the vast blame it is going to have to shoulder in the next decade or two. And give all you can heap up to the general abandonment of religion."

Many critics, particularly among the clergy, attributed the youthful rebellion principally to the decline of "that old-time religion." Actually, there is no evidence of a decline in church membership in the 1920's, although there are no national statistics available on church and Sunday School attendance. It was not necessarily true that Flaming Youth was godless. Rather, they disagreed with the fundamentalist interpretation of the Bible, and, more strongly, with the puritanical concept of right and wrong. In the eyes of a Methodist minister dancing and going to the movies were sinful. With this, his younger parishioners refused to agree. They danced—in what oldsters considered a most shocking manner—and they went to the movies in great droves. Some of the cry of juvenile delinquency at the time was directed against such "sinful" practices.

An interest in the new psychology was another explanation offered for the wild behavior of kids. This was the era when Freudian concepts were glibly tossed around by pseudo-intellectuals. Jane Addams spoke of the influence of the psychoanalyst: "The Freudian theories as to the dangers of repression were seized upon by agencies of publicity, by half-baked lecturers and by writers on the new psychology and finally interpreted by reckless youth as a warning against self-control. All of this profoundly influenced the attitude of children to parents and the attitude of the sexes toward each other." Another writer expressed the schoolgirl's perversion of Freud as the understanding that "all the miseries of the world are caused by self-control," and quoted a young Freudian disciple, who said, "Far be it from us to dispute your delightful theory that life is unrestrained self-expression, that the suppressed wish is the root of all evil, and that the only right way of living is to want what you want when you want it, and see that you get it in full measure.

Thanks very much; now we know exactly where we are."

Aside from the opinions and theories of experts and clergy, the position of parents in the 1920's was very much the same as that of parents in the 1960's, as younger grandparents of today's teenagers should remember from their own teen-age days. The Lynds found that in their Middletown "a 'date' at home is 'slow' compared with motoring, a new film, or a dance in a nearby town. It is not surprising that both boys and girls in the three upper years of the high school marked the number of times they go out on school nights and the hour they get in at night more frequently than any other sources of friction with their parents. . . . With the diminishing place of the home in the life of the child comes the problem of 'early sophistication,' as business class parents put it, or 'children of twelve or fourteen nowadays act just like grown-ups' in the words of workers' wives." One Middletown mother expressed her problem in words that have a familiar ring today: "You see other people being more lenient and you think perhaps that it is the best way, but you are afraid to do anything very different from what your mother did for fear you may leave out something essential or do something wrong. I would give anything to know what is wisest, but I don't know what to do."

The wild kids of the twenties had much to say in their own defense. College students in particular were articulate in throwing the ball back to the older generation, which they said had created conditions that made the youthful rebellion inevitable. One wrote: "I would like to observe that the older generation had certainly pretty much ruined this world before passing it on to us. They give us this Thing, knocked to pieces. Leaky, red-hot, threatening to blow up; and then they are surprised that we don't accept it with the same attitude of pretty, decorous enthusiasm with which they received it 'way back in the eighteen-nineties, nicely painted, smoothly running, practically foolproof. . . . As they look back on it, they see their youth through a mist of muslin, tennis, bicycles,

Tennyson, Browning and the Blue Danube Waltz. The other things, the ugly things that we know about and talk about, must also have been there. But our elders didn't care or didn't dare to consider them, and now they are forgotten. We talk about them unabashed, and not necessarily with Presbyterian disapproval, and so they jump to the conclusion that we are thoroughly bad, and keep pestering us to make us good."

That was the voice of the "Lost Generation" speaking—the youngsters whose ideals had been shattered by the social upheaval of World War I and who affected a "tomorrow we die" attitude. Their name was supposedly given them by Gertrude Stein and their principal prophets were the young writers, F. Scott Fitzgerald and Ernest Hemingway, whose novels *This Side of Paradise* and *The Sun Also Rises* had great influence upon the more intellectual jazz-age youth. As Mark Sullivan wrote: "Many a father had to tolerate a conversation overheard in the sitting room between eighteen-year-old Nelly and her beau, a conversation which shocked the old gentleman—because a man he never heard of named Hemingway wrote a book he never heard of called *The Sun Also Rises*."

There was a definite relationship between Flaming Youth and the Lost Generation. The groups that had arbitrarily been thus dubbed were not the same, although they talked alike and acted alike in ways which oldsters deplored, and overlapped to some extent. In general the Lost Generation were the youthful intellectuals, mostly of college age. Flaming Youth included this age group and extended down into the early teens. The young intellectuals forcefully expressed their credo of rebellion, which condemned puritanism, Victorianism, fundamentalism, prohibition, censorship and all repression by legislation or the will of the great bourgeois majority. Few high school kids fully understood the revolutionary ideas of the intellectuals. They merely said defiantly: "I have a right to do anything that doesn't harm any one else." "That was heard often by parents of the twenties," said Mark Sullivan. "It was a kind of slogan of the adolescent. . . . the twenties were a hard time for raising children."

Literate members of the Lost Generation read the works of such creditable writers as Hemingway, Fitzgerald, Theodore Dreiser, John Dos Passos, Somerset Maugham and D. H. Lawrence—whose books were frequently concerned with sex. For less erudite Flaming Youth, there was a flock of tawdry sex novels by hack writers that were devoured by unsophisticated youngsters who sought to learn the ways of the world. The heroines of Warner Fabian's *Flaming Youth* were three motherless girls who were exclusively concerned with sex, alcohol and nude moonlight bathing. Sex in Paris was exposed in *The Bachelor Girl,* whose heroine maintained an apartment in which she entertained a series of men. Sex in college was the subject of *The Plastic Age;* sex in the desert was covered in *The Sheik*. The seduction of a young boy in a midwest town by a glamorous foreign countess was the long-drawn-out theme of *The Tattooed Countess.*

Much trash was written and published in the twenties, all of it read avidly by youngsters, particularly girls, seeking knowledge and a vicarious thrill in the description of sexual experiences. The most popular writer of the era with this group (and with many older women who should have known better) was Elinor Glyn, who changed the meaning of the simple pronoun "it." In a short story, "The 'It' Girl," Miss Glyn created the sex symbol of the decade. If a girl did not have "It" (sex appeal), she was "out." Miss Glyn's heroine was immortalized in celluloid by Clara Bow, the "It" girl of the silver screen, in a series of pictures which were solely concerned with drinking from silver flasks, doing wiggling dances on tables, and the removal of clothing.

Vying for popularity with sex novels were trashy sex magazines. Of such cultural fare Frederick Lewis Allen wrote in his history of the twenties: "As the revolution began, its influence fertilized a bumper crop of sex magazines, confessions magazines, and lurid motion picture magazines, and these in turn had their effect on a class of movie goers who had never heard and never would hear of Freud and the libido. The publishers of the sex adventure magazines . . . learned to a nicety the gentle art of arousing the reader without arousing the censor."

In their study of what Middletown youth was doing with its leisure time, the Lynds reported: "While four leading motion picture houses were featuring synchronously four sex adventure films, *Telling Tales* on the Middletown news-stands was featuring on its cover four stories, 'Indolent Kisses,' 'Primitive Love,' 'Watch Your Step-Ins!' (Irene didn't, and you should have seen what happened), and 'Innocents Astray.' The way Middletown absorbs culture about (to quote the advertisement of a local film) 'things you've always wanted to do and never DARED' was suggested by the coverless, thumb-marked condition of the January, 1925, *Motion Picture Magazine* in the Public Library a fortnight after its arrival."

Movie producers, then as now, were dependent on juveniles to fill the seats in their plush, new cinema palaces. Of the influence of the movies on the minds of their juvenile audiences psychologist Dorothy Bromley, in a study entitled *Youth and Sex,* wrote: "The movies' direct influence on the new sex mores through their preoccupation with the more star-spangled aspects of sex is generally recognized. The crudity of the Hollywood accent on sex becomes tiresome to a sophisticated audience. For young men and girls who have not yet had time to discover the comparative scale of values which life offers, the lush sensuality of these shows, night after night, may be very disturbing. The movies have taken off the bed-room doors for young people and turned life into a French peep-show."

Those who now complain of the frankness of modern films as having a pernicious influence on the impressionable minds of the young are fortunate that they did not bring up children in the twenties. Compared to the offerings on the silver screen at the time, a film such as "Lolita" is tame, chaste and respectable. The type of movie fare prevailing then is indicated by the titles of the four films mentioned above, which were running simultaneously in Middletown. If a boy did not want to take his girl to "The Daring Years," they had a choice of "Sinners in Silk," "Women Who Give," or "The Price She Paid"; and next week they could see "Rouged Lips," "Queen of Sin," or "Name the Man—a story of betrayed womanhood." In making their selection of what to see, they might study advertisements. The producers of "Alimony" proclaimed that their epic offered "brilliant men, beautiful jazz babies, champagne baths, midnight revels, petting parties in the purple dawn, all ending in one terrific smashing climax that makes you gasp." Or perhaps the youngsters might prefer "Flaming Youth," which offered "neckers, petters, white kisses, red kisses, pleasure-mad daughters, sensation-craving mothers, by an author who didn't dare sign his name; the truth, bold, naked, sensational."

The effect of such fare on the young was described by one sixteen-year-old girl who testified: "Those pictures with hot love-making in them, they make girls and boys sitting together want to get up and walk out, go off somewhere, you know. Once I walked out with a boy before the picture was over. We took a ride. But my friend, she all the time had to get up and go out with her boy friend."

The tumult of indignant complaint from churchmen, educators and parents at the things that youngsters were seeing in the movies induced Hollywood to appoint a moral czar, Will B. Hayes, President Harding's Postmaster General. Mr. Hayes placated the oldsters with speeches like this one: "The industry must have toward that sacred thing, the mind of a child, toward that clean virgin thing, that unmarked slate, the same responsibility, the same care about the impressions made upon it, that the best clergyman or the most inspired teacher of youth would have." To effectuate this the Hayes office promulgated a "code" which, if anything, worsened the situation, since it made it mandatory that every picture have a moral ending. The screen continued to present all kinds of sexual misconduct which, youngsters learned, was all right so long as virtue triumphed in the end. All of the pictures and advertisements quoted above were released after the Hayes office came into being.

To put into action the ideas that they gained from sex novels, sex magazines and sex movies, youth had a fine new tool—the automobile. During the twenties the automobile changed from a semiluxury to a necessity; thirty-one million of them were produced in that decade. Then, as now, a boy had to have "wheels" or he was "dead." The horse and buggy and the bicycle built for two could not take Flaming Youth to dances and road houses far from parental supervision or the eyes of tattle-tale neighbors. A bulwark of American morality had always been the difficulty of finding a suitable place for misconduct. Now the car on a dark deserted road provided the privacy of a bedroom.

In his study of gangs in Chicago, Thrasher wrote: "There is a common practice among young men in Chicago, and this is by no means confined to boys of the gangs or the underprivileged classes, of picking up girls, utter strangers, on the street and taking them for a ride in an automobile. During the course of this ride it is customary to indulge in passionate petting, and often the affair culminates in the sex act. If the girl refuses, it is commonly supposed that she is put out of the car some place in the country and asked to walk back. So widespread is this practice that allusions to it have become a common joke on the vaudeville stage. Many a girl voluntarily or involuntarily begins a delinquent career in just this manner; in some cases she is made the victim of a brutal attack after accepting such an invitation."

There were many who insisted that the car was the principal factor in the juvenile immorality current during the twenties. One juvenile judge castigated the automobile as "a house of prostitution on wheels" after nineteen of thirty girls, who came before him for sexual offenses in a single month, admitted that the misconduct had taken place in a car. The main use to which youth supposedly put automobiles was depicted in a cartoon which showed a boy and a girl talking to a policeman, the boy carrying the cushion of the back seat of a car under his arm, with the caption: "We want to report a stolen car."

MOST OF THE CRITICISM OF ADOLESCENTS in the twenties was directed at the female of the species, the "flapper," who burst, as from a cocoon, on the national scene in the immediate postwar years. The name "flapper" did not derive from a sail or a sheet flapping in the breeze. Rather, quite appropriately, it was based on the definition of a fledgling bird which, too young to fly, could only flap its pin-feathered wings. The genesis of the flapper actually went back to the war years when patriotism justified young girls, unchaperoned, passing out flaglets and badges on the streets in a worthy cause. The girl might even talk to a strange boy if he was in uniform; nothing was too good for "our boys." After the war the flapper maintained and enlarged upon her new freedom to the point that one contemporary writer noted: "Never since civilization began has the girl in the early teens seemed so self-sufficient and sure of herself, or made such a break with the rigid traditions of propriety and convention which have hedged her in. From this, too, it follows that the tension which always exists between mothers and daughters has greatly increased, and there now sometimes seems to be almost a chasm between successive generations."

The accusation was widely made that the girl, rather than the boy, was the leader. The flapper, it was said, not only permitted the boys to take liberties, but she also encouraged them. The *Southern Baptist Review* reported that "one hears it said that the girls are actually tempting the boys more than the boys do the girls, by their dress and conversation. Not all of the boys and girls are bad, but evil is more open and defiant of public opinion and restraint. The situation causes grave concern on the part of all who have the ideals at heart of purity and home life and the stability of our American civilization."

One certain invitation to misbehavior, in the minds of the older generation was the way in which the flapper dressed. In most past eras, even as today, age has criticized the costumes of youth for their slovenliness, sloppiness, or unconventionality. But, in the twenties the charge was made that girls were dressing in a manner that was not only immodest, but also indecent and immoral. The principal point of attack was the short skirt. It had literally taken centuries for women's skirts to get to the top of high-buttoned shoes. In five short years, 1920 to 1925, the flapper took them to the knee and defiantly held them there for four years despite the anguished protests of her elders.

The President of the University of Florida declared: "The rolled hose and short skirts are born of the Devil and his angels and are carrying the present and future generations to chaos and destruction." In New York a group of women, current social leaders, including Morgans, Harrimans, Phipps and Roosevelts, proposed an organization to discourage fashions involving "an excess of nudity." In Philadelphia a committee, after querying 1,000 clergymen, designed a "moral gown" with a hem that was seven and one-half inches from the floor. It was endorsed by ministers of fifteen denominations. The YWCA conducted a national campaign against immodest dress among high school girls. In several state legislatures bills were introduced to make short skirts illegal. Utah proposed a fine and imprisonemnt for anyone appearing on the streets in "skirts higher than three inches above the ankle." Ohio wanted to set the skirt's limit for any female over fourteen at "that part of the foot known as the instep."

None of this had any effect on the flapper. She brazenly continued to flaunt her kneecaps to an anguished nation, and she won her revolt. Perhaps on the theory, "If you can't lick 'em, join 'em," mothers started to expose their adult calves. In the early twenties Paris decreed that skirts should be longer, and American retailers loaded their racks with long-skirted garments that nobody would buy. The long-range result of this aspect of the revolt of youth in the twenties is the bikini, which is today universally accepted, and the mini-skirt which, at this writing, is only mildly censured in some quarters.

With the short skirt the flapper combined short hair. "Woman's crowning glory" was scattered on the floors of countless barber shops—establishments which, prior to the twenties, no young lady would think of entering. The adolescent did not originate bobbed hair; this is attributed to the dancer Irene Castle. But it was the adolescents who made Miss Castle's innovation an enduring style.

To bobbed hair, the teen-aged rebel added costume jewelry— rings, bangles, bracelets, beads, wrist watches, pendants and earrings in great profusion—and perfume in an assortment of scents, frequently worn at the same time. To complete the picture of a shameless and brazen hussy, the flapper painted her lips and rouged her cheeks, usually after she left home for school. The only unladylike thing that flappers did not do was chew gum. For some reason this habit was "out" among the young "in" people of the twenties.

In all her glory the flapper danced endlessly. But before she danced she removed her corset. In the early years of the era she usually had to wear this garment when she left home, for mothers seemed to feel that it represented protective armor against the prying hands of boys. When she arrived at the dance, however, the flapper parked the offensive garment in the ladies' room, and when a boy put his arm around a girl to dance he got an armful of girl rather than of stiffened cambric and steel stays.

An indecent and outrageous style of dancing was one of the most common charges against the young people of the twenties. It was performed to the barbaric strains of the saxophone rather than the romantic tones of the violin, and the mildest description of it was "syncopated embrace." Boys and girls danced body to body and check to cheek as if glued together, in a manner that was variously called "impure, polluting, corrupting, debasing, destroying spirituality, and increasing carnality." The *Catholic Telegraph* said, "The music is sensuous, the embracing of partners—the female only half dressed—is absolutely indecent; and the motions—they are such as may not be described with any respect for propriety, in a family newspaper. Suffice to say that there are certain houses appropriate for such dances, but those houses have been closed by law." Dancing and accompanying activities of adolescents were so offensive to the conservative oldsters that dancing was prohibited entirely in a leading boys' preparatory school, Phillips Academy.

After the dance and/or sometimes between dances or without dancing the kids "petted" in dark corners of rooms, on lawns, or in parks, or any place where they could find reasonable privacy—preferably in a parked car. In the Roaring Twenties the petting party replaced the more decorous "spooning" of the preceding generation. Whether it was any worse than, or different from Colonial bundling is a matter of opinion. Certainly the word "petting," meaning the stroking, patting or fondling of an animal, had a horrifying connotation to parents of young daughters.

The Lynds tried to determine the extent of petting among junior and senior high school students in the midwest city that they surveyed. In reply to the statement, "Nine out of every ten boys and girls of high school age have 'petting' parties," 48 per cent of the boys and 51 per cent of the girls answered "true." There may be some significance in the fact that more girls than boys answered this in the affirmative, although in the reasons given by girls who admitted petting, only 48 per cent said that they did it for a "good time," and 36 per cent said that they allowed boys to pet them for fear of being unpopular if they refused. The Lynds summarized their findings this way: "There is a small group of girls in the high school who are known not to allow 'petting.' These girls are often 'respected and popular' but have less 'dates'; the larger group (many of them from the 'best families') with whom 'petting parties' are not taboo, are said to be much more frequently in demand for movies, dances, or automobile parties."

Mothers of Middletown, at least the mothers of Middletown's boys, were convinced that the blame of petting and general licentiousness could be laid squarely on the girls. They made such statements as: "Girls aren't so modest nowadays; they dress differently." "It's the girls' clothing; we can't keep our boys decent when girls dress that way." "Girls have more nerve nowadays—look at their clothes!" "Girls are far more aggressive today. They call the boys up to try to make dates with them as they never would have when I was a girl." "Girls are bolder than they used to be. It used to be that if a girl called up and asked a boy to take her somewhere, she meant something bad by it, but now they all do it." "When I was a girl, a girl who painted was a bad girl, but now look at the daughters of our best families!"

A college humor magazine summed up adult opinion of the girl of the twenties in this couplet:

> When they're good, they're very, very good,
> But when they're bad, they're torrid.

Another relationship between boys and girls that became prevalent in the twenties and is disturbing parents of younger adolescents today, was "dating." Before this time, well-brought-up boys and girls did not go out alone together, or even sit in the parlor alone together unchaperoned, until they were engaged. Being alone together was one of the final steps in an orderly process of courtship.

The adolescents of the twenties brashly repudiated this convention. Having a date with a boy was a lot more fun than pulling taffy with a group. The new relationship of the sexes was explained by Willard Walker, professor of sociology at Barnard College, as follows: "The decay of this moral structure has made possible the emergence of thrill-seeking and exploitative relationships. Whether we approve or not, courtship practices today allow for a great deal of pure thrill-seeking. Dancing, petting, necking, the automobile, the amusement park, and a whole range of institutions and practices permit or facilitate thrill-seeking behavior. . . . For the average student a love affair which led to immediate marriage would be tragic because of the havoc it would create in his scheme of life. . . . The sexes associate with one another in a peculiar relationship known as 'dating.' Dating is not true courtship, since it is supposed not to eventuate in marriage; it is a sort of dalliance relationship."

By today's standards few of the juvenile activities in the relations between the sexes in the twenties that have so far been discussed would be considered delinquencies. The youth of that era won most of the points in their battle for freedom and forced the acceptance of a more lenient code. But it was widely claimed that the indecent dress, the cheek-to-cheek dancing, the dating and petting were but the outward manifestations of a moral decadence that went much deeper, that kids were not only discussing sex interminably and experimenting tentatively, but they were, in great numbers, indulging in complete sexual experience.

There were no reliable statistics then, as there are none now, on how many youngsters completed their teens as virgins. There was no factual support, as there is none today, for the charge of widespread misconduct. There were indications that many more "well-brought-up" girls had sexual intercourse before they left high school than in previous times. This was what was causing so much alarm. Previously, there had been very little public concern about the girls from the slums, the daughters of immigrants, the servant girls and factory girls who went astray; such delinquency was brushed off with the "what can one expect" attitude. When high school girls started to be swayed by their biological urges, it was claimed that Flaming Youth was setting new records for immorality.

Denver's Judge Ben Lindsey quoted some statistics and estimates for his own city on this subject, and there is no reason to believe that Denver differed from other urban areas. Lindsey was in a unique position to express expert opinion. The kids of the community considered him their champion in their revolt against the old code. They talked to him freely, and in great numbers. In his book, *The Revolt of Modern Youth,* he concluded there were three steps in their sex experience:

"The first item in the testimony of these high school students is that of all the youth who go to parties, attend dances, and ride together in automobiles, more than ninety per cent indulge in hugging and kissing. This does not mean that every girl lets *any* boy hug and kiss her, but that she *is* hugged and kissed. . . . The testimony I receive regarding this estimated ninety percent is practically unanimous. If it is true it means that these young people have more or less definitely come to the conclusion that this minor form of sex experience may be legitimately indulged in. . . .

"The second part of the message is this: at least fifty percent of those who begin with hugging and kissing do not restrict themselves to that, but go farther, and indulge in other sex liberties which, by all the conventions, are outrageously improper. . . .

"Now for the third point of the message. It is this: fifteen to twenty-five percent of those who begin with hugging and kissing eventually go all the way. . . . To most persons reasonably well acquainted with girls and boys of high school age that estimate will doubtless appear excessive. I can only say that the estimates came from high school students and that they are the most conservative estimates I have received from that source."

As to boys only, the students' estimates of the percentage who had sexual intercourse while in high school varied widely from thirty to ninety. Said Lindsey: "My opinion is that fifty percent is a safe and conservative estimate for all classes of high school boys averaged together."

As is often the case today, much of Lindsey's more sensational reporting was based on records of individual cases, which were probably far from typical. There was a seventeen-year-old girl who came to him for advice and made him "a list of fifty-eight girls of high school age, known to her personally, who had at least one or more sex experiences with some youth." The judge called some of the girls in to talk to them. "One of these girls, aged sixteen, had had relations with twenty boys. . . . Nine of the girls had gone the limit with an average of five boys each. These nine had had such relations, collectively, more than two hundred times." This was Flaming Youth with a vengeance, but it is extremely unlikely that most youth flamed to this degree.

The use of contraceptive devices by teen-agers of the twenties was a major scandal. In *Youth and Sex,* Dorothy Bromley wrote: "Censorship has concealed the rapid expansion of the distribution of contraceptives. In a small, conservative Eastern college town, the best hotel provides in its men's washrooms a slot machine which sells a contraceptive device for a quarter. It is no longer necessary to find a drugstore. Today gasoline stations, tobacco stores, confectionery, grocery, dry-goods stores and pool rooms are stocking this type of contraceptive and they combine to sell a larger share of the total output than the drugstores." Lindsey added: "But of 495 girls of high school age—though not all of them were in high school— who admitted to me that they had had sex experiences with boys, only about twenty-five became pregnant. That is about five percent, a ratio of one in twenty. The others avoided pregnancy, some by luck, others because they had a knowledge of more or less effective contraceptive methods—a knowledge, by the way, which I find to be more common among them than is generally supposed."

There were girls who carried in their compacts a contraceptive device, to be used by boys. As one teen-aged miss said, "A girl would be a fool to be caught without one." Lindsey wrote, with unconscious wit, "No such wholesale rebellion against conventions of sex has ever been known before in the history of our civilization. The reason is that this civilization is the first of its kind. No other civilization, for example, had rubber. Rubber has revolutionized morals."

The fact that high school girls were misbehaving in greater numbers during the twenties did not prove that there was an overall increase in sexual juvenile delinquency during those years. More "good" girls were behaving like "bad" girls, but it is very likely that there were fewer of what had previously been considered as "bad" girls. Juvenile prostitution had been sharply reduced, principally because the brothel had been forced underground in most places and more aggressive action was being taken against procurers and white slavers who had been responsible for the delinquency of many girls. Also, with the relative decrease in the impoverished slum class, not so many girls were forced into prostitution for economic reasons. Wages were higher. If a girl had to support herself, she had more chance of doing so by non-delinquent means.

Another class of female, the teen-aged domestic servant, who had contributed a great deal to sexual delinquency, was disappearing. In the early years of the century most middleclass families had a servant girl, usually a farm girl who had come to the city, or an immigrant girl. Completely unsophisticated, these girls were extremely vulnerable. As in Victorian England, many were seduced by the master or by a teen-aged son of the family. They either gave themselves willingly or through fear of losing their jobs and being cast adrift in the strange city where they would have little chance of supporting themselves except through prostitution. One federal report stated that approximately half of a large number of prostitutes studied gave domestic service as their previous occupation. By the 1920's servant girls in middle-class families were the exception rather than the rule. There were no immigrant girls who would work for a pittance, and far more farm girls were getting jobs in towns near their homes to which they traveled by bus.

The situation seemed to be that boys who previously had sex experience with girls of a lower class or with prostitutes were now consorting with girls from their own "peer group." The relative number of boys who had their first sex experience with prostitutes had certainly declined. When Denver still had a red light district, Judge Lindsey made a survey of two groups of high school boys. Of forty-one boys in a certain high school, all but three had been in the red light district, at least to see what it was like. Twenty-six had been inside a brothel, and twenty-two—more than half—had relations with prostitutes there. Of a group of about one hundred boys in another high school, "over half admitted to me that they had had relations with women, mostly on Market Street." By the 1920's the red light district was gone and the remaining prostitutes were getting a lot more amateur competition from high school girls. Lindsey's comment on this was: "A red-light district in Denver might have saved those girls from these experiences, but it would not have saved the boy—nor the prostitutes, who have as good a right to be saved as anyone else. There can be no doubt, I think, that since the red light districts were abolished far more good girls than formerly have had sex experiences. But, curious as it may seem, fewer girls have been ruined and lost."

ANOTHER ASPECT OF JUVENILE DELINQUEN-cy in the twenties which was highly controversial was youthful drinking. Flaming Youth was charged with an appalling lack of sobriety. Certainly a lot of kids were doing a lot of drinking, but whether more kids were drinking than before or the drinking was merely done by a different type of kid can never be resolved.

The Volstead Act took effect on January 16, 1920, and the imme-diate effect of prohibition on youthful drinking was unquestionably a good one. The disorderly saloons that served liquor to minors and were associated with sex delinquency were closed, as were most of the dance halls where youth drank so freely. These, catering to large crowds, could not sell liquor clandestinely and liquor sales were their main source of revenue. Far fewer slum kids were drinking, because the places in which they drank were gone, and the cost of illicit liquor was beyond their means.

But, after the first year or two of prohibition, the situation changed. The speakeasy came into being. This was usually too expensive for youthful patrons, although the most famous of them, The Stork Club, catered chiefly to boys from the Ivy League colleges, to whom its proprietor sent cards of admission. The places most closely resembling the old dance halls as a source of delinquency were the roadhouses frequented by adolescents which, wrote Jane Addams, "were notorious for their prostitution. . . ." Automobiles, she pointed out, "make it possible to quickly transport patrons to these disorderly roadhouses—also affording concealment for the intoxicated young people returning together." After a survey of Cook County roadhouses made by the Juvenile Protective Association the conclusion was reached that they "constitute a decided menace, offering untold temptations to young poeple and not only moral but physical hazards. . . . There was a time when city dancehalls were as dangerous to boys and girls as the road-houses of today through a tieup with vice and liquor interests. They have been under supervision, by and large, but through the automobile their old problems have been widened out beyond the cities where control by parents, authorities and public opinion is even more difficult than in the cities themselves."

In addition to drinking and, for a few juveniles, criminal associations with bootleggers, liquor during prohibition presented other opportunities for juvenile misbehavior. Acquiring it involved delinquency. Despite the legend of the hip flask containing hard liquor, it is probable that the beverage most widely consumed by youngsters was domestically made rot-gut wine, some of it fortified, obtained from a bootlegger. Such vicious vintages sold, in New York, for seventy-five cents to a dollar a quart. In small towns and rural areas fortified hard cider was the common tipple. In addition to buying cheap liquor, kids made it and filched it from their parents.

A few teen-aged boys built stills or stole them from the school chemistry lab, and tried their hand at distilling, producing weird varieties of brandy from fruit juice, "Jersey Lightning" from sweet cider, and whiskey from assortments of grain mashes. Some kids made potent "home brew" by fermenting malt and hops. Such activities involved the collusion of parents, if carried on at home, because of the odor, to say nothing of blowing caps and explosions now and then. A high percentage of parents considered it almost a duty to violate the Volstead Act, so permission for such illegal manufacture was frequently given, and some youngsters manufactured liquor for the family.

A more popular beverage than any of these concoctions was "bathtub gin," which could be made almost anywhere quickly and without special equipment. This merely involved mixing 40 per cent purloined or otherwise illicitly obtained grain alcohol with 60 per cent water and adding a few drops of oil of juniper and glycerine, both legally obtainable in drug stores. The more sophisticated added a couple of drops of vegetable coloring from the kitchen shelf to give the end product the yellowish tinge associated with good English gins. The grave danger here was that kids would use denatured or wood alcohol instead of grain alcohol. Hundreds were made blind and scores were killed as a result of using denatured alcohol. Contrary to legend, bathtub gin was seldom made in a bathtub. The usual container was a two-quart pitcher or a gallon pot.

The symbol of Flaming Youth's drinking was the hip flask which was filled with liquor stolen from the supply that papa had obtained from a bootlegger, water being added to the remainder to disguise the theft. Flasks were in evidence at most juvenile dances and their use was a not uncommon prelude to the parked car petting party. Judge Lindsey found that "no petting party, no roadhouse toot, no joy ride far from the prying eye of Main Street, is complete unless the boys carry flasks. There are no actual statistics to be had on these matters, but it is very clear in my mind that practically all cases where these boys and girls lose their judgment in Folly Lane, involve the use of drink." Headlines on juvenile drinking were made when the principal of Lawrenceville School, an eastern preparatory school for boys, wrote a widely published letter to the parents of all his students, calling their attention to the prevalence of drinking by schoolboys and requesting their cooperation in suppressing the evil at Lawrenceville.

Jane Addams, who had a somewhat different view on juvenile drinking in the twenties, wrote: "Many young men are very eager to demonstrate their superiority to law, and consider this demonstration a very sporty thing. We know indeed that a great many young people are drinking at the present moment solely from a sense of bravado. Each generation looks for a method with which it may defy the conventions and startle its elders. The present generation seems to have settled upon the obtaining and consuming of illicit liquor. The motive is so cheap and superficial that it is almost impossible to place the situation in the area of morals or any other human field."

Flaming Youth was wild; of that there is no doubt. They probably drank more—or, at least, more unwisely—than kids today. But whether the consumption of alcoholic beverages by *all* kids in the twenties was greater than the consumption by *all* kids in previous eras is subject to question. The same is true of juvenile sex. Despite the great uproar about juvenile delinquency in the twenties, there is no real evidence that, in terms of all types of delinquency by all types of kids, it was as great or any greater than in most earlier times.

Looking back on the Roaring Twenties, H. L. Mencken in 1931 discoursed on the demise of Flaming Youth. Mencken was a sophisticate, a cynic and a moral liberal whose views did not coincide with those of more conservative commentators. His championship of the youth of the day was not endorsed by the "Bible belt" (a phrase which he coined), but he did strike a blow for the youngsters in relation to their critics when he wrote:

"The late pious bellowing against the crimes and carnalities of Flaming Youth seems to be dying out: one hears a great deal less talk than aforetime about gin-toting and necking in shady lanes. This is a welcome relief, and perhaps shows that there is such a thing, after all, as human progress. It would be curious and instructive to examine the business historically, and find out who set up the first alarums. My guess is that they came from oldsters, male and female, whose own youthful conduct was anything but chemically pure. Find me an active moralist and I'll point out for you a fraud who has something to conceal and forget. . . .

"The truth is that the moral divagations of the youth of today probably do not differ three percent from those of the youth of yesterday. When I was a youngster, which was very long ago, with Victoria in full blast upon her throne, great numbers of boys were diligent lushers, just as they are now: the only difference I can make out is that they then drank beer, which was relatively harmless, whereas they now have to put up with bootleg gin, which often makes them sick.

"There was necking, too, in my early days, and all of it that the traffic would bear. . . . A little necking, I am convinced, does no normal and healthy girl any appreciable harm. On the contrary, it tends to improve her, if only by ridding her of groundless fears. . . . In case the business goes further than mere necking there is some ground, of course, for sociologists to intervene, but I doubt that it goes further today any oftener than it did yesterday. The notion that it does is simply a delusion spread by two classes of nuisances: parents who forget what they did themselves when they were young, and professional moralists who live by unearthing and denouncing sins which do not exist. Such moralists are always reckless pornographers."

9

Wanderers
of the Depression

A FREIGHT TRAIN BUMPS AND CREAKS TO
a stop at dusk in the railroad yard of a midwest division point
town. Promptly from the doors of boxcars and over the sides of
gondolas a little company of forty to fifty males drop to the cinders
beside the track. There are a few older men in the group, traveling
alone—perhaps ten in all. The majority of the company are
ragged boys, from twelve to twenty years of age, traveling in gangs
of ten or twelve members. As the assemblage starts to leave the
yard, straggling toward the main stem of the town, two cars shoot
out to block the street in front; a truck pulls up behind the group.
Five men step from the cars in front, an equal number from the
truck behind, all carrying ominous-looking pick handles. The head
of the column of youngsters halts. The men at the rear prod the
laggards forward, herding them like sheep into a compact mass.
A heavy-set man facing the silent group flashes a sheriff's badge in
his hand as he addresses the congregation:

"You're under arrest boys, but don't let that scare you. We aren't
going to be tough on you unless you make us tough. We're not

going to put you in a rotten old jail all winter or in a chain gang on the roads if you behave like we tell you. But you can't panhandle this town, boys, remember that. That freight you got off is the last tonight. There'll be another at eight tomorrow morning. Now we're going to give you a nice supper, a chance to wash up, a warm place to sleep, and a good breakfast. Then we're going to march you back to the yards in time to catch that freight in the morning, and, if you don't give us any trouble, nobody's going to get hurt."

Scenes like this were enacted in hundreds of cities and towns throughout the United States in the early 1930's as the nation faced a type of delinquency that was new to America. Vagrancy had been a problem in Europe as far back as the days of the Roman Empire. At one time during the war-torn era that preceded feudalism it was estimated that almost half of the population of western Europe had become wanderers. In the United States boys had always run away from home, but they seldom became vagrants. Some went to sea; others took Horace Greeley's advice, "Go west, young man." For a youth of fifteen or sixteen to run away from home to seek adventure, excitement and opportunity in distant places was not considered delinquency. Huckleberry Finn, who took off for the open road when faced with the prospect of adoption, epitomized an American ideal of the independent, self-sufficient American youth, able to hold his own against the world.

In the 1930's there was no longer a frontier to give youth a goal, and there was a depression that deprived youngsters of opportunity at home. By the hundreds of thousands they took off to wander aimlessly, seeking they knew not what. By 1932 it was estimated that the number of homeless juveniles on the move throughout the land exceeded a quarter-million. This figure was quoted as a "conservative" estimate, although it was, in truth, little more than an educated guess, because the kids never stayed still long enough to be counted. The extent of the increase of transiency was indicated by one social agency in Los Angeles which served 360 homeless boys in 1928 and 4,400 in 1932. Five Los Angeles agencies gave 225,927 nights' lodging to boys during that year, although the majority of the wanderers avoided the relief agencies whenever possible, preferring to beg or steal their food and to sleep in hobo jungles. Approximately one out of twenty of the transients was a girl.

The kids soon learned what to expect from the relief that was grudgingly doled out by the communities. The "nice supper" that the sheriff promised the group described above consisted of a cup of cold canned tomatoes, a boiled potato, and a slice of stale bread; the "good breakfast" was a cup of watery cornmeal mush and another slice of stale bread; and the "warm place to sleep" was the concrete floor of a detention cell and the corridor leading to it. Relief agencies, public and private, were not heartless; they were simply incapable of handling the vast horde of transients on top of the load of local relief cases created by the depression. The wanderers were not welcome anywhere. Few communities would feed or shelter them for more than one night, or two at most. The policy was to run them out in the morning, hoping that they would move on to become some other community's headache.

A feud developed between the "town clowns," as the transients called local police, and the railroad "bulls." The latter wanted the kids off the trains because of the danger to themselves and to freight. There was normally not much for kids to steal in freight cars, but the youngsters frequently broke the seals on refrigerator cars, causing the loss of all perishable goods. The local police wanted the kids back on the trains going some place else, they cared not where. The young wanderers were bounced back and forth like a volley ball between the public and private forces of law.

Although there was little record of major crime associated with the juvenile wanderers, all of them were delinquent in that necessity compelled them to steal food or clothing, and most kids did not consider it criminal. After all, one had to eat to live and must have protection from winter's bitter cold. Most of them begged in preference to accepting the slops that passed for food in most missions and other relief agencies. For every nineteen boys who were vagrants, there was only one girl. These girls, traveling and living with boys, were all sex delinquents by choice or necessity.

Except for these youthful transients, juvenile delinquency was not a problem in the thirties; at least, very little was heard about it. This seems somewhat paradoxical in view of the relationship that had always existed between poverty and delinquency, and the fact that the work of juvenile courts and other youth agencies designed to curb delinquency was drastically restricted by the depression that pared their staffs and budgets. But the type of poverty brought about by the depression was different from the permanent pauperism of city slums that had formerly bred so much delinquency. These were "hard times" rather than poverty, and in a great many cases the financial difficulties tended to draw families closer together. As on the farm and the frontier, children of middle-class families that were facing difficulties had opportunities to share in coping with problems and overcoming obstacles, and this has always been a deterrent to delinquency. There were also fewer broken homes, another factor associated with delinquency. There was a sharp decline in the divorce rate during the depression. Perhaps marriage partners working together in facing problems had something to do with this; certainly there were many who may have wanted a divorce, but simply could not afford it.

There was also a change in the kids themselves. The youth of the depression did not flame. They did not even give off a sickly little glimmer. The outstanding characteristic of this generation was apathy. Eleanor Roosevelt applied to them the same name that Gertrude Stein had given their predecessors, the "lost generation," but Mrs. Roosevelt did not mean the same thing. Miss Stein's lost generation had lost its ideals and rebelled against the social system that had permitted their world to shatter. Mrs. Roosevelt's generation was lost in terms of having no place in the economic scheme of things. They did not rebel against anything. They resented and mistrusted an economic system that left them sidetracked, but they could not blame parents or church or school authority as the cause. There was nobody to rebel against. Some who sought an active means of opposition to the scheme of things espoused Communism, which made considerable headway among the young during the middle and late thirties.

Pearl Buck did a little expertizing on the younger generation in *Harper's Magazine* in 1935: "They have been given in the United States an amazing amount of deference and freedom to do what they call living their own lives. Indeed, to the observer from elsewhere the attitude of the average American parent toward his child, or even of the adult toward youth, is one of pathetic deference. The effect upon the child would be amusing were it not so alarmingly bad, for it bestows upon the youth a spurious superiority which he has done nothing to achieve and robs him of the enthusiasm for life which is the right of every individual. . . .

"They are so charming, they are so mild, they are so unconsciously and completely selfish, they are so sophisticated with a sort of pseudo-sophistication which is touching in its shallowness, they are so docile, docile to their parents or their teachers whom for the most part they ignore, and docile toward life; and nothing is so unhealthy in the young as docility. When I say they are docile toward their parents and teachers, I do not mean that they listen to their parents and teachers with any interest or respect, but they do not rebel against them as they should. . . .

"Our young people now, therefore, show the signs of not having their inalienable right of rebellion. They exhibit all the physical and mental restlessness of the teething child who cannot find anything upon which to set down his sore and swollen gums. They are vaguely rebellious; for, of course, they cannot help being rebellious against something, and they are rebellious not against their natural enemies, their parents and their teachers, but against life itself."

Another contemporary writer, Maxine Davis, put it this way in a book entitled *The Lost Generation*: "We of previous generations were not willing in our young years to accept life as we found it. Whether we wanted change in the conduct of our personal affairs or in the whole social structure, American youth has always been inclined to take the bit in its teeth. It has never been submissive to the current conditions. Youth today, we note with trepidation, accepts its fate with sheep-like apathy.

"It is easy to observe this in its attitude toward public problems. Dixie's youth today would never fire on Fort Sumter. British tea and King George's taxes would be unloaded without protest by the young men of Massachusetts and Vermont. The Declaration of Independence is a page of fine type in the back of their history books. . . . There would be no Lexington and Concord, no Vicksburg or Bull Run. They would not fight for states' rights or any rights, because they have no interest in them."

In a sense, the hundreds of thousands of youthful wanderers were rebelling in rather a passive way merely by leaving home, but for most it was an act of necessity rather than opposition. The principal authority on the youthful transients was young sociologist Thomas Minehan who, disguised as a tramp, traveled with them for two years, sleeping and eating in jungles, missions and flophouses. He interviewed in depth or secured complete case histories of 1,377 boys and 88 girls, something more than half of 1 per cent of the total number of transients, if the quarter-million estimate is accurate. Minehan reported that 83 per cent of the children whom he interviewed told him that they left home because of some variation of "hard times." One boy said of his father: "He didn't exactly kick me out, but he gave me plenty of hints. He hasn't worked steady in the last three years. There's seven of us kids at home, and

I'm the oldest. I'm seventeen. . . . Last fall they cut down on our relief. We had to go to bed because our house was so cold. I cut nine cords of wood for a man. He gave us two. That wasn't so bad, and I thought I'd stay until Christmas. I got the kids a duck, too, for Christmas, but I ain't saying how I got it. Then, before the old man could start giving any more hints, I scrams."

Said another youngster: "I couldn't go back to high school in these pants. What the hell, I'd rather take to the road. The old man? I don't know where he is." One fifteen-year-old lad reported: "Geez, it's two years ago since I left home, and I ain't never wanted to go back yet. No, sir, the old road looks good to me. Square meals don't come every day, but I eat better than I ate at home and no grief about the old man being out of work all the time and how he used to do so much when he was as old as I was, and then the snoopy old social worker coming around asking questions and the cops waiting for a chance to hang something on you. If they do give me a rap now, nobody knows about it and if I haven't got a clean shirt there ain't nobody else showing off his new sport roadster."

To which another tramp replied: "Yes, and I'll bet you're glad you beat it. I know I am. Work! Work! 'why don't you get work?' That's all I hear from the old man for a year. Cripes! What does he expect a kid to do? I try a job cleaning a shoe store every morning from four to six o'clock for a buck and a quarter a week. And one morning my mother forgets to wake me. And I'm canned. The old man goes nuts for a while. So finally I asks him, 'Why the hell don't you get work yourself for a change? You ain't done nothing now since the war!' Then he bangs me with a chair, and I lams it."

The stories of the girl tramps usually indicated a somewhat greater prerunaway delinquency, such as this one who said: "I didn't have any clothes to wear to school. So one day a guy says to me, 'Get wise, sister, get wise.' So I got wise. And the old man catches me taking my first two bits from a fellow and he goes kinda nertz. He calls me down on my knees in the kitchen and Ma comes in and takes my part. 'Why shouldn't she take two bits?' Ma says. 'Somebody in this house has to earn something.' And the old man slams the door and goes out to get drunk. 'Gimme that two bits,' Ma says. 'Gimme that two bits, you dirty slut, before I kill you.' So I says, 'Like hell you will.' And I scrams."

Those kids, comprising 17 per cent of juvenile vagrants, who did not connect their wandering with the depression told stories of the brutality of step-parents, or dislike of school. For instance, "Nothing I did ever satisfied anybody in school. I hated them all." Others simply had a desire to travel: "I always wanted to go swimming in the middle of winter, so when I got a chance to go to Florida, I went." But the usual reason among the older boys who were not victims of the depression, was girl-trouble. One boy explained, "We were all in it. Drunk. And we went to a cottage after the football game, but it was my old man's cottage, so I got the heat. Everything would have been all right then, but one of the dumb clucks had to start making coffee about five o'clock in the morning. Her guy was sick, and she got up to make some coffee. The kerosene stove exploded and set fire to the place. We got out but none of us had any clothes on. One girl was burned pretty bad. We had cars, all right, and we could have ducked into them, but the cars were locked and our keys were inside our pants in the cottage. Everybody blamed me: all the mothers of all the girls and the school principal and my old man. So before they got a chance to kick me out of school or anything, I says 'To hell with you!' and I hitch-hikes to Los Angeles."

In the early days of the depression many of the kids hitchhiked, but for several reasons most later turned to the railroads for transportation. A hitchhiker must make a fairly good appearance to get rides, for few motorists will pick up a ragamuffin. After even a short spell on the road, not many tramps could maintain a sufficiently neat appearance to get rides. Also, the depression caused a decline in motor traffic while the number of transients increased. The main reason, however, for giving the trains preference was that most youthful tramps wanted to travel with a group of their peers, both for protection and companionship. Hitchhikers had to work singly or in pairs, which made travel lonely and dangerous. The isolated youngster was vulnerable to the law along the road.

Most popular with the free riders were empty boxcars. The kids would sneak aboard one when it was standing in the yards or on a siding and wait for it to be picked up by a train. This involved luck in avoiding the railroad police, except in some instances when the officers turned a blind eye to the practice. These humane men allowed the youths to board an empty car so long as it was standing still. But such humanity was exceptional. Usually the kids had to board or leave the train while it was in motion. They waited at the edge of the yards, beyond the patrol area of the police, or at the first upgrade that would compel the train to slow down. A favorite "flipping" place was a grade near a block signal where the train might stop.

While boxcars were preferred, kids rode anywhere that they could: between cars, on top of cars, in gondolas, in "reefers" (refrigerator cars) and with the stock in cattle cars. There were a few "passenger stiffs" who considered themselves the elite of the tramps because they would ride nothing but through trains. These boys were always "loners" who would endure cold, hunger, privation and considerable danger to gratify their mania for speed. When possible, the passenger stiff rode the blinds, the closed door in the front end of a baggage car. But sometimes they clung to roofs, crouched on steps, or wherever they could find a hand- or foothold.

The young tramps covered much ground on foot, walking perhaps eight hours a day on the average. They usually had to board trains several miles from the town or city limits and, in larger cities, it was more miles to the downtown section where the missions or other relief agencies were located. They walked miles, begging from door to door. The cops were forever moving them on. If they could not find a place to bed down, they frequently "carried the banner" all night, that is, walked the streets.

A few youngsters ranged widely. New York was a magnet for some from the West and South and Los Angeles for some from the Midwest and East. Some went south for the winter, returning north in the spring. In the early part of the depression southern California was a lodestone for many, until Los Angeles, deluged by transients of all ages, sought to solve the problem of homeless youths by putting them in work camps under semiprison discipline.

These widely traveled tramps were in the minority. Most of the youngsters stayed within about 500 miles of their homes. Within this area they developed routes, moving from place to place in a circle and hitting the same spots, which they came to know, over and over again. In the summer they favored small towns and rural areas. Here there were no tax-supported relief stations or soup kitchens, but housewives were more sympathetic and food could always be worked for, begged for, or stolen from farmers. Haystacks, barns or open fields served as sleeping places in mild weather, and rural jails would usually bed down a boy without the necessity of registration or fumigation.

IN THE WINTER THE TRANSIENTS WERE forced into the cities to rely reluctantly on bread lines and soup kitchens for at least some of their sustenance and missions for shelter. Incredibly, the relief agencies were much less lenient with youthful transients than with mature ones. Whereas an adult tramp might receive six meals and two nights' lodging, the youngster was usually restricted to one or two meals and a single night's shelter. The presumed explanation of this is that the relief people believed that by forcing the child out, they would compel him to go home.

In reality, since most of the young tramps had no homes in which they would be welcome, the relief agencies were simply fostering further delinquency.

For most of the young tramps, missions, "Sally" (the Salvation Army), community welfare stations, and all other relief agencies were refuges of last resort. When a boy arrived at one of these places he was registered for identification and usually given something to eat, although some made him work for even this first meal, and all agencies required him to work for two to four hours before he could have a second meal. The first handout was usually a bowl of soup, "invariably thin, watery, lukewarm, tasteless, and served without even stale bread, and never with soda crackers. A portion equals about a small cupful and no second bowl is ever given."

The food varied in different places, but the staples were commonly soup, meatless stew, and watery beans. This was supplemented with stale bread and sometimes stale cake and rock-hard doughnuts. The only use of the undrinkable coffee was for dunking the stale baked goods. "Sundays or holidays, being days of joy and feasting, a dish of prunes or rice pudding might be served with the doughnuts." Although pie is traditionally associated with mission meals, Minehan never saw a piece in his two years of travel with the tramps, "nor have any of the boys and men to whom I have talked ever encountered a mission meal with pie, save one old hobo. He asserts that on Christmas in Chicago in 1911, he received a small piece of mince pie in a mission, but his memory—rapidly failing—cannot recall the place, he is not sure of the time, and it may not have been mince pie after all."

The beds in most welfare centers were reserved for local relief cases, and there were no beds for transients, who slept on the floor or, if they were lucky, a wooden bench. Minehan described the sleeping accommodations in one typical establishment: "It is a large room, eighty by one hundred and fifty, low-ceilinged and outlined rather than lighted by a dozen small-watt bulbs. Every available space large enough to contain a man's body on the floor is occupied. In the dim light you feel before you see the forms curving away from the desk and entrance aisle. A half-circle ten or fifteen feet in radius is clear. And in all the remainder of the room you cannot see a space large enough to spread a newspaper. Benches follow the walls, pewlike seats stand in the center of the room. On every bench there is a reclining form. Feet to feet, and head to head they sleep. Some have removed shoes. One or two have checked damp overcoats. Here and there a man has opened the belt of his trousers, a boy has thrown off his cap. The majority sleep in their outdoor clothes, caps or hats pulled down over their heads, legs outstretched, faces to the floor. . . .

"We stumble to a vacant spot in the room, at the rear. It is not a happy place nor one in which a man might wrap the mantle of his cloak about him and lie down to pleasant dreams. A door opening directly into a small toilet greets us. The stench of chloride of lime and of latrines is nauseating. Here, if we wish, with the drunks and late arrivals, we may sleep."

Frustrating to many of the hungry and homeless youths was the religious aspect of the missions which, they said, were "places where you get sermons and sour stew." Below the sign on the mission wall that proclaimed: "It's never too late for Jesus," some kid invariably scrawled: "But it's always too late for a bed." Before the depression the missions were the only agencies to deal with the problems of homeless men and their purpose was to "convert and feed." Now, food was the greatly enlarged problem, but in the eyes of many of the men who were running the missions, religion was still the most important objective.

In some missions, relief recipients were required to attend a service of prayer, hymns, and a sermon before they could eat. As a group, the young transients were not religious; in fact, they were probably antireligious because of the experiences of hardship in their young lives. And even if they had open minds the religious fare was rarely suitable for such an audience. The clerics were used to sermonizing to confirmed bums, long gone in rot-gut whiskey. To such they enjoined repentance for the past sins that had reduced them to such straits and for the money that they had squandered on harlots and riotous living. Few of the boys had such sins to repent. Even the more reasonable preacher who appealed to the boys to go home to their sorrowing mothers and aging fathers seldom reached the youthful audience, most of whom knew quite well that they were serving their parents far better by remaining away than by going home to become one more mouth to feed.

Some of the boys became quite adept in following the lead of older tramps in the hope of getting better treatment in the mission. Many of the old rummies made a point of standing up at the proper point in the service and announcing, with tear-dimmed eyes, that they had been saved and were ready to come to Jesus. They had learned that this sometimes earned them a second bowl of stew. Smarter youths joined the ranks of the "pork chop Christians," although it seldom, if ever, got them a pork chop.

Away from the missions, in the hobo jungles, the boys sometimes held their own irreverent parodies of religious services, singing hymns such as:

> I don't care if it rains or freezes,
> I'll be safe in the arms of Jesus.
> I can lose my shirt and britches,
> He'll still love us sons of bitches.

Then all joined in the chorus:

> Am I Jesus' little lamb?
> Yes, you're goddam right I am.

Hobo jungles offered the young tramps a way of life that was far preferable to that of the welfare centers. Most jungles were merely outdoor clearings where tramps congregated to cook, wash, repair their clothing and tell tall tales. The best ones had been established years before by older tramps with whom the youngsters shared the space, although with the advent of swarms of youthful tramps many new ones were started that were patronized exclusively by kids. A jungle was preferably near a good flipping point on a rail line, near enough to a community or a farming area to permit begging or stealing food, but not too near other human habitation. There was an inviolate rule among the tramps against panhandling in the immediate vicinity of a jungle. If the kids did not pillage the neighborhood, the cops would usually leave them alone.

Water and fuel were necessary in a jungle, and grass and trees were highly desirable. Old pots, pans, pails and tin cans used for cooking and eating were left at the jungle and used by its successive occupants. Failure to take care of this equipment, to wash it after use and turn the containers upside down to drain was a cardinal sin in hobo-land. Jungles in the outdoors were favored for other than winter use, although there were some in caves, deserted ice-houses, empty buildings or sheds and other shelters that, with stoves, could be used year round. Minehan described a scene in one outdoor jungle:

"It is the middle of September and already a tinge of winter haunts the air in spite of the mellow sun of autumn and the warmth of the early-changing, reddening leaves. Twelve boy tramps and three little girl companions sit in a natural clearing in a woods a hundred yards from a railroad grade fourteen miles south of Chicago. A spring bubbles from the ground in one corner, running away in a tiny stream to the woods. Here the child tramps wash their clothing. Bushes are hung with drying shirts, socks, underwear, and pants. Two boys try to bend a shoe nail with rocks as last and hammer. A Titian-haired girl of fifteen, extremely pretty and extremely thin, sews a patch on the seat of a boy's pants. The boy stands very still on a hummock. The girl sews very business-like, as she turns in the edges of the patch and reenforces the center. A second, blond girl boils coffee and potatoes and directs the barbecuing of a small hog. Except for the disproportionate ratio of boys to girls, the drying clothes and the deshabille of many, the gathering seems very much like a high school wiener roast, or a Sunday school barbecue. Nature has been kind to the farmers, and the farmers, with crops rotting in the fields, have been kind to the child tramps. There is food enough in the jungle to feed forty. Vegetables have been collected by the sack. Cantaloupes and apples stand in a pyramid on the ground. The hog, of course, was not a gift. But, then, he might have been hit by a truck."

When there were girls in a jungle, they almost invariably did the cooking and superintended the housekeeping, ordering their male companions to secure fuel, carry water, and scour the containers in the sand. The boys supplied the food. In the jungle described above, two of the boys had approached a farmer who was digging potatoes a couple of miles from the jungle and said: "Will you give us a few, please, mister, if we dig three or four bushels for you? We ain't had nothing to eat since last night." Such an appeal was usually effective. In this case the farmer's wife fed them lunch and, after they helped him load a truck, they departed with two burlap sacks filled with potatoes, apples, three cabbages, a loaf of homemade bread and a jar of jelly. Back at the jungle they found another boy had secured four fish from a sportsman and another three chickens, which had probably been obtained in the same way as the pig.

Although some food was secured in the country through a little work for farmers, much of it, sad to say, was stolen. When produce was ripe, orchards and fields were raided regularly and any chickens, ducks, turkeys, or little pigs that strayed far from the farmhouse became victims of nimble boys who lay in ambush. In towns and cities the kids could seldom get work. They might cut or rake a lawn occasionally or clean a garage, but, in the main, they had to depend on begging or stealing for their sustenance.

Bakery trucks parked early in the morning before stores, and produce trucks going to market were handy targets for the young
thieves. A couple of boys could dart out of a culvert when a truck
was going slowly up hill, leap aboard and be gone with enough
produce to feed the jungle before the driver knew that he was
being raided.

BEGGING TECHNIQUES WERE SIMPLE, BUT
varied. The children begged for money on the streets, for food at
back doors of houses, bakeries, butcher shops and restaurants, and
for clothing at homes. Begging on the main stem was the most
dangerous, for the youthful vagrant had to keep one eye peeled
for the hostile cop. The advice of one youth was: "Fast and hard
you want to hit the stem, no use arguing. Don't let them see you
first. You size them up and then surprise them by saying, 'please
mister give me a nickel for some food.' If they see you first they
get ready for you and say no, but if you hit 'em fast-like the
chances are they shell out." Another with a different technique
said: "Hit the cars. If there's a parked car with a woman alone in
it, she'll pretty near always give you something. If there's a man in
it, stay away." A third advised: "Straight, I always plays it. Tell
'em you're hungry and want something to eat."

Equally important as the manner of approach was the careful
selection of potential donors. Old ladies, who might have adolescent
grandchildren, were very good, but not in great supply. Young
or middle-aged single women were not usually generous, but young
married women ranked high, as did prostitutes, who would always
give a kid something if they had it. Best of all, in the opinion of
one lad, were Negro women. "I never asked a black woman for
anything yet that I didn't get it," he said.

In selecting men, "Pick out a working stiff with poor clothes,"
said one boy, "and it's all the better if he's young. He likes you
to think he has a dime." Another experienced beggar found that

"fat well-dressed men have been hit so hard and so often since the depression that they are becoming tough. Poorly dressed men with a grouch and a mean look are often the best prospects because they don't get hit so much."

In hitting the houses it was also important to be selective. "Look for a yard with a kid's toys in it," said one expert panhandler. "If the grass is cut in front and there's toys in the backyard you're sure to get something." Another tramp judged prospects by clothes on wash lines: "A good day to hit a house is when there is a lot of washing on the line. You're sure the woman is in and has got something ready to eat, and, if there are a lot of men's clothes, she's probably a good cook. If there's nothing but woman's clothes, ask for a dime instead of food."

The proper way for a beggar to behave was explained by one fourteen-year-old this way: "If she asks you in the house to eat always wipe your feet on the stoop and don't say much at first. Take off your hat and act scared, kind of. Wait until you've finished eating and she is sitting down looking at you. Then she asks you something and you answer polite-like. Then she asks you something else and you begin to tell a story. If she's a fat lady and sitting down you can tell her anything. Pretty soon she will be bawling and you can have the house."

It was also good technique not to ask for too much. "Hit a guy for a nickel and he'll give you a dime. Hit him for a dime or a quarter and you'll get a stony stare," said one. Another offered: "Ask a woman in a house if she's got anything left over and pretty soon she'll be cooking you a meal. Ask her for a meal and she'll slam the door."

An expert on panhandling from stores explained: "I always ask a baker if he has any old half-loaves that he is going to throw away. He pretty near always gives me something good. I even get pie slices that way. Ask a butcher for some old scraps of dog meat and first thing you know he'll be handing you a ring of fresh bologna. I went into a swell joint in Chicago one time and asked the cook if I could clean up the plates that were coming back from a banquet upstairs; the stuff the big guys weren't eating. First thing you know I'm having chicken, ice cream and pie. And before I left I got a buck from a big, fat guy."

Clothing, which was almost unobtainable by transients from relief agencies, was secured by begging and stealing, preferably the former. A snowy day was a good time for the thinly garbed kid to beg for clothes and, as to places, "Flats where a lot of young married people live are the best. A young married woman is good that way, she'll pretty nearly always give you an old shirt of her husband's." Another youth favored "a woman who's kinda old— you know, about forty—and who lives in a house." One lad, a shrewd psychologist, reasoned that the best time to ask people for clothing was when they were wearing their best. "I wait until after church on Sundays and when I see a woman going home I follow her and hit her for some clothes and lots of times I get a big dinner and some spiffs too."

The easiest place to steal clothes was from clothes lines and the best time was immediately after dark, when a pair of boys going through an alley were inconspicuous and housewives, busy with dinner preparations, may not have gotten around to taking in the wash or clothing that had been put on the line to air. Some thieves used a pole six or eight feet long, with a hook on the end, which could be carried openly as though it were a play spear. They used it to lift clothing from fire escapes or pushed it through a fence to take clothing off a line. At night, boys who stole by choice rather than from necessity used this technique to lift pants, handbags or wallets through open bedroom windows. They pawned the articles and kept only whatever money they found.

There was, on the whole, little crime for the sake of crime perpetrated by the young tramps. There were some who travelled from place to place in stolen cars, and who supported themselves by looting tires, generators, spark plugs, etc., from parked cars and disposing of them to dishonest garage men. These out-and-out thieves were a small minority. Most of the boy tramps had respect mounting to reverence for big-time gangsters and machine-gun bank robbers, but although they avidly read about and discussed their exploits, they showed no inclination to follow in their steps. Perhaps the general apathy of the group had more to do with this than high standards of morality.

Girl tramps had a far more difficult time in securing food, clothing and shelter than boy tramps. Most welfare agencies were closed to transient girls; the missions were for homeless men only. About the only place a girl could be sure of getting shelter in a city was in the women's house of detention, and this might lead her to juvenile court. In begging, men were frequently more generous to a girl than to a boy, but this was more than compensated for by the strange attitude of most women, who might become tearful over a wandering boy but were stony-faced to a wandering girl, who, they were sure, was "no good." The girl had one advantage over the boy in that she could trade the use of her body for a meal or the money to buy one. Under the spur of necessity many did this but, on the whole, the girl tramps, although they were all sex delinquents, were not active prostitutes.

A few were sexually delinquent to the point of depravity, and this may have been their main reason for being on the road. Minehan recounted one case of two girls in their mid-teens who came into a jungle where about thirty men and boys were preparing a lunch of mulligan stew. The young misses made a frank and straightforward proposition. There was an empty box car on a nearby siding. If the men would give them lunch and dinner, the girls would repair to the box car and receive the men in pairs during the afternoon. No monetary payment was required, but the girls made it clear that they would appreciate small donations to buy one of them a pair of shoes. They stipulated that they must have dinner at six o'clock as they wanted to catch a freight that went through shortly after. Throughout the afternoon the men lined up for their turns in the box car, most men going through both lines. Promptly at six the girls quit, ate a hearty meal, and departed with seventy cents contributed for shoes to catch their train.

Most girl tramps fell into one or another of three classifications. One kind of girl traveled with a single boy who was her lover and protector. She may have met him on the road or she may have left home with him. In more fortunate circumstances and at a more advanced age, he might have been her bethrothed or ultimately her husband. These couples, if they traveled alone, had certain advantages. Train crews were inclined to be lenient with them, perhaps out of a romantic regard for young love. Posing as brother and sister when begging, they aroused the sympathy of many housewives, who saw in them a personification of the Babes in the Wood legend.

Sometimes these couples joined a gang of wandering boys, in which the girl was the only female member. She functioned as a housewife for the gang, doing the cooking and sewing, but was a wife only to her boy friend. In most cases the other members of the gang respected her lover's exclusive rights and, unless the boy chose to lend her, the other boys did not molest her. If her initial companion deserted her, she usually became the mistress of the rest of the gang, unless another boy who had strong enough fists to assert his exclusive rights became her protector.

Other girls traveled, sometimes singly but more frequently in pairs, with a particular gang of boys. These served as housekeepers and mistresses to the entire gang, who, in turn, fed and clothed them and protected them from other males. About one gang in five of the juvenile tramps had permanent female members. When new members were accepted into the gang they were, perforce, accepted by the girls as well. The system of sex mores here was very similar to that of the bachelors' huts of some primitive tribes.

Finally, there were the girls, like the two in the boxcar incident described above, who joined a gang temporarily or entered a jungle and offered their bodies in return for food and clothing. Sometimes they stayed in one jungle, serving successive groups of transients; sometimes they traveled with a gang for a short period and then moved on. These girls were in the nature of semiprofessional prostitutes with a wanderlust, rather than the housekeeping-mistress type who stayed with one gang.

All of the juvenile wanderers had a completely pagan attitude toward sex. They were amoral rather than immoral. Sex was a normal part of existence, a fact of life to be accepted without question. So far as the girls were concerned, regardless of their personal feelings toward or desire for intercourse, it was necessary to compensate for their inferior capabilities as tramps. For the boys, continence was governed entirely by the absence of opportunity. Morals or virtue did not enter into the matter. There was no stigma attached to a girl who was promiscuous. In a society in which males outnumbered females nineteen to one, the females obviously had to be shared. If a girl made her way by offering herself on the main stem the boys might comment that "she's a whore," but they would say it in the same way as they might say: "She's a nurse," or "She's a school teacher."

A sex problem for the boys was the prevalence of homosexuals among the older, long-time tramps. Before the depression vagrants had been almost exclusively a male group and, as in any one-sex society, homosexuality was commonplace. A few boys willingly teamed up with older men, accepting their protection and, in return, catering to their aberration. These were rare. Most of the boys, who saw nothing wrong in normal sex relations, had a horror of perverted sex. Many of them were brutally seduced by older men in empty boxcars and elsewhere, but if such a boy was a member of a gang it went hard with the older "wolf," if the gang caught him. The best he could expect was to be beaten into insensibility. In a few cases, the homosexual did not survive the beatings.

By the third year of the depression the boys and girls of the road had developed a unique tribal society. Wrote Minehan: "Driven out of homes, unable to find work or live in normal ways, they are developing, in the face of necessity, their own means of sustaining life and their own social habits, justifying their actions through their own folkways and systems of morals. Within a year I saw Texas [a boy tramp] change not only physically but mentally. From a bright, witty American schoolboy, full of dreams and vigor, he had turned into a predacious, cunning person, whose habits and actions differed as much from those of the American schoolboy he had been as the habits and actions of a member of one African tribe differ from those of another. He had, in fact, dropped out of one tribe or nation and gone into another where the tribal life is different."

The basic unit of the wanderers' tribal life was the gang, which was its principal point of similarity to the life of delinquent youngsters who stayed at home. The tramp gangs were not organized primarily for purposes of delinquency other than stealing and begging from necessity. Nor were they basically dedicated to defying adult authority and customs. Rather, the gang was essential in a nomadic existance for reasons of survival and protection. A railroad cop might freely use his club on a single youth, or even two or three, but he would hesitate to face twelve teen-agers acting in concert. Numbers saved them, too, from the homosexual wolf.

The ideal size for a gang was about a dozen. Smaller units would not be sufficient for protection; larger ones invited organized opposition from the law enforcement officers. A jungle of a dozen kids would usually be left alone unless their actions were too delinquent. A jungle of fifty or more would probably be raided and broken up, on the theory that such an aggregation was a threat to the neighboring community.

In most gangs there was a division of labor. In those that did not have girl members one or two boys did the cooking; another might do most of the tailoring. The majority spent their time getting food, and here there might be a division between thieves and beggars. This division of labor was determined by ability and interest, and by the gang leader. In every gang, as in the primitive tribes that this society somewhat resembled, there was a chief. He was not necessarily the strongest boy, or the eldest, although he might be. Usually he secured the position by inherent gifts of leadership and courage which had become evident in a crisis. Under his leadership the tribe was communistic, in that the wealth and the food of the group were shared equally. A member who chiselled or held out faced the rigid discipline of the group, which might mean a beating, expulsion, or, for minor offenses, "being sent to Coventry"—isolation.

Fighting was frequent in the jungles, for any reason or for no reason, but these fights were between individuals of the same gang or of different gangs. There was virtually none of the fighting between gangs that marked juvenile society in the cities. In a sense, the wanderers formed a natural group, of which the gangs were units. War between the units was frowned on as being destructive to the total group. Also, there was little racial prejudice among the child tramps. Whites and Negroes, Christians and Jews lived together on a basis of absolute equality.

When the housekeeping in the jungle was finished, the youngsters talked endlessly. The subjects that interested the stay-at-homes of the same age had little part in the tramps' conversations. There were no sports, movies, dances and dates in their lives. They talked of clothes—how to get them, not what to wear. But most talk was about food and the various means of getting it. They had a keen interest in politics, not in terms of parties, but of a system of government. The one that we had, they were sure, was rotten. They looked forward to a revolution which would result in a new type of society, of which they would be an accepted part. Who would revolt or who would lead they knew not.

Their attitude toward the police, as revealed in their conversations, was somewhat surprising. To their city counterparts the cop was an enemy. To the tramps, cops were sometimes friends. True, they had all been chased, some beaten and others jailed by police, but many officers had more sympathy for the wanderers than they had for local delinquents. Most of the tramps had had experience with at least one cop who had helped them to obtain food, clothing or shelter, such as one girl who said: "A great big cop takes me into a restaurant and says, 'Here, Bill, give this girl all she wants to eat and no funny business, understand.'" Of course, there were cops and cops. One boy asserted: "You don't have to be afraid of a fat cop, unless he is drunk. He'll always give you a break," while another observed: "When you see a small cop who isn't shaved, look out; he's tough."

BY THE END OF 1932 THE ARMY OF WANDERING juveniles was a major national concern. Congress held hearings on the subject and considered ideas that ranged from putting them on farms at government expense to providing shelter, sustenance and a training program aboard refurbished unused battleships. The Senate finally passed a bill appropriating twenty-two million dollars to open the Citizens' Military Training Camps to homeless boys between the ages of fifteen and twenty. This created a furor. The word "military" was unfortunate; the attitude of the nation was extremely pacifist at the time. The proposal to send thousands of boys to some of the mammoth training camps left over from World War I and put them under army supervision and military discipline, smacked of the European conscription of youth as cannon fodder. (A peacetime draft would have been unthinkable in the thirties.)

The proposed legislation was condemned in hundreds of headlines like "Prison Camps for Homeless Boys," and the Secretary of New York's Children's Aid Society vigorously condemned the plan: "Because the boys will be virtually prisoners we believe a single question will reveal its fallacy. Suppose one of our American boys placed in such a cantonment is dissatisfied or gets homesick and decides to leave and the camp guards pursue him to bring him back and he refuses to stop—will they shoot him?" The Senate bill expanding the CMTC died in the House.

In the spring of 1933 the CCC, the Civilian Conservation Corps, came into being to provide work for young men under twenty-one. In camps run by the army and supervised by the Department of the Interior, youths labored in the national forests on conservation and reforestation projects. This was supposed to help correct juvenile transiency but, in fact, it had little bearing on it. It covered only boys, and the minimum age was eighteen, which ruled out well over half the young tramps. Also, an applicant to the CCC had to have a residence and references, two things that few of the tramps possessed. Some boys joined; perhaps as many deserted to swell the ranks of the transients, who did not like the discipline of what they called "Roosevelt's roosts" or "army chain gangs." Probably most of the young wanderers did not know exactly what they wanted, but they did know that they did not want to be put in work camps.

No positive action ever subdued the widespread juvenile vagrancy of the thirties. It subsided when the condition that caused it was removed. In the late thirties, as jobs became more plentiful, the need for leaving home lessened, and many of the tramps became wage earners. By the early forties they were all working except those who were fighting on Iwo Jima or the beach at Normandy.

10

Children
of Mars

"A WHOLE NEW UNDERWORLD OF BEGGARY
and lawlessness existed in Europe at the end of the war. It was
inhabited by children, hordes of children whose moral natures
seemed to have disintegrated under the impact of the conditions
in which they lived. Nothing was safe from their depredations.
They cheated, smuggled, stole. They snatched food from market
stalls, lorries and shops, clothing from back-yards and bicycles and
motor-cars from the streets. Money and small possessions were
stolen in schools and collective homes. Children smashed windows
or climbed into damaged houses and looted the rooms. Even protected children, living with families among whom such misdemean-
ours would once have been undreamed of, did these things, while
swarms of homeless youngsters who begged or scavenged every
day, like lost dogs, for their bread, stole what they dared when
begging and scavenging failed. Every kind and degree of juvenile
delinquency was practiced, from mere childish defiance to prostitution and organized crime. In France and other Western countries
three times as many minors were brought before the courts as had

been usual before the war, while facilities for dealing with them had decreased. Statistics meant little; while many of those charged were far from being common offenders, innumerable hardened young malefactors were never charged."

So wrote Dorothy McArdle in *Children of Europe,* after World War II. She continued: "The number of these delinquent children, their hardihood, their ingenuity, defeated the police, while the question of what was to be done with them if they were convicted baffled the magistrates. . . . The police of many states had to be advised by the courts to let all but flagrant cases alone."

Juvenile delinquency of all kinds has always rocketed during and after a war. This was probably true of the Punic and the Peloponnesian wars. It was certainly true during the almost constant warfare of the Middle Ages in Europe. The report of a London Committee in 1816, quoted in the first chapter of this book, blamed the wave of juvenile delinquency at that time on the Napoleonic Wars. Many blamed the Flaming Youth of the 1920's on World War I, although most thoughtful socioligist pointed out that the seeds for this particular youthful rebellion were planted during the prewar years and the war merely hastened their full fruition.

Russia had its great spurt of juvenile delinquency in the early 1920's, during and after the civil war that followed the revolution and the resultant agrarian collapse. Tales are told of half a million or more *besprisoryni,* homeless children, who roamed the country in bands, killing for food or loot. A commentator thus described the Russian delinquents at that time: "Year by year these wanderers became older, smarter, tougher. Soon Soviet Russia had an army of street savages on its hands. Outcasts, forgotten and untrained, with no regular habits of getting a living, it was natural for these young savages to take to crime. . . . Living free from all control, they came to love their liberty and resented efforts to limit it. They developed a liking for their own hard life, with its fights, adventures, and perils. They stole and they begged. Drunkenness and drug habits spread rapidly among them. Sex relations were uncontrolled. The wandering children became like a foreign army."

By its very nature warfare justifies many forms of peacetime delinquency. In war, killing, vandalism, and all kinds of deception are approved activities. In past centuries, looting and rape were also accepted as prerogatives of the soldier. These are supposed to be outlawed in modern warfare, but by most accounts the Russian army raped its way through Germany in World War II, and, in 1946, the American market was flooded with cameras that G.I.'s had "liberated" in Berlin. The same soldiers who did these things were held up as heroes to youth. It is only natural that young people became confused.

Other primary causes for an increase in juvenile delinquency in wartime are obvious. When a father goes to war, he breaks up the home temporarily. Starting with World War I, when automatic machine tools made it possible for a woman to do a man's work, this aspect of war became much worse, because the mother frequently went to work and there was no real home. War creates an atmosphere of excitement as well as of anxiety, both of which aggravate natural youthful tendencies toward undisciplined behavior. The Children's Bureau explained: "Millions of youth, feeling the restlessness, excitement and anxiety that war brings, lack both effective means of sharing in adult concerns and opportunities for wholesome fun and companionship."

War stimulates the adolescent's desire for independence. In previous times many whom we now consider juveniles participated in the fighting. As recently as the Civil War, fifteen-and sixteen-year-olds were not uncommon in the armed services; in fact, three boys of those ages were awarded the Congressional Medal of Honor. In twentieth-century warfare, the urge for independence may be satisfied by the jobs that a wartime economy creates for adolescents. During World War II some sixteen- and seventeen-year-olds earned more than their fathers, and a psychologist pointed out that: "At a time when the boy has a strong desire to enjoy and assert his independence, it is clear that a family situation has been created that may prove troublesome to all concerned. If the boy's sense of responsibility to his family is slight and he has already tasted precociously the enticements of vice, he is likely soon to illustrate the way in which the war can become a menace to young people who would under normal circumstances escape immoral and anti-social behavior." The other side of this particular coin is that war-time employment opportunities for youth usually do not continue in a postwar era. Boys who have left school for work are reluctant to return. They join the dropouts who are rightly accused of a disproportionate share of delinquency.

Modern war contributes to the conflict between generations because of its scientific nature. In olden days the grown male could brag about his prowess with a musket, bayonet or saber and be listened to with awe and respect by youth. Today junior high school kids can lecture their elders on rocketry, electronics and radar. In wartime such knowledge is a prime interest, and when the child knows more than his father about what is currently considered the most meaningful things in life, the child is going to be hard to control.

After a war a new kind of separation of the generations takes place. Since the older generation is held responsible for the catastrophic blunder of war, youth is less willing to accept its teachings and accord it infallibility. There is some question in the minds of juveniles as to whether adults who bring on a war are worthy of respect. During World War II, a child prodigy of thirteen, Elizabeth Benson, then a college sophomore, wrote: "The war is responsible for our discovery that our parents are not supercreatures of infallible judgment, that our government is not the divine impregnable institution that we had been taught to consider it when we practiced the flag drill in grade school." She continued with more specific charges: the unlovely passions and bitter prejudices shown by adults during the war; the restrictions on free speech and imprisonment of conscientious objectors; the profiteering; the misleading propaganda; the pettiness of men in high offices. She concluded: "We never really had a chance to venerate our elders."

PERHAPS WORLD WAR II CAUSED MORE EXtreme types of juvenile delinquency in Europe than any war since the almost constant combat of the Middle Ages. This actually started in Germany in the years before the war, when an entire generation of youngsters were taught to be delinquents, if judged by any civilized standards, as part of their training for warfare. In fact, the German youth movement, which had been influenced by two wars and finally culminated in a roundabout way in the Hitler Jugend, began at about the turn of the century when the Wandervoegel made their appearance.

The Wandervoegel were kids who took to the road in protest against the crash program of industrialization of Germany after Bismarck. They broke their home ties to find freedom by getting back to nature. Dressed in distinctive costumes—velvet shorts and jackets for the boys, peasant dresses for the girls—and usually hatless and sometimes barefooted, they wandered through the countryside in groups of mixed sexes, singing folk songs and sleeping under the stars. A eulogy of the beginning of the German youth movement says: "They revolted against the strict conventional rules for the relations between boys and girls. Now, on the road they were free companions. They tramped and swam together, slept side by side in all sorts of shelters or in the open fields. They developed a fine comradeship which young Germans had never known before."

The early Wandervoegel were not vagrants in the meaning of disorderly persons. Rather they were somewhat like Boy Scouts and Girl Scouts on extended camping trips, except that Boy and Girl

Scouts do not sleep side by side. The German youth movement was accepted without much criticism by society at the time, and state-owned youth hostels were built to provide the wanderers with shelter. These were later tremendously expanded as part of the Nazi youth program.

The original wandering juveniles were absorbed by World War I. After that, a new generation of Wandervoegel, their ideals shattered, intensified and extended their rebellion. In a typical statement of protest a German youth of that time said: "We felt stifled and unfree in the atmosphere of the home circle, where we were never taken seriously, were compelled to conform to the whims of our elders. . . . We will no more stand the buffoon at a desk who compelled us to cramp body and mind bending over books. Who gave them the right to call us names, insult us, hammer into us their mechanical nonsense? We will no more go back to the prison they call the school!"

In the early 1920's this widespread rebellion of youth overlapped into political areas. Conditions at that time in Germany were similar to those in America during the 1930's, although more acute, and youth sought some kind of a change in a state and a society which offered them no opportunity. Naturally they turned to radical political movements, and the one that promised them the most in a new Germany was National Socialism. In 1926, the Nazis organized boys from fourteen to eighteen into the Hitler Jugend, which became an important factor in the victory of the National Socialists over the Communists. Twenty-six of them died in the street fighting that resulted in the complete suppression of the German Communists.

An interesting story of the importance of youth in Hitler's rise to power involves the Institut fur Sozial Forschung (Institute for Social Research). In the late twenties this organization made a sociological study that it published under the title, *Authoritut and Familie* (Authority and Family). This disclosed that the Nazis were successfully undermining the authority of the parent and transferring it to the state, and from it the Institute accurately predicted the course of the National Socialist movement. It is said that the study inspired these social scientists to escape from Germany in time to salvage the endowment on their Institute.

Some historians maintain that Hitler's success would not have been possible without the support of the country's youth, a factor which the Fuehrer realized when he wrote: "Whoever has the youth has the future." No effort was spared in organizing the children and shaping them to the dictator's purpose. Dorothy McArdle said in her study: "These were Hitler's first victims—the children of Germany. Fired to a white heat of devotion, they were then hammered and twisted, like iron on the anvil, into weapons for his ends. Such a calculated distortion of human minds is not recorded elsewhere in history, and, in fact, it could not have taken place at any much earlier date, since the psychological knowledge and the resources for mass suggestion by means of which it was accomplished were comparatively new."

During the 1920's the Hitler Jugend was an underground movement, illegal in most sections of the country. When Hitler came to power in 1932, it numbered only 35,000. Three years later the Hitler Jugend and associated organized groups of girls and younger boys numbered 6,000,000, some of them among German minorities in fifty-three countries outside of Germany. Ultimately there were three youth organizations for boys and two for girls. The Pimpfs were boys from six to ten, the Jungvolk from ten to fourteen, and the Hitler Jugend from fourteen to eighteen. German girls from ten to fourteen belonged to the Jungmadel, those of fourteen to twenty-one to the Bund Deutscher Madel. At first it was claimed that membership in these organizations was voluntary, but the Nazis quickly suppressed all other youth groups that they did not absorb into their own. By the late 1930's, membership in the state-controlled groups was, in fact, compulsory for all, except Jewish children.

It was a prime objective of the Nazis to train children for only one purpose: strict devotion to the aims of the party. In *Mein Kampf* Hitler had written: "Beginning with the primer, every theater, every movie, every advertisement must be subjected to the service of one great mission, until the prayer of fear that our patriots pray today: 'Lord, make us free,' shall be changed in the mind of the smallest child into the cry: 'Lord, do Thou in future bless our arms.'" The basics of the training for this purpose were hate and brutality. In a state turned topsy-turvy, the children were taught that everything was permissible that was good for Germany and in accordance with the Fuehrer's will, and all else was bad. Hitler boasted: "My magnificent youngsters! In my *Ordensburgen* [leadership schools] a youth will grow up before which the world will shrink back. A violently active, dominating, intrepid, brutal, youth—that is what I am after. Youth must be all those things. It must be indifferent to pain. There must be no weakness or tenderness in it. I want to see once more in its eyes the gleam of pride and independence of the beast of prey."

To accomplish their purpose the Nazis had to undermine three influences in the child's life that were directly counter to their ideology: the home, the school and the church. They started with the home even before their rise to power. The Hitler Jugend were taught that the authority of their parents was subordinate to the will of their youth leaders. Obedience to or respect for parents was not necessary, nor was it good unless the parents were dedicated Nazis whose teachings conformed to those of the party. Hitler said of the older generation: "We will take away their children. We will not allow them to lapse into the old way of thinking. . . . They shall not escape us."

Erika Mann, daughter of novelist Thomas Mann, tells the story of a birthday party that a doctor arranged for his twelve-year-old son. Six boys were invited and five arrived promptly to stand around in their brown shirts and swastika armbands, awaiting the final guest, the fourteen-year-old leader of their particular band of Jungvolk. Of great appeal to youngsters of the Nazi youth organizations was the fact that their immediate leaders were not adults, but boys slightly older than themselves.

When the leader arrived, he demanded to see the father of the host. The mother explained that he was busy, but the son pleaded with his mother to call his father. When the man came, the youth leader asked for an explanation of why the son had missed the last youth meeting. The father explained that the boy was sick with a cold. "But," said the fourteen-year-old, "he went to school that day and the next, did he not?" The father admitted that he did. "Then," said the youth, "you kept him away from the meeting. I shall have to report this." After much pleading from the son, the leader agreed that he would not report the incident if the father promised that it would never happen again. Knowing the consequences to both himself and his son if the incident were reported, the father, in front of the room full of children, apologized to the fourteen-year-old and assured him: "Certainly it will never happen again."

Immediately after Hitler's assumption of dictatorial powers, the schools were brought under the complete control of the party. Teachers taught what they were told to teach and, aside from this, had no authority over their charges. School ended shortly after noon and the rest of the day was devoted to youth group activities aimed at creating good Nazis. There were frequent assemblages of youngsters called by the party, such as parades, marches, and convocations of all kinds. When kids missed school to attend these, teachers were not permitted to require them to make up the work. What they learned in the school was of little consequence; what they learned in the youth group was of vital importance.

Children were influenced to deride and mock their teachers—an

attitude that had great appeal to youngsters. Every issue of the
Jungvolk, a magazine published by the state for boys, contained
articles, letters and essays presenting teachers as spineless and totally
inadequate individuals who must be made to learn that academic
educators could not be allowed to interfere with the will of the
youth leaders. "There is but one point on which we are sensitive,"
began one article, "and that is when people mix into our affairs;
when they try to palm off their old-fashioned ideas on us as though
they were timely and up-to-the-minute." It concluded: "Our advice
to this sort of 'educator of youth' is this: Hands off the leadership
of youth."

Much training involved activities for the development of physical
fitness—organized sports, long hikes and camp-outs, junior war
games, target practice, Volk-Festa, fire rituals and other exciting
events. The encouragement to defy normal adult restraints of home
and school was heady stuff, as were the parades and mass meetings
with their banners and martial music. It was a proud day in the
life of a ten-year-old member of the Jungvolk when he passed his
initial physical tests and was given a dagger to wear. It was a still
prouder day when, at fourteen with the high-ranking members of
the party looking on, he was promoted from the Jungvolk to the
Hitler Jugend in a soul-stirring mass ceremony. It would have been
hard to find a more contented and arrogantly self-satisfied juvenile
generation than the German youth of the 1930's.

By the Nazi standards there was no juvenile delinquency in Germany during that time. The only form of delinquency that was
recognized, other than major crime, was infraction of or complaint
against the party dictates. There was very little of this, and it could
usually be corrected merely by ostracism. To lose his good standing
in his youth group condemned a child to a lonely and miserable
existence.

The persecution of Jews was a favorite sport for the Jungvolk
and the Hitler Jugend and was encouraged even for the Pimpfs.

Gregor Ziemer, the director of the American School in Berlin, starts his book, *Education for Death,* by describing an incident when his primary kids were dismissed at the same time as the Pimpfs from a German Volksschule across the street. The foreign children were driven back into their school by a hail of stones from the Nazi youngsters in their party toggery to the cry of *"Juden— Amerikdanische Juden—Laestige Auslander."* [Jews, American Jews, meddlesome foreigners.] Ziemer called the principal of the German school to remonstrate and was told that he could not interfere, even if he wanted to, with such a "popular spontaneous demonstration." Besides, said the German: "You have Jewish students and we teach our students that the Jews are our greatest enemies."

Jungvolk, in the years before the war, were encouraged to commit vandalism on Jewish property. They vied with each other in creating obscenities which they scrawled or painted on Jewish stores or houses. They were aided in this by what they read in *Der Stuermer,* a pornographic paper that was circulated in the schools and which contained articles and pictures to prove that Jews were completely depraved. Catholic priests were also a target in *Der Stuermer,* which accused them of rampant sexual misbehavior.

The Hitler Jugend, under the direction of the older Storm Troopers, were active in burning synagogues and looting Jewish businesses. Beating up Jews was fine sport, as was parading a captured Jewish girl shamefully through the street. Until the war, Jewish children were permitted to attend schools, where they were isolated on the back benches and used as examples by the teachers in lectures on the superiority of the pure Aryan race.

All juveniles were taught to spy on their parents and inform on them for any criticism of the government or any activity counter to the dictates of the Nazis. Edward Hartshorne, now a professor of sociology at Harvard and one-time Fellow of the German Social Science Research Council, recounts this incident of Nazi informers of tender years:

"A six-year-old girl was playing at home with a friend. In an adjoining room the girl's father was overheard making various critical comments about the government. 'Oh,' said the little friend, 'your father shouldn't say things like that. It is not loyal to the *Fuehrer.* You must report him to the police.' 'Oh no,' said the daughter, 'I couldn't do *that.* I love my father. Why should I tell on him to the police?' 'Because,' answered the friend, 'my brother, who's in the *Hitler Jugend,* says a good German's loyalty should be first to his *Fuehrer,* and second to his relatives and friends. If you don't tell the police about your father, then I shall have to do it, and that would be worse for all of you since I'm not in your family. It will be much better for your father if you do it.' So the six-year-old girl visits the police, and the police summon the father and reprimand him."

For every German kid who actually informed on his parents or his teachers there were scores or hundreds who used the threat to do so for blackmail. A charge laid by a child, real or trumped up, could send an adult to a concentration camp. The juvenile line in many homes was, in effect: "If you don't let me do what I want to do I'll report you to the Gestapo."

In Nazi Germany, education for girls, who were educated separately from boys, was primarily concerned with instruction in housekeeping, eugenics, and physical conditioning that would make strong bodies for child-bearing. A girl's mind was of no importance; only her body and her ability to serve man sexually and for his comfort. This theme was repeated constantly in school, newspapers, plays, books and films. Girls were told: "The healthy girl of eighteen who is not already a mother is lacking in a sense of her social duty." Inducements and opportunities were offered by the state to girls as young as fourteen to become pregnant. "The number of illegitimate pregnancies and births among the members of the 'State Youth' is tremendous." The party line on extramarital sex was set forth by Professor Ernest Bergman in an essay, "Knowledge and the Spirit of Motherhood," in which he wrote:

"Life-long monogamy is perverse and would prove harmful to the spirit of our race. Were this institution ever really enforced—and fortunately this is almost never the case in reality—the race must decay. Every reasonably constructed State will have to regard a woman who has not given birth to a child as dishonored. There are plenty of willing and qualified youths ready to unite with the girls and women on hand. Fortunately, one boy of good race suffices for twenty girls."

Said one anti-Nazi mother, "Young German girls have been deprived of mental life and turned into breeding beasts. Every vicious instinct has been loosed. . . . Young boys have been taught that it is right and smart—yes, and *patriotic*—to despoil young girls in the name of the *Fuehrer*." An old-fashioned father, on learning that his teen-aged son was responsible for the pregnancy of a young girl, thrashed him. The boy denounced his parent to the Gestapo, who sent him to a concentration camp. The boy was awarded a Hitler Jugend decoration.

Girls were given ample opportunity to fulfill their patriotic duty to have sexual intercourse. The Bund Deutscher Madel hiked and camped to strengthen their bodies for motherhood. Their overnight camps were usually near enough to those of the boys' so that the sexes could mingle. When a girl became pregnant from such nocturnal fun, she was envied by her comrades and praised by her leaders. The younger Jungmadel were prepared for this sexual self-sacrifice. Ziemer tells of observing a group of twelve-year-old girls who were beating one of their number. When he stopped the fight and asked the cause, he was told that the victim had insulted the sister of one of the assailants. She was so lacking in her concept of duty to the Fatherland that she had ventured the opinion that it was not right for the sixteen-year-old sister to become pregnant.

The educator also told of attending a girls' meeting at which the guest of honor was a seventeen-year-old who had just had a baby out of wedlock and who made a speech to her contemporaries describing what a wonderful experience it was and how well she was treated in the state home in which she spent her pregnancy. When her young group members gathered around to ask questions the new mother told them: "Go ahead. Do it yourselves. The *Fuehrer* wants us to."

The state homes in which unmarried girls spent the months of their pregnancy, of which there were sixty scattered throughout the country, were confiscated estates or lush ex-resort hotels. They were idyllically situated on lakes, at the seashore, in picturesque valleys or the beautiful Harz Mountains. Here the girls did no housework, prepared no meals. They ate much better than at home and lolled on the grass or the sand when they were not listening to lectures on Nazi ideology. When her baby was born, the girl could keep it, if she had the means, or turn it over to a state nursery to be raised as a good Nazi while she went on her way with another boy.

During the war similar ideally situated relaxing establishments were maintained where members of the S.S. and Luftwaffe spent leaves. It was a great honor for a teen-aged girl to be selected as a temporary mate for one of these heroes. Frequently the choice was made by the girl's youth group leader—a reward for her accomplishments in the group. Sometimes a girl was specially honored by being permitted to pick the young man whose leave she would brighten from photographs, and always she was given an allowance for beauty parlor and wardrobe to make herself a more attractive courtesan.

By the time the war started millions of German boys with up to seven years of Nazi training were ready for the armed forces, and during the six years of conflict other millions matriculated. It was their training as juvenile delinquents that made it possible for these young men to later carry out the unspeakable cruelties of the Germans in occupied countries and the sadistic tortures perpetrated by the S.S., calmly and without apparent reluctance or distaste. They saw nothing wrong in the extermination of millions of Jews or the mass murders of civilians in Poland, Czechoslovakia and Greece. Under the code that they had learned as children, it was *right* that these inferior people be eliminated or enslaved.

MOST CHILDREN OF THE NAZI-OCCUPIED countries also learned to be delinquents. Defying the authority of the occupying forces became an act of patriotism. Children were taught to lie and steal, commit vandalism and sabotage to this end. They had to learn to be quick-witted in giving lying answers to the questions that the Germans asked. When the diet of the native population was reduced below subsistence level, the nimble young made the best thieves and beggars.

Many youngsters actively participated in the resistance movements, the younger ones serving as guides and couriers, the older ones as saboteurs. Kids stole material and made explosives. They acted as look-outs while their elders prepared to derail a train or blow up a bridge. They cut communication lines, blew up ammunition trucks, and stole hand grenades to make booby traps. Many a German sentry died with a knife in his back, stuck there by a teen-ager. Dorothy McArdle wrote that "respect for human life was deteriorating among the young people and so, as was inevitable, was respect for property. People who see themselves robbed by the officials of the State need a strong sense of discrimination to refrain from repaying themselves as they can, and discrimination is a thing that children do not often possess. As deprivations increased many of them became reckless as to how and where they secured fuel and food."

The wartime activities of children of all ages in occupied countries that most closely resembled an indoctrination in delinquency were in the nature of tormenting or heckling the occupying forces and showing contempt for the adult conquerors. This was particularly true in Denmark, Norway and Holland. The Germans considered the blood of the Nordic and Dutch people as acceptable and hoped that these might become citizens of a Germanized Europe who would be only slightly secondary to pure Germans, as opposed to Slavs and Poles, who would be useful for nothing except virtually illiterate slave labor. In these favored countries their occupation policy involved persuasion and propaganda backed by slight force, as opposed to the naked force employed in other lands. As an instance, in Poland teen-aged girls were rounded up and carted away, presumably for a labor force. After screening, some were used as labor, some marked for extermination and the most suitable placed in brothels. In Norway and Denmark girls of the same age were offered inducements, financial and otherwise, to mate with Germans to produce offspring for Nazi training.

In Norway and Holland branches of the Hitler Jugend were organized, with distinctive uniforms and extra food rations for the children of collaborators, and in Holland, for the offspring of the considerable German minority. For boys of parents who forbade their children to join the Nazi youth groups, there was a secret organization, the Juvenile Companionship, whose un-uniformed members served the Germans as informers. Collaborating juveniles were offered higher education in Germany and the promise of future leadership in their own countries. Beating up these wartime youthful collaborators became a form of postwar delinquency.

Few children of the favored countries were taken in by the blandishments of the Nazis. Most developed ingenious schemes to thwart and embarrass them. Dutch kids secured buckets of orange paint and decorated official German cars with a gaudy W, for Wilhelmina, and it was even more fun to put a pool of orange paint in the back seat of the car, hoping that a German officer would sit in it. Norweigian kids scrawled patriotic slogans on walls and fences and a defiant symbol of an H with a 7 on the crossbar for King Haakon the Seventh. Danish kids developed the best stunt: little ones roamed the streets with water pistols filled with corrosive acid stolen from school laboratories, and when a German's back was turned squirted him. The German felt nothing, but when he took his coat off it fell apart in his hands. In a single day 220 German soldiers stationed in one Danish town reported the ruin of their uniforms.

In all countries youngsters organized packs of "bicycle commandos" who pedalled innocently along with their lunches in bundles on the handle-bars. When they passed a place that catered to Germans, they hurled their "lunches" of paper-wrapped bricks through the windows. Or they might start a near riot by pausing in a square to shout "Down with Hitler" and "Drive out the German swine." By the time the Gestapo arrived, the boys had raced to the other side of town. Putting sand in the gas tanks of German cars was a favorite juvenile sport, as was the "potato trick" practiced in Norway. In this a pretty teen-aged girl was the bait. She seemed to be supervising the play of some smaller children near a group of German cars. When the young German guards tried to strike up an acquaintance she did not rebuff them, as did most Norwegian girls. She was surprisingly friendly and so enticing that the Germans were distracted from the activity of her younger companions. These worked in pairs; one kid put potatoes into the exhaust pipe of a car while the other pushed them far up the pipe with a stick.

The youngest saboteur on record was a five-year-old Danish boy named Erick who was a member of a tiny-tots' underground which had its headquarters in a railroad culvert. Erick was intercepted trying to derail an ammunition train. His demolition material consisted only of sticks and stones, but with the idea of sabotage he had placed them carefully and with the proper technique. Probably because he was a Dane, the Gestapo returned him after interrogation to his parents; had he been a Slav, he would undoubtedly have been shot.

After pointing out that the incidence of juvenile delinquency in

the Scandinavian countries had always been the smallest in the
world, Swedish writer Arnold Haverlee, who had observed the
occupation in Norway and Denmark, continued: "It is impossible
to shield a child from the effects of invasion. . . . He has heard his
parents rejoice over sabotage of trains, bridges and factories; he may
suspect they have shared in this destruction. He has learned vandalism in a land where formerly a vacant house could stand for years
without having a window wantonly broken. He has seen teachers
and clergymen, former examples of rectitude, defy every rule laid
down by the Gestapo. In his direct childish mind any who wears
a uniform represents authority, and he has grown up in a hatred
and contempt for all authority. The result is a complete reversal
of morals, an increasing indifference to all authority. . . . It is now,
and will be in the postwar years, one of the most tragic consequences of the New Order."

Haverlee's postwar prediction could not have been more accurate.
After living for five or six years in a society where breaking the
law was encouraged by adults—where lying, cheating, deceiving,
stealing and defying authority were brave and admirable things to
do—children could not adjust to peacetime morality. The behavior
that they had learned during the war was antisocial and these habits
prevailed to become the basis of peacetime crime and immorality
long after all pretext for defying authority had gone.

The postwar European wave of juvenile delinquency was ag-
gravated by the millions of homeless and orphaned kids that the war
had created, most of whom became vagrants. UNESCO estimated
that there were 350,000 orphaned or morally neglected children in
Greece alone, one-quarter of the juvenile population under nineteen years of age. One hundred and eighty thousand vagrant and
street children were counted in the Italian cities of Rome, Naples
and Milan. The efforts of the various nations and the liberating
forces to care for these children were commendable, but far short of
the need. Most of these youngsters had to fend for themselves by

begging, stealing, black market trading, or prostitution. As time passed, the total number of uprooted young strays diminished as facilities to care for them were developed, but the number of confirmed delinquent vagrants seemed to increase. There was no question that many of the war-trained kids liked this kind of life.

The problem was more acute in defeated Germany than in any of the liberated countries. In a report published in 1950 UNESCO surveyed the first four postwar years. Although it was admitted that there were no reliable statistics, it was estimated that there were between four and five million wandering German youngsters, some with families or relatives but many alone, "homeless and without papers, supporting themselves by black marketing, theft and prostitution. Some even committed murder in order to get food cards. At that time there were considered to be a good many more vagrant girls than boys . . . . Children and adolescents took to the roads and formed groups which from time to time became bands of gangsters."

Their Nazi training made it more difficult for the German youngsters to adjust to peace. They had been taught that they were members of a master race that would be all-powerful through force. Now, said UNESCO, "the disillusionment and confusion created by the sudden destruction of all they had seriously and fervently believed in caused the more forceful characters among the young to feel a profound distaste for civilization and organized society."

Kids as young as kindergarten age were useful as smugglers, sometimes under parental guidance, more often as agents for older youths. Household articles or items stolen from the occupying forces could be traded in Holland and Belgium for cigarettes or coffee, which could in turn be traded to German farmers for food. Little kids could slip across the borders more easily than adults. Older youngsters, too, organized smuggling bands, frequently with girls who used their sex to distract the guards while their young male compatriots crossed and recrossed borders. More serious problems were the gangs of boys who armed themselves with weapons that were easily obtained from deserters, and stood ready to shoot it out with the border guards if they were apprehended.

The children of Germany's defeated allies were no better off. Of the children of Vienna it was said: "Boys and girls who had been impregnated with the teaching of Nazi schools and youth organizations were floundering in a morass. . . . With all that they had built upon overthrown, they could find no foundation on which to reconstruct their lives. . . . Girls of fifteen were prepared very soon to become mothers, but expected to have no necessarily permanent relationship with the father of their children and no responsibility for the children. The presence of soldiers of four different 'liberating' armies, all with cigarettes or candy bars or other precious goods to spare, and all susceptible to Viennese charm, helped to induce in young, hungry girls a reckless unconcern with anything beyond momentary pleasure or the satisfaction of an immediate need. Children went out into the streets with one purpose only—to bring something edible home, and no one at home asked too many questions as to how it had been obtained."

In Hungary, "homeless children living in streets of the capital and neighboring towns numbered thousands—fifteen to twenty thousand was the estimate in March, 1946. Their gangs were augmented during the daytime by children in whose homes there was no fire and no food. These young derelicts, desperate for clothing, sometimes fell upon passers-by after dark and stripped them. People were murdered by boys of fifteen. Girls of thirteen were brought to hospitals for venereal disease. These young delinquents were unfit to be sent to families or placed among other children. Because there were no institutions in which they could be cared for, the police were not required to arrest them."

Children were an important factor in the black markets that were a way of life in all European countries after the war. Many operated on their own, stealing from the occupying forces or performing services for soldiers in return for cigarettes and other merchandise that they could convert into a profit. More were agents for big-time adult black market operators who trained and supervised them and disposed of stolen merchandise. Values fluctuated wildly in various occupation zones, and trading became an exciting gamble at which even twelve-year-olds were expert. In France, particularly, children acquired a mania for selling and cared little as to how they acquired the merchandise that they sold. The French Ministry of Education finally ruled that no child might have more than fifty francs in his pocket at one time.

The most widely known postwar juvenile delinquents were the children of Italy—the *sciuscia* (shoe shiners) who were romantically and sympathetically portrayed in a film by Vittorio de Sica. Of these youngsters a UNESCO observer wrote: "Morally, their condition was lamentable, for their native vivacity, heedlessness and lightness of heart made them easily led into desperate enterprises. Children of six hired themselves out to gangsters of every description, while hardier lads formed their own rackets and gangs. Girls of fifteen took to prostitution."

Alone or in groups, the hundreds of thousands of *sciuscia* were formidable delinquents, mostly from necessity, partly from choice. Talking of a particular quarter on the fringes of Milan where there were over 2,000 such children, an Italian social worker said: "No one controls them or takes care of them. . . . They grow up like savages and regard everything advantageous to themselves as good and just, and everything impeding them as bad and unjust. They have no sense of right and wrong and if, one day, they came up against the law they do not realize why it is. They do not steal, they simply 'take' what attracts them, and if necessary they share the spoils of their thievery with their playmates and companions in adventure. Wasteland and the dark corners of cellars are their sexual playgrounds. These children are not organized in groups; they act singly or, if need be, in small bands."

Every European city was plagued by gangs of postwar delinquents, but the situation seemed more acute in the major Italian
cities where such gangs were more plentiful and more skilled in
delinquency. Some operated independently, some were linked from
city to city, and many were agents for or were supervised by adult
criminals. Theft was the principal delinquency of these groups;
there was little vandalism, mugging or street fighting.

An Italian sociologist, describing the situation in Genoa, said:
"These children who are aged ten or eleven meet in casual shelters
or at the communal tables of the charitable institutions that give
them soup. . . . Gangs of youths aged from thirteen to seventeen,
real delinquents, make use of these 'tyros' who at that stage are
easily persuaded that theft is a job like any other. We have heard
them saying, 'We shall be robbers, just as some men are doctors
and others priests.' . . . Their rendezvous are not always the same.
Sometimes they sleep at home, sometimes with friends, sometimes
under bridges. They cannot be said to have a leader, but three or
four of the older or cleverer ones apportion tasks to the juniors
(who sometimes are no more than eight years of age), which result
in the latter, unwittingly or in exchange for a cigarette, doing them
some valuable service. Girls of thirteen, women before their time,
similarly go to the bad. They . . . frequent the harbors and later,
perhaps in an outburst of revolt, leave home to work 'for themselves' with boys of their own age, or a little older, with whom
they live as their mistresses."

Sadly, American G.I.'s were a factor in the juvenile delinquency
of occupied countries. Much has been written about the kindness
and generosity of our troops to foreign children and the time they
spent in trying to improve the lot of the youngsters—and all of it
is true. Yet the G.I., in most cases unwittingly, did much to corrupt
the youth that he at other times tried to help. With his numerous
possessions he represented great material wealth to the deprived
European kids, and he was easy to steal from. Also, he was the best

market for certain stolen goods. The American boys wanted souvenirs of their stay in Europe, and they could acquire them readily for candy or cigarettes from the small fry who were always hanging around. In Germany the Leica camera was in great demand by G.I.'s—a demand which youngsters were happy to fill. The American haggled about how many packs or cartons of cigarettes a certain camera was worth, but seldom bothered to inquire as to where a twelve-year-old got a Leica camera.

G.I.'s played an important role in the sexual delinquency of young girls in occupied countries. Glamor was responsible for some of this; girls in the liberated countries who would never have associated with Germans were proud to be seen with American soldiers, and the ardors of the times overcame all restraints. Many of the G.I.'s were themselves upper-age juveniles. Girls of sixteen or younger were sexually attractive and were readily available for a pack of cigarettes that could be traded on the black market, or sometimes a candy bar. The American boys were young, away from parental restraint for the first time, and felt that they were entitled to relaxation after the victory. The extent to which American boys were trading with ex-enemy males and sleeping with ex-enemy females in Germany became so distressing that rules were formulated to forbid "fraternization." These regulations were notoriously ineffective in preventing a boy from getting a fraulein when he wanted one, and a goodly share of the willing frauleins were juveniles.

BACK HOME, THE INCREASE IN WARTIME delinquency was much less marked, but it was far above prewar years and continued into the postwar years to become the foundation for the situation that is today causing such concern. In 1943 the FBI summarized the increase in juvenile delinquency in a statement: "For the first time in twelve years, age 17 predominated in the frequency of males arrested, and age 18 predominated in the frequency of female arrests. Boy arrests under 18 increased 23.4 per cent and girl arrests under 21 years of age increased 47.9 per cent. Arrests of females under 21 years of age for offenses against common decency increased 56.9 per cent, for crimes against property 30.1 per cent, and for miscellaneous violations 53.2 per cent. . . . Arrests of males under 18 years of age increased 39.8 per cent for rape, 39.0 for robbery, 27.7 per cent for burglary and 23.4 per cent for auto theft. . . . The seriousness of the problem of juvenile delinquency is more clearly seen when it is noted that compared with arrests in 1941, the figures for 1943 show that arrests of girls under 21 years of age increased 130.4 per cent."

Sexual misbehavior loomed large in the wartime delinquency. The *Annals* of the American Society of Political and Social Science reported that adolescent girls "are likely to feel, more than boys of the same age, that they are left out of the adventure and excitement associated with the carrying on of the war; and, more than boys, they have one resource on which they can count as giving them the means of escape from this isolation. This, of course, has to do with sex. . . . The record shows that this delinquency among girls has become a more serious problem than in any other of our war crises. The increase in this type of delinquency has been startling. The young girl has become a serious problem even in the transmission of venereal diseases. It would be a great mistake also to suppose that these girls who are offering themselves to soldiers and sailors come only from homes of poverty and ignorance. . . . every experienced social worker will bear testimony that they also come forth from families that are of high quality."

A minor phase of this sexual misbehavior had to do with farm work. With a wartime shortage of farm labor, teen-agers were taken from the cities at harvest time to "save the crops." This was thought to be fine for the kids physically, mentally and morally, but an appalling number of the girls came back pregnant. According to one report, "this belief that the child weeding on a truck farm or picking strawberries necessarily works in a favorable environment is the result of ignorance and misunderstanding of the way in which rural surroundings favor certain sorts of misbehavior, particularly of a sexual character. The isolation easily had in the country, especially where there is access to pasture land and woods, provides privacy that the teenage child cannot so easily have in the city without attracting an attention that is likely to bring his misdoings into the open."

Another factor in the increased delinquency of the war years was a resurgence of the juvenile transiency which had subsided in the late 1930's only to become more acute in the early 1940's. Some kids not yet in their teens left home in great numbers, stimulated by excitement and hope of high adventure. Older ones, fifteen and up, departed to seek jobs in centers of war industry. Here was an exact reversal of the situation of the previous decade, when youngsters had left home because there was no work. Now one study reported: "Opportunities for work, instead of being hard to find, beckon to youth from all sides. But for both groups [the adventure seekers and the job seekers], living conditions are no better than in the 1930's, the hazards of undesirable companionship are just as great, and the effect of complete release from parental authority and supervision is just as dangerous."

The great symbol of World War II juvenile delinquency was the "latch key" children, or the "eight-hour orphans." These were the offspring, of all ages, of working mothers. During the war there was a great propaganda campaign to induce housewives to take jobs in industry, featuring such headlines as "Why be baking biscuits when you could be building bombers?" Women responded by the millions, some for the high wages offered, others out of patriotism. By 1944 there were almost 17,000,000 working women, one-third of the labor force and 41 per cent of all women of working age.

Obviously, working mothers had little control over or knowledge of what their children were doing. Little ones were taken care of by relatives, neighbors or siblings, or put in nursery schools. Older ones were the latch key children who were given a key with which to unlock the door to an empty house when they came home from school. What they did until mama came home from work—if she was not on the night shift—was their own business, and much of it was business of an undesirable nature. The hut where the gang hung out became the youngster's home away from home in a more real sense, and, without parental supervision, the members of the gang became increasingly involved in delinquent practices. Most of this was not very serious and involved mainly petty shoplifting, minor burglaries, car stripping, etc., and some sexual experimentation. But it laid a foundation for delinquent conduct that carried on into the postwar years.

11

Is This
the Wildest Generation?

A FEW YEARS AGO A TEAM OF PSYCHOLO-
gists undertook a study to compare the emotional adjustment of
adolescent children of dominant parents with those of permissive
parents. To secure fifty children in each group, they went to West-
chester County in New York where, they assumed, a more liberal
attitude toward child-rearing prevailed than in most localities. With
the help of churches, schools, child guidance clinics and other
agencies, they searched for a year for fifty children who, by their
standards, were permissively raised. They then lowered the standards and, by the end of another year, they found thirty-seven; they
never did find fifty.

This incident is not quoted to question parental authoritarianism
or to endorse permissiveness, but rather to make the point that
youngsters today are subject to more complete adult domination in
more areas and for a longer period than kids were at most times
and in most places in the past. And, in some ways, the adult code
of conduct that we would impose on our children is confusingly

contradictory. If an American mother is asked how she wants her children to behave, she may well answer that she wants them to be "free, natural and spontaneous," and then add, "and obedient." Obviously if a child is obedient in all things he is not going to be free, natural and spontaneous. And, when a child reaches the end of its teens, we no longer want it to be submissive. We do not want to raise docile, meek adults with no wills of their own; yet for the first twenty years of their lives, we put great emphasis on training our children to play such a spineless role.

Most behavioral scientists—psychologists, psychiatrists, psychoanalysts, and sociologists—do not agree with the lay "experts" that leniency of parents is a prime cause of delinquency. Many take the opposite view and hold that extreme aggressiveness that results in major delinquency is far more characteristic of the children of dominant parents. In fact, social scientists are far more concerned about the shy, timid, withdrawing, morose, docile and troubled child that usually results from complete submission to adult will than they are about the healthy-minded young rebel, some of whose behavior society may now label delinquency.

There has long been a cliché that "there are no delinquent children, only delinquent parents." Unlike many lay experts, most serious behavioral scientists do not endorse this view, although one sociologist, Dr. James Bassard of the University of Pennsylvania, made an amusing point that may represent a minor cause of the conflict between the generations when he wrote: "One senses today a somewhat pronounced even if indefinite tension between generations in regard to the identification of their respective age stereotypes. Each accuses the other of not acting its age. Much of this seems to spring from the widespread effort of middle-aged persons, with the aid of physicians, vitamins, and beauticians, to retain the looks, the vigor and the ways of youth. . . . Some way or other, many parents seem envious of youth, and resent the growing up of their own children, for grown children are such undeniable evidence of what they seek to hide. Adolescents resent this effort on the part of middle age. Overtly, they see older persons acting kittenishly or childishly; vaguely they resent the loss of the comforting parental stereotype. The modern mother, with her vivid slacks and streamlined hairdo, may look like an attractive companion for her daughter, but the child may sense the lack of a historic and traditional pattern. One recalls here the plaintive cry of Abby to her mother, 'You don't knit, you never make cookies, and you haven't any bosom.'"

A fairly recent development in American society that affects today's kids is the emphasis on the organization of their activities. In this era of the "organization man," totally adjusted to the demands of industry, unions, state agencies, councils and committees, there may be an effort to create the organized child. If his activities are not organized, they are not wholesome. Baseball is a glaring example. Sandlot baseball used to be an American tradition. All boys played on scratch teams that they chose themselves. There was much loud wrangling, occasional fist fights, and a lot of fun. Now the sandlot is buried under a high-rise housing project or a phalanx of spilt-level ranch houses and replaced by the Little League field, build by adults and maintained by adults, where the game is strictly supervised by what one writer has cynically called "middle-aged Peter Pans." In the old days a kid could take a swing at an umpire if he did not like a decision. No more—the umpire may be somebody's father.

It used to be that if a high school had facilities for sports most of the students would play. Today the emphasis, imposed by adults, is often on "making the team." This type of adult-controlled and adult-dominated activity can be frustrating for kids. There is no freedom in it, and it is not really play. For the minority of boys who are selected for teams (by adults), every move that they make must be in accord with the dictates of an adult. The majority of boys who do not make teams may sit on the sidelines and watch, or go out and do something unlawful.

Even casual play is organized. A recent book, *The Tired Adult's Guide to Backyard Fun with Kids,* offers "hundreds of games, stunts, activities for relaxed and happy times together." Kids cannot just play in the yard anymore; they must play games that have been organized and imposed on them by adults! It is getting to the point that anything they can do or want to do without adult supervision may be questioned. Some who advocate this playful togetherness of father and son stress how the boy will benefit if the father is his buddy. But some small fry ask: "Who wants a forty-year-old buddy?"

In our modern society the trend is toward creating public services that can assume some of the responsibilities of the parental role in controlling children, and to give existing services more authority in this area. In some places, particularly in many suburban towns, it is said that the police spend more time chasing kids than chasing criminals. If a youngster lives in a housing project, the Housing Authority has a statutory right to keep his morals under scrutiny. If his family receives financial aid from the city, a welfare worker checks up on him. If he is taken to a clinic, the admitting officer asks questions. The school guidance counselor is a new monitor, and directors of neighborhood community centers report his conduct to the proper authorities, which brings a youth board worker into play. Fifty years ago almost all children went through life without meeting any of these watchful individuals.

An example of the use of police authority is the juvenile curfew that has been established in some communities. The police, either of their own volition or under pressure from a committee of citizens, ordain that children on the streets after a certain time of night are incipient delinquents. The Children's Bureau opposes extensive interference by public agencies with the rights of both children and parents. They consider that a publicly imposed curfew, for instance, is not only improper, but illegal, maintaining that "the most effective curfew regulation is applied by the parents. Children are more likely to obey this. It can be flexible to meet different circumstances. Certainly, parents have the legal right to insist that they and not the police have the authority to allow their children to be out at night for legitimate reasons."

Forty-odd years ago Judge Lindsey, the champion of youth in that era of revolt, had much to say on this subject. It was his opinion that trying to thwart the youthful will for freedom, the demand to be different, by a multitude of edicts and prohibitions was not only ineffective, but most harmful to youth. He wrote: "The damnable and destructive thing about this multitude of taboos and these varied censorships of the most minute details of conduct is that it removes from individuals all real responsibility for their own conduct. They make no choices. It also relieves the church, school, and home of responsibility simply by saying a sweeping 'Don't' to every practice in life that is capable of abuse or misuse. It is like putting a man's arm in a sling and expecting it to be strong. It is like putting the whole human race on crutches."

The multitude of rules under which today's kids live, and for the violation of which they may be labeled wild, are far more stringent than those which governed their grandparents. Indeed, the biggest factor in current juvenile delinquency is the current concept of what constitutes delinquency. A good part of the increased "case load" of probation officers and social workers in the juvenile court consists of youngsters who have committed acts that would have been considered as pranks or serious mischief in their grandparents' day and would not have been of major concern to public authority other than the neighborhood policeman.

Juvenile courts now distribute a pamphlet printed as a public service by Kiwanis International to explain the laws governing various types of delinquency. It is a good piece of well-written information for kids, and much of it deals with obvious delinquency:

joy-riding, rifling school lockers, shoplifting, vandalism, etc. But one section headed "disorderly conduct," cites examples:

"Larry and Joe began to play catch with their books in a crowded bus after school one day. They shoved and disturbed the other passengers. They meant it all in fun, but actually they were guilty of disorderly conduct. Other examples of disorderly conduct are shouting or making noises outside a building at night, loitering around a school without permission, pushing and shoving in a crowd, and causing a crowd to collect." This section concludes with the warning that "in some states it [disorderly conduct] may be punished by imprisonment for six months."

Another section on "unlawful assembly" gives this instance: "While Jack and Dick were walking down the street on Friday night, they met some of their friends standing on the street corner. These boys were planning to crash a dance being held at the Y.M.C.A. . . . . A policeman came along and ordered the group to break it up and move along. The boys refused to leave. Jack and Dick just stood there with their friends. 'This is a free country, isn't it? We don't have to move for nobody.' They thought they were treated unfairly when the policeman took them all down to the station house."

A third section tells about Larry and Joe who were playing at being snipers with an empty .22 rifle. A letter carrier at whom they pointed it called the police. "Larry and Joe were taken to juvenile court."

In addition to "disorderly conduct" and "unlawful assembly," "disturbing the peace" contributes to the increase in the number of cases of reported delinquency. Swelling the ranks of wild kids are children who have been brought into court for ringing door bells. Youngsters have been referred to the courts for shouting disrespectful remarks at adults whom they dislike. Kids are hauled into court for publicly showing a lack of respect for policemen, although taunting the "fuzz" has traditionally symbolized youthful rebellion.

Minor offenses against property, which used to be considered mischief and were handled by parents and the cop on the beat, are now called vandalism and bring the youngster to juvenile court.

It may be that kids today are really misbehaving themselves in far greater numbers than those of yesterday, but it may also be that the increase is due to the fact that more of them are getting caught and becoming the concern of public authority. There has been a nationwide propaganda campaign during the last decade to "curb juvenile delinquency," and law enforcement agencies, special youth services, boards and bureaus, community committees and other groups have made this a subject of special interest, as have private citizens. There has been so much publicity that many good citizens believe that it is their duty to be the keepers of their youthful brothers and sisters, and more of them than ever before call the police to report juvenile misbehavior. The public and public agencies demand that the police curtail the actions of youngsters who do not conform to the dictates of adult society, and the police shovel non-conformers into the juvenile courts.

In a recent speech addressed to representatives of all public facilities concerned with youth, the senior probation officer of the Connecticut juvenile courts pleaded for help for the courts which, he said, are facing an almost insurmountable problem because individuals and community agencies are referring kids to them for every conceivable type of misbehavior. He spoke humorously of private citizens who seemed to feel that the function of the courts was that of protecting them from annoyance by children, and told of a woman who called a court probation officer to say: "You have to do something. That boy is on my lawn again." This drove home his point with regard to the growing trend to classify as delinquency all youthful conduct that displeases adults.

INFLUENCING THE BEHAVIOR OF TODAY'S teen-agers is the scarcity of jobs for youths. As recently as forty years ago every store had a delivery boy who worked after school, on Saturdays, and during vacations. Every office had an office boy who ran errands, kept the stockroom neat, and went out for coffee. Every small and suburban town had a multitude of paper routes served by boys on bicycles. Boys in their mid-teens could get jobs helping artisans in the building trades. When a motorist stopped for gas, it would quite frequently be pumped by a teen-ager and sometimes by a pre-teen-ager. These and various other jobs were filled by kids of thirteen or fourteen and up since there was no prohibition regarding children of that age working after school.

In the 1960's all this has changed. No business will hire a youngster under sixteen, and the unions in the construction trades would be horrified at the idea of a mid-teen-aged helper. In the suburbs, twelve- to sixteen-year-olds can do little except mow grass, a most boring and depressing occupation for any age. In the cities there is little or nothing that they can do to gainfully pass their free time. And there are few jobs for sixteen- to eighteen-year-olds. The few stores that make deliveries do so by car, as do most distributors of newspapers. There are virtually no more sixteen-year-old office boys, and few businesses will consider taking on a kid in any capacity who has not finished high school. In the modern service station, an adult in uniform pumps gas; he has made a career of it, after taking the oil company's training course.

In the business world there is no place for youth. Those in their teens have few meaningful objectives. They do not have the opportunity to be useful or to accept responsibility. They are expected to occupy themselves with the many activities that oldsters have organized for them—activities which offer little opportunity for the expression of initiative or individuality and small chance for freedom. They are told that they have to wait until they grow up before they can do anything meaningful. In truth, they *are* grown-up biologically. As one sociologist puts it: "In terms of growth, strength, fecundity, and mental capacity, full maturity tends to be attained only a short time after puberty; but socially the adolescent still has a long way to go, in most cases, before full status is reached." They are prohibited from doing a multitude of things because, they are told, they do not have the experience to make decisions; then they are prohibited from getting that experience.

History gives no exact answer to whether modern youth represents the wildest generation or not; whether juvenile delinquency is more commonplace today than it was in many past eras. The change in the society makes true comparisons impossible. Two hundred years ago the United States was a small settlement, over 90 per cent agrarian, on the edge of a vast frontier. One hundred years ago it had started to become urbanized and industrialized, and the cities were largely peopled by a vast flood of foreign-born of low educational and economic status. Today the frontier has vanished, the rural civilization is relatively inconsequential, and the immigrant class, with one exception, has disappeared. The society is becoming increasingly concentrated in central cities and sprawling suburbs. The latter, as an important factor in American society, did not exist fifty years ago.

Politically, America has changed from the worship of rugged individualism to a reliance on centralized government. And despite claims that ours has always been a classless society, it was not until World War I that the great leap forward was made to convert the bulk of our total population into a middle class occupying what would have previously been considered a highly privileged economic position.

There is one area in which some comparison might be made— the behavior of urban Negro youth today and the behavior of immigrant youth in the past century. In a sense the bulk of the Negro population in northern cities are first- or second-generation immigrants from the agrarian society of the south. Negroes constitute about 12 per cent of the population and account for about 25 per cent of juvenile arrests. In terms of so-called major crime they represent almost one-third of juvenile arrests; in three classifications—murder, rape and assault—Negro youths account for over 50 per cent of all arrests of those under eighteen; in robbery the figure is over 60 per cent. *White children living under the same conditions in the past behaved the same way.*

Negro children in urban areas are subject to all the classic causes of delinquency of the past: congestion, poor housing, lack of education, etc. There is a high percentage of broken homes and illegitimacy. There is an absence of job opportunities for men, and most mothers work. One hundred years ago all of this was true about the offpsring of most white immigrants in the large cities. They swarmed in slums, which were not yet called ghettos, in which entire families shared a single room with the rats. They were the children for whom there was no room in the schools. Their mothers scrubbed floors or labored in sweat shops; their fathers sought release in saloons. Economically they were victims of discrimination against nationality rather than color, and signs reading: "Men wanted—no Irish" were common.

The Irish kids of the slums, and later the Italian and Polish kids, had the same feeling towards their homes, their families and the society that oppressed them as Negro kids have today, and reacted to it in much the same way. It is said that they were virtually *all* thieves, although their thefts of food and fuel were not then included in the national statistics on larceny. Many were accomplished pickpockets, bag-snatchers and burglars. Many boys belonged to gangs which made headlines for fighting, mayhem and vandalism. Many slum kids drank, illicit sex was part of their lives, and, if we believe Jane Addams, the use of dope was a serious problem. At times the white slum teen-agers were the action arms in riots that terrorized cities, just as some Negro teen-agers are in the riots of the 1960's. The casualties of all of the Civil Rights riots of this decade are insignificant compared to the casualties of the Draft Riots of one hundred years ago.

Those who feel that today's youth may be the wildest generation quote statistics. In determining the wildness of modern kids it is worthwhile to examine two of the government sources of statistics on juvenile delinquency: the 1967 report on crime by the President's Commission on Law Enforcement and the Administration of Justice, and the brochure, *Juvenile Court Statistics,* issued annually by the Children's Bureau of the Department of Health, Education and Welfare.

On the surface, the statistics compiled by the President's Commission on juvenile crime are alarming. But when its figures are analyzed in relation to those of the Children's Bureau, a much different picture emerges.

The leading classification of juvenile crime, according to the President's Commission, is auto theft with 61 per cent of those arrested for this offense in 1966 under eighteen. The Children's Bureau also lists auto theft in its breakdown of offenses for which juveniles are referred to court, but it breaks it down into subclassifications, "unauthorized use" and "other," this latter being the actual theft of a car. Eighty-five per cent of the referrals are in the former classification. Almost nine out of ten youngsters whom the President's Commission classifies as car thieves are, in fact, kids who take a car from point A to point B and abandon it, or are apprehended while so doing. The motivation here is not theft but adventure and excitement and, since no harm is done to persons or property, such cases are not properly classified as "major crimes."

The same is true, to a lesser extent, of the next largest classifications, larceny and burglary. The President's Commission reports that 49 per cent of the arrests for larceny are juveniles between the ages of eleven and seventeen. The Children's Bureau breaks this down into "under $50" and "$50 or more." Over 75 per cent of the youngsters brought into court for larceny are in the former classification, which includes those who have stolen a toy or a tool from a shop counter, hardly a major crime. According to the President's

Commission, juveniles in the above age group account for 47 per cent of the arrests for burglary, but to this classification the Children's Bureau adds the words "breaking and entering." If kids break into an empty house or store, they are guilty of burglary, even if they do not take anything, or take nothing of more consequence than a flashlight or a transistor radio. The great majority of the offenses which cause youngsters to be accused of almost half of the country's major crimes are by no stretch of the imagination major crimes.

The treatment which these offenders get in juvenile court confirms this. In a year when the FBI reported 377,579 juvenile arrests for major crimes, there were a total of 686,000 juvenile court referrals (excluding traffic) of which only 9 per cent, less than 62,000, were committed to corrective institutions, and this included commitments for sex delinquency, vandalism, incorrigibility, and numerous other offenses that are not in the major crime classification. It is beyond credibility that, if there really are almost 400,000 young major criminals, the courts are turning all but a handful of them loose.

Actually, over 50 per cent of the youngsters referred to juvenile courts never come before the courts. Their cases are handled nonjudicially by a probation officer or a social worker, but they still swell the total in juvenile delinquency statistics. Over two-thirds of all cases are dismissed or the youngsters involved are placed on probation or under informal supervision. The balance of those not committed are referred to other agencies, guidance clinics, psychiatrists, etc.

But, if this is not the wildest generation, why are juvenile arrests reaching new peaks, and increasing faster than total arrests? The President's Commission states: "Young people commit a disproportionate share of crime . . . Although the 15- to 17-year-old age group represents only 5.4 per cent of the population, it accounts for 12.8 per cent of all arrests. Fifteen- and 16-year-olds have the highest arrest rate in the United States." A typical FBI report states: "Arrests for all criminal acts, excluding traffic, increased 5%. For persons under eighteen arrests were up 17%; in suburban areas 21%." Juvenile court referrals have increased from 200,000 in 1940 to over a million in 1964 (including traffic in both cases), an increase of 500 per cent during a quarter-century in which the juvenile population increased only by 50 per cent.

It is a fact that an incredibly high percentage of kids in this generation see the inside of a juvenile court. The Children's Bureau estimates that "11 per cent (or about one out of nine) of all children will be referred to juvenile courts for an act of delinquency (excluding traffic) prior to their eighteenth birthday. Considering boys alone, the probability is much greater—about one in every six; for girls alone, much less—one in twenty-three." Nothing like one out of nine youngsters were involved with the juvenile courts a couple of generations ago. Is it because more kids are delinquent today, or because there are more juvenile courts and other public agencies to control youth?

Originally juvenile courts were located in large cities and dealt principally with slum children who were flagrant offenders. Even in cities where such courts existed, relatively minor delinquencies of children in so-called better neighborhoods were usually not referred to the court, but were handled in the neighborhoods where the offenders lived.

Today the juvenile court system covers nearly all children. Over 60 per cent of the courts are in communities of less than 100,000 population. Before this expansion, police officers seldom arrested youngsters for minor offenses, if only because there was nothing to do with the culprits except take them into an adult court that had no proper facilities for handling them. A circuit court judge or a magistrate could either scold the young offender and dismiss him or send him to a reformatory. He had no juvenile probation officers and social workers to administer a middle-ground treatment.

Is This the Wildest Generation? 281

In former years, the cop, if he became involved at all in cases of minor delinquency, usually bawled the youngster out, possibly at the police station, and then turned him over to his parents. Today it is customary for an officer to arrest the young offender and fill out a form in triplicate. One copy stays at headquarters, one goes to the juvenile court, and the third to a record bureau; thus the youngster becomes part of the national statistics on arrests and the Children's Bureau records on juvenile delinquency.

TODAY'S YOUTH ARE ACCUSED OF EXTREME wildness in two areas other than criminal delinquency: drinking and dope. The press regularly reports instances of teen-age drinking parties and of youngsters getting high on "pot" or pushing needles into their arms, and from such instances the inference is drawn that like conduct is common for the younger generation. For some less sensational and more basic enlightenment on this, we might turn to the Armed Forces Examining Stations, which handle a great cross-section of boys who are called up for the draft at the end of their teens. It would seem that if a high percentage of these have been hitting the bottle or taking drugs in the few years before they are examined there would be a significant number of rejections for alcoholism and narcotics addiction. Apparently there are not. The Armed Services are not backward in publicizing the appallingly high percentage (57.9) of young men who are rejected for mental and physical causes, but they make no mention of alcohol and dope as factors in rejections, as they surely would if they had any significance.

Colonel George Walton, who published a study of the Armed Services rejections in a book, *The Wasted Generation,* had this to say about juvenile drinking: "The sociologists insist . . . that there is less drinking among our young people today than in the nineteenth century and considerably less than during the flaming twenties of the prohibition era. This is confirmed by the draft rejections for alcoholism. Separate records are not kept on those so disqualified, but it is probably less than one-tenth of one percent." And of dope he wrote: "The little information currently available from the Armed Forces Examining Stations indicates that youthful drug addiction is principally confined to urban areas, particularly such large cities as New York or Los Angeles. Addiction is confined largely to certain minority, racial, or national groups."

And then there is sex. Perhaps the concern about the sexual wildness of modern youth should be seen in the context of this quotation from Dorothy Bromley's study of the subject, *Youth and Sex:* "Whether there have been significant changes in mankind's attitudes and mores about sex is a very old subject of debate, about which universal agreement is still lacking. It is perennially argued that youth *now*—'now' being any particular time set for the intellectual battle-royal, from the age of Pericles to the present—are behaving differently and much more scandalously than their elders did when they were young."

There are no reliable facts on the sex mores of the modern younger generation, nor are there reliable indications that they differ from those that were established in the 1920's, when there was a breakthrough in the double standard. Prior to the 1920's better-class girls were all supposedly as pure as the driven snow, but we know that the facts were somewhat different during the Victorian era. As to teen-aged boys, it seems unlikely that their sex lives are very different today than from those in the past, except that they may be more moderate and the sexual companion is more likely to be a member of their peer group than a prostitute, a servant, or a female who is socially inferior.

A prime reason for the belief that today's youngsters are setting new records for misconduct is the way in which their behavior is sensationally reported. Juvenile delinquency is "hot news"; it makes headlines, sells articles and books for writers, gets engagements for speakers. To be kept busy with bookings from women's clubs.

P-TA's, church groups and service clubs, a speaker does well to polish a talk on some aspect of the growing wave of juvenile delinquency, and he can command capacity audiences if his speech is advertised with a startling charge against youth.

To announce a symposium of a Yale Medical Society, the University News Bureau started its release with the sentence: "One out of six teen-aged girls in Connecticut was illegitimately pregnant in 1965." The release was used by almost every paper in the state, without any question as to the validity of the charge. When traced down, it was found that Yale had misquoted the Connecticut Health Department, which had said that one out of six girls would be illicitly pregnant during her teens—not in any given year. Further, this statement was a projection from a small sample that might not be accepted as valid by competent statisticians and in which girls in their late teens who subsequently married the man predominated. Thus the true situation is very different from that publicized in the news, from which one might envision teen-aged girls promiscuously dropping illegitimate babies throughout the Nutmeg State. Yet the "one out of six" charge was used to headline an article in the *New York Times Magazine.*

Writers of sensational articles accusing youth of flagrant delinquency can find a market in almost every general interest publication or women's magazine. *McCalls Magazine,* in two successive issues, carried articles headlined: "The Answer to Youthful Drug Addiction" and "Our New Drug Addicts." The first article did not even mention the only addictive drug in common use, heroin, but "Youthful Drug Addiction" is a fine headline and the article would probably not have been published unless it was designed to startle the reader. The second article based its charge that juveniles are "Our New Drug Addicts" on a statement by a police officer which the writer used as a springboard to imply that tens if not hundreds of thousands of teen-agers throughout America are regularly puncturing their skin with dope-filled needles. A police lieutenant in

Yonkers, New York, "revealed" that there were 100 juvenile heroin addicts in that city of 200,000. If this is correct, *juvenile* addition in Yonkers, as indicated by a comparison with the figures of the Federal Narcotics Bureau, is relatively ten times as great as *total* addiction for the country as a whole, a most unlikely situation, particularly in view of the opinion from all responsible sources that juvenile addiction is largely confined to the ghettos of major cities.

The *Reader's Digest* carried an article on youthful drug addiction under the title "An American Tragedy." The writer supported his charge of the widespread use of drugs by juveniles by three instances of individual teen-agers who had been ruined by drugs, quotations from local police officers, and statistics for which no reputable source was given. At about the same time that these several articles were published, the New York County Medical Society made a thorough study of the use of heroin in New York high schools and released a statement that they could find no evidence of it beyond a few isolated cases in three schools. This report made no headlines.

Many of the startling statements about the infamy of youngsters come from departments, bureaus and agencies that are part of a political structure, and voluntary organizations that seek publicity to build prestige, attract attention, raise funds, or support requests for larger budgets. Statements on the appalling extent of juvenile delinquency will make the headlines and will get the agency issuing them into the press, frequently with the implication that if it had more money, more workers, more power or more facilities, or, if its recommendations were followed, the situation would be greatly improved.

All of this can add up, in effect, to a "witch hunt" with today's youngsters as the victims. Are they more sinned against than sinning? Sinned against by a society which prolongs their period of juvenile submission and makes more demands for obedience to adult-imposed codes on more details of their conduct than at any time in history? Behavioral scientists stress the importance of individuality in the child, but society seems to be more interested in emphasizing the importance of the youngster's conformity.

History suggests that there is no difference in the basic behavior of modern youth from that of youngsters through the ages. Youth has always rebelled and, hopefully, it always will. Any society in which youth does not rebel against the status quo has started to decline and is doomed to collapse. Today, more than before, more aspects of this rebellion are being labelled delinquency. But there is little evidence that today's younger generation is wilder than youth of most periods in the past. Indeed, history—as we've seen—suggests that the extent and gravity of their wildness is more moderate than the general standard of behavior of other times.

All things considered, today's youth is probably far from the wildest generation. They are doing what youth has done since the dawn of time—doing it more extensively than in a few eras, doing it more moderately than in most eras. They will grow up to inherit the society that now seeks to control them, just as their parents did, and their grandparents, and their great grandparents. With few exceptions, they will become worthwhile members of that society and perhaps their youthful rebellion will equip them to improve it.

Perhaps this generation may carry out the hope that Judge Lindsey expressed for their grandparents when they were in rebellion over forty years ago, when he wrote: "That the Youth of today makes mistakes disturbs me somewhat but not excessively. That it is honest heartens and delights me much. Here it comes, with its automobiles, its telephones, its folly and its fun, and its open and unashamed refusal to bow down to a lot of idols made of mud, and it makes me hope. This revolt of youth, with a scientific and mechanically grounded civilization back of it, offers the world more hope than anything that has happened in centuries. About once in so often, the human race rediscovers Fire. This younger generation, Prometheus-like, is doing it now."

Acknowledgment is made for permission to quote from the following sources:

Our Times, by Mark Sullivan, published by Charles Scribner's Sons.

Coming of Age in Samoa, by Margaret Mead, published by William Morrow and Company, Inc. Copyright 1928, 1955, 1961.

The Gang, by Frederick Thrasher, published by The University of Chicago Press. Copyright 1927.

Material quoted on pp. 42-43 from *Folkways: A Study of the Sociological Importance of Usages, Manners, Customs, Mores and Morals,* by William Graham Sumner, published by Ginn and Company.

Only Yesterday, by Frederick Lewis Allen, published by Harper & Row, Inc.

Youth and Sex, by Dorothy Bromley, published by Harper & Row, Inc.

Material reprinted with permission of The Macmillan Company from *Twenty Years at Hull House,* by Jane Addams. Copyright 1910 by The Macmillan Company; renewed 1938 by James W. Linn.

The Spirit of Youth and the City Streets, by Jane Addams, published by The Macmillan Company. Permission to use granted by the Stanley Linn Estate.

Gangs of New York, by Herbert Asbury, published by Alfred A. Knopf, Inc.

Excerpt from editorial by H. L. Mencken, quoted on pp. 214-215. Permission by Alfred A. Knopf, Inc.

Where Are the Young Rebels? Copyright 1935, 1963 by Pearl S. Buck.

Cooperation and Competition Among Primitive Peoples, by Margaret Mead, published by Peter Smith.

Boy and Girl Tramps of America, by Thomas Minehan. Copyright 1934, 1962 by Thomas Minehan. Reprinted by permission of Holt, Rinehart and Winston, Inc.

Children of Europe, by Dorothy McCardle, published by Victor Gollancz, Ltd.

Middletown, by Robert S. and Helen Merrill Lynd, published by Harcourt, Brace and World, Inc.